MOUNTAIN REBELS

MOUNTAIN REBELS

East Tennessee
Confederates and the
Civil War, 1860–1870

W. TODD GROCE

The University of Tennessee Press / Knoxville

Copyright © 1999 by The University of Tennessee Press / Knoxville. All Rights Reserved.
Manufactured in the United States of America.
Cloth: 1st printing, 1999.
Paper: 1st printing, 2000; 2nd printing, 2001; 3rd printing, 2004.

The paper used in this book meets the minimum requirements of ANSI/NISO Z39.48-1992
(R 1997) (Permanence of Paper). The binding materials have been chosen for strength and
durability. Printed on recycled paper.

Library of Congress Cataloging-in-Publication Data

Groce, W. Todd.
Mountain rebels : East Tennessee Confederates and the Civil War, 1860–1870 / W. Todd
Groce. — 1st ed.
p. cm.
Includes bibliographical references (p.) and index.

ISBN 1-57233-057-0 (cl.: alk. paper)
ISBN 1-57233-093-7 (pbk.: alk. paper)
1. Tennessee, East—History—Civil War, 1861–1865. I. Title.
E579 .G76 1999
973.7'468—dc21
99-6207

To KCG

She kept the faith

Contents

Illustrations

Tables

Preface

On May 4, 1865, Confederate president Jefferson Davis and his escort rode into the village of Washington, Georgia. Behind them lay the ruin of the Confederacy: Lee's and Johnston's armies had surrendered, the Confederate capital had been captured, and most of the South had been overrun by Union forces. The four-year struggle for Southern independence was clearly at an end. Davis and his small band were the last diehards, still hoping somehow to continue the fight. Among this determined group of last-ditch holdouts was Brig. Gen. John C. Vaughn and the remnant of his Tennessee brigade. The image of a defiant Davis, the symbol of states' rights and secession, surrounded by East Tennesseans as he fled the Federals seems almost bizarre. How could soldiers from a section of the South known for its intense loyalty to the Union be among the last defenders of the Confederacy, fighting on when no hope was left, long after men from states more fervently secessionist had already surrendered?

The answer is simple: Vaughn and his men had no place to go. Having staked everything on a gamble which placed them at odds with their neighbors who opposed secession, these East Tennessee Rebels faced a bleak future. To return home, as other Confederates, meant confronting a victorious and vengeful Unionist majority. Facing the Yankees and an uncertain future with Davis seemed better than confronting William G. "Parson" Brownlow and his supporters. So they stayed with their president, following him until ordered to abandon the retreat and give themselves up to their foes.

Most of them had entered the fight reluctantly. Only after President Abraham Lincoln issued his call for volunteers to suppress the insurrection in the Southern states did East Tennesseans who had developed ties with the Deep South and Virginia move into positions of leadership and organize volunteers from their region to resist Northern invasion. Motivated by what they perceived as a threat to the lucrative trade in foodstuffs with neighboring states, which the railroad had accelerated and strengthened, and hoping to turn secession to their economic advantage, town-based merchants and professionals took up the sword to fight alongside Georgians, South Carolinians, and Virginians in an effort to win Southern independence and continue their new-found prosperity. Although not among the first to clamor for the Confederacy, they were certainly among the last to fight for it.

It is the story of these mountain Rebels that this study seeks to tell. Few historians have been attracted by their tale of defeat, suffering, and banishment. Most writers interested in the mountain South during the period between 1861 and 1865 have focused on Unionists and their attempt to obstruct and undermine the Confederate war effort. With few exceptions, they have either ignored mountain Rebels or viewed them as shadowy characters operating on the fringe, rather than at the center, of events. They have assumed, when recognizing East Tennessee Confederates at all, that these Rebels were little different from other Rebels across the South, and thus they have dismissed them as unimportant or labeled them a mere aberration—a deviation from the staunch Unionism considered more typical of the region.

The extremely complex nature of the war in Appalachia has also discouraged scholarly inquiry into the roots of secessionist sympathy among the mountain populace. East Tennessee history is particularly filled with the sorts of sandbars, whirlpools, and shoals that make navigating a clear and convincing course difficult at best. The ease with which one could run aground has forced many writers to focus their interest on people and regions less treacherous to discern. Certainly it is much easier (and less dangerous) to understand how and why a cotton planter living in Marshall County, Mississippi, for instance, could have favored secession and enlisted in the Confederate army than to discover why a young merchant or lawyer in the hill country village of Sweetwater, Tennessee, would fight under the same banner.

Only recently have historians such as John Inscoe, Gordon McKinney, Phillip Paludan, Jonathan Sarris, and Kenneth Noe begun to acknowledge the existence in sizable numbers of Confederate sympathizers in the Southern highlands and to examine the role played by these mountaineers in the sectional conflict. Inscoe's, McKinney's, and Paludan's works on western North Carolina, Sarris's on northern Georgia, and Noe's on southwestern Virginia are broadening our view of Appalachia during the Civil War and are exploding some previously cherished myths about Unionist solidarity in the region. It is hoped that as this work attempts to answer questions about what was happening on the Tennessee side of the mountains, it will add to the debate about the Civil War experience in the Southern highlands generated by these scholars.

The experience of Confederate sympathizers in East Tennessee was in many critical ways unique. Like characters in a Greek tragedy, they found themselves in 1861 on the verge of an odyssey that would scatter them across the South and elsewhere, banished from their homes by former friends and neighbors. Caught up in a war that most neither sought nor started, East Tennessee Confederates faced challenges little imagined by their fellow Rebels in other regions. They not only were opposed by Northern armies in the field and threatened with Federal invasion but also had to contend with the additional burden of an unfriendly administration in Richmond and a hostile Union majority in their very midst. For them, the war would have to be waged on three fronts. As their sons fought in the hills of Middle Tennessee and the delta bottoms of Mississippi, East Tennessee Confederates battled for support from Richmond while struggling for political domination and survival at home.

When they were unable to overcome the opposition from without and within and came to the realization that secession was destroying, rather than enhancing, their prewar prosperity, many East Tennessee Confederates simply lost the will to continue the struggle. Defeated on the battlefield, suspected of disloyalty and abandoned by their national government, occupied by Northern forces, and unable to quell the largest domestic rebellion within the borders of the Confederacy, the Rebels saw their hopes for Southern independence and economic fortune crushed and watched as their commitment evaporated. Worst of all, many were condemned to exile, refugees from the Yankee invader and the vengeful hand of Union vigilantes. The Federal columns that marched triumphantly into Knoxville and Chattanooga in the late summer and fall of 1863 ushered in a period of terror and banishment that only intensified after the shooting formally ended at Appomattox. The resulting social chaos and dislocation resembled a mountain feud on a grand scale, continuing the violence and uprooting hundreds of families already torn apart by the war.

In the process of telling their story, I have tried to let these people speak for themselves. For this reason I have quoted extensively from the primary sources and attempted to weave the words of my subjects into the text as often as possible. The reader should be warned that I have preserved the original spelling and grammar but avoided using the term *sic* in order not to disrupt the flow on the narrative.

The roots of this book go back to my youth. Although a native of

Virginia, I grew up in Memphis, Tennessee, a particularly unreconstructed town situated in the heart of the South's cotton belt. As a child, I could not help but be exposed to the lingering Confederate heritage of the city, little dreaming that there could be people in the same state who sided with the Union during the "late unpleasantness," as it is still called by some Memphians. Upon moving to Knoxville to attend graduate school, I heard so much from West Tennesseans about the hard-shell Unionism of East Tennessee that I verily expected to be bushwhacked by guerrillas concealed along I-40 as I crossed the Cumberland Plateau.

Thus I was convinced, like so many others, that East Tennessee was simply a den of Unionism, a solid phalanx of bridge-burning Brownlow-ites. And yet, as I studied the history of my new home, I kept coming across references to people who had sided with the South. I was intrigued. Who were these mysterious and now-forgotten Confederates, and why had they fallen into such obscurity? Still curious, and searching for a Ph.D. dissertation topic, I came across an essay written in the 1930s by Samuel Cole Williams urging some historian to examine the region's Confederate leadership. Considering such a study long overdue (it had been six decades since Williams issued the call) and hopeful of the rewards promised by Williams, I set out to answer several basic questions: Who were the secessionists of East Tennessee? Why did they chose separation over union? What happened to them during and after the war that had made them so invisible to us today? While I did not always find clear or definitive answers, I at least hope my quest will rescue these Southerners from their ill-deserved obscurity and create a more complete picture of what happened in East Tennessee during the tumultuous and often bloody ten-year struggle for control of the region. Undoubtedly there will be those who disagree with my conclusions, but then, that is what the history profession is all about.

It goes without saying that this book never would have happened without the assistance and encouragement of many people who gave of their time and various talents. Foremost among those I need to thank are the archivists and librarians who assisted me in my research. James B. Lloyd and the staff of the Special Collections Library at the University of Tennessee and J. Stephen Cotham and the staff of the McClung Historical Collection were particularly instrumental in locating key primary material and in furnishing a quiet, friendly place in which to work. Bill Eigelsbach and Nick Wyman of UT's Special Collections are the kind of archivists that every historian loves: once they understood my topic, they just kept finding materials buried in their collection. It was like having my own research assistants. Wayne Moore and Marylin Bell Hughes of the Tennessee State Library and Archives played a crucial role in helping me sift through their vast collection and in suggesting East Tennessee materials rarely used by researchers. Any praise for the research that went into this project goes to these dedicated professionals.

Other good and generous people assisted in a variety of ways, both large and small. The Board of Directors of the East Tennessee Historical Society and of the Georgia Historical Society generously provided time to work on the manuscript as I sought to fashion a dissertation into a readable publication. Graciously granting permission to publish photographs in their collections were several institutions and individuals, including Dr. Anthony Hodges, Chattanooga, Tennessee; Scott Van Ness, Fairfax, Virginia; the Georgia Historical Society; Knoxville Chapter No. 89 of the United Daughters of the Confederacy; the McClung Historical Collection; the Special Collections Library, University of Tennessee; and the Thomas County (Georgia) Historical Society. Betty Broyles of Dayton, Tennessee, kindly offered access to her research notes and rich collection of primary materials and pointed me toward important sources on Rhea County soldiers. I would be remiss if I did not mention four East Tennesseans—Namuni Young, Cherel Henderson, David Babelay, and Malcolm Rogers—and three Georgians—Jim Ogden, Frank Wheeler, and Deborah Cahill—who helped out along the way during the ten years it took to write the dissertation and then transform it into a book. And Jennifer Siler and the staff of the University of Tennessee Press have been simply great. I appreciate their professionalism and skill, but mostly I appreciate their patience.

I owe an intellectual debt to many teachers, friends, and colleagues. Historians Durwood Dunn, John Inscoe, R. B. Rosenburg, Bill Harris, Ken Noe, and Tracy McKenzie offered insightful suggestions and comments that contributed more than they could ever know. As a Civil War historian venturing into the field of Appalachian studies, I quickly realized my painful lack of familiarity with sources and historiography. These learned gentlemen supplied helpful criticism and direction which added to and strengthened the project. John Inscoe's work on North Carolina had a profound impact on my own research and made me curious about what was happening on the Tennessee side of the Smoky Mountains. Our good friend Durwood was always after me to keep going and revise my dissertation before someone encroached on my topic. I cannot thank him enough for pushing. And although they are not Civil War or even Southern historians, my old friends and former office mates at the University of Tennessee, Wayne Morris and Ralph Brown, deserve special mention and re-membrance for our long discussions and debates over the meaning and use of history, all of which taught me more than any classroom experience.

My family, of course, played a seminal role in this book. My parents affectionately instilled in me at an early age a passion and a respect for the past, through the Sunday afternoon drives down Monument Avenue in Richmond, the battlefield tours of places like Shiloh and Appomattox, and the gift of Douglas Southall Freeman's *Lee's Lieutenants* on my eleventh birth-day. My mother in law encouraged my scholarly pursuits and challenged me to become a historian. And my darling wife, Karen, was my moral and financial pillar of support during the long years in graduate school and beyond, always urging me onward. She knows that I could not have done this without her devotion and her love.

The greatest debt of all, however, is due my dissertation director and mentor, Paul H. Bergeron, longtime editor of the *Papers of Andrew Johnson.* Paul's skill as a writer, editor, and historian attracted me to him when I first entered graduate school, and my admiration of him has only grown through the years. Our friendship was a great source of strength for me during my graduate career and tenure as director of the East Tennessee Historical Society. His guidance, patience, and unfailing belief in me and my ability makes this work as much his as it is mine. Only the errors be-long to me.

A Land that Can Flow
with Milk and Honey

Early on the morning of May 14, 1858, excursion trains chugged out from the depots at Bristol and Knoxville and wound their way slowly through the rolling green hills of the Valley of Tennessee. As they approached each other from opposite directions, they stopped at a spot two and a half miles west of the village of Blue Springs in Greene County, Tennessee, where the last remaining rail of the East Tennessee and Virginia Railroad lay beside the grading, waiting to be heaved into place. Work on the 130-mile road had begun nearly seven years earlier and had progressed steadily but slowly, its promoters battling adverse financial conditions and the skepticism of many East Tennesseans all the way. Now, at last, the line was complete. At the appointed hour, a group of dignitaries, including the railroad president, directors, engineers and contractors, and various other onlookers gathered to witness the driving of the last spike. As the hammer came down, John McGaughey, former state senator and railroad director, stepped forward and declared that East Tennesseans, "after a bondage of 88 years, since the germ of a civil community was first planted upon the banks of the beautiful Watauga, have . . . crossed the Jordan to till the land, that can now be made to flow with milk and honey."[1]

The completion of the East Tennessee and Virginia Railroad was the culmination of a major campaign to link East Tennessee with the important markets and cities of the Atlantic seaboard and Deep South. The need for a predictable and inexpensive line of communication with the outside world had become painfully clear to many residents of the Great Valley by the 1830s.[2] Most of these "boosters" realized that the serious economic problems facing East Tennessee during the first quarter of the nineteenth century were the product of the region's mountainous geography. More remote from major markets than other parts of Appalachia, such as the Valley of Virginia or western North Carolina, East Tennessee was literally hemmed in on its eastern and western frontiers by high mountain ranges that restricted access to markets and channeled the trade of the first settlers back into Virginia and down the Shenandoah Valley to the port city of Baltimore. Faced with these restrictions, the new residents of what was then almost the entire state of Tennessee began to search for interregional avenues of trade. It was the hope of some that the Tennessee River, which flows southward through the heart of the Great Valley, would become a suitable route. Surplus farm produce was loaded onto flatboats and then floated down the river for sale in markets in New Orleans and, as the cotton culture spread into northern Alabama, in the Tuscumbia–Florence area.

This water route, however, only partially alleviated the problem of geographic isolation. It was not only long and roundabout but also seriously hampered by numerous "sucks," sandbars, and narrow gorges, and worst of all by the difficult passage required at Muscle Shoals. When the flatboats reached the dangerous waters of the Shoals, they were unloaded and their cargo then transported overland by wagon, a laborious process that only added to the time and expense of transportation to market.[3]

Turnpikes and roads offered a better, albeit still imperfect, alternative to reaching markets at great distances, especially when it came to transporting livestock and grain. Knoxville, situated in the heart of the Great Valley, became the trade center from which routes radiated like spokes on a wheel, stretching out to the cities of the lower South and Virginia. The Carolinas were reached down the valley of the French Broad River and into Asheville, where the road branched, moving on into eastern North Carolina or passing through the Saluda Gap and along the Saluda River into the Palmetto State. Access to Georgia was gained via the Tennessee River near Chattanooga or to the east of that city through Unicoi or Woody's Gap. It was also possible to enter Georgia by crossing into South Carolina and then swinging back to the west across the Savannah and Tugaloo Rivers. Drovers could reach Alabama or southwestern Virginia and the cities of Lynchburg and Richmond by herding livestock directly north or south along the Tennessee Valley.[4]

Hog driving was a more economical means by which to get grains, especially corn, to market. Since hauling corn out of East Tennessee was a long and expensive process, most of what was grown was fed to hogs, which in turn were driven to the cities of the southern Atlantic seaboard. Other corn was grown and sold to drovers from Kentucky as feed for their animals as they passed through the region.[5] During hog-driving season, thousands of bushels of corn were consumed as the columns of pork were headed down the valley. In the French Broad alone, it was estimated by tollgate keepers that anywhere from 150,000 to 175,000 hogs a year were herded

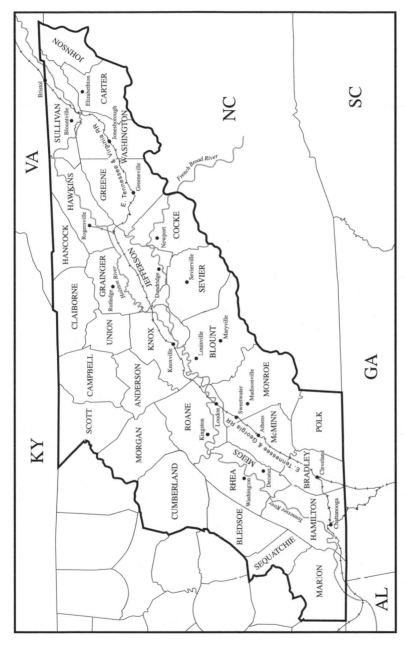

East Tennessee in 1861. Map by Deborah Cahill.

into the Carolinas.[6] To one observer along the French Broad, viewing the "parade of hogs as they gathered from far and near," it appeared as if "all the world were hogs and all the hogs of the world had been gathered there, destined for the Carolina slaughter pens and the cotton growers smokehouses."[7] Indeed, so much pork was raised in Tennessee before the Civil War that residents of the state became known, somewhat derisively, as "the hog drivers."[8]

Yet even if they were superior to water communication, roads and turnpikes were still a slow and difficult, not to mention expensive, way to reach distant markets. Dirt roads received only minimal maintenance; their condition was described by one observer as "execrable." This was especially true of intraregional routes, those that connected towns and villages with rural districts. Wagons and teams easily broke down or wore out as they strained up and down the hilly countryside or became stranded in the ruts which invariably developed along the uneven surfaces. Surprisingly little attention was paid to building macadamized roads, though rocks were abundant. According to Killebrew, only one macadamized route, from Morristown to Cumberland Gap, had been completed by the time of the war.[9]

Although it is clear that East Tennesseans were sending hogs and corn down the Tennessee River and various roads to cities in the Deep South and along the Atlantic seaboard, it is less clear what markets were actually consuming this produce. Traditionally, scholars have argued that by the mid-antebellum period, East Tennessee had become a major source of pork and corn for vast sections of black-belt Alabama, Piedmont Georgia, and the plantation districts of the Carolinas, areas which produced little foodstuffs.[10] Not only could farmers and planters in these regions ill afford to shift valuable land out of cotton production into food, but also Tennessee hogs and corn were inexpensive enough that it was more efficient to buy what they needed rather than raise it themselves. "The more fertile a district," William L. Barney has observed, "the greater was the specialization in staple crop production." Barney figured that no more than one in twenty of Deep South planters met their own food needs. Instead, they alleviated their deficiencies in corn and meat by importing these products from the upper South.[11] More recently, Robert Gallman, William K. Hutchinson, and Diane Linstrom have argued that the Deep South in general and the plantation districts specifically were self-sufficient in foodstuffs, despite the vast acreage committed to cotton production in these areas. These researchers have suggested that, rather than reaching hungry planters and slaves in the black belt, corn and hogs from the upper South made their way to either the urban centers in the Gulf states and along the southern Atlantic seaboard or markets in New York and Europe (the Crimean War increased food demand for armies fighting across the Atlantic).[12]

The debate generated over markets for upper South foodstuffs is important but in the end not necessarily pertinent to this study. What does matter is this: Regardless of its final destination, the produce of East Tennessee was, in general, carried to ports (and eventually railheads) in Virginia, South Carolina, Alabama, and Georgia, economically linking the towns and villages of the Tennessee Valley to cities such as Savannah, Richmond, Charleston, Montgomery, and Augusta, and the commission merchants located there, as a cursory reading of market reports and advertisements in any antebellum East Tennessee newspaper makes perfectly clear.[13] That the foodstuffs of the Great Valley might have been eaten by Southern urban dwellers or planters or New Yorkers or Europeans is not as important as the fact that East Tennessee's trade was sought and captured by the factors of the Atlantic seaboard cities. Most East Tennesseans involved in this trade only knew or cared that a commission merchant in Augusta or Charleston was interested in purchasing their produce.

So while restricted access to markets made trade difficult, it did not prevent the integration of antebellum East Tennessee into the Southern economy. Contrary to the popular notion that a self-sufficient form of agriculture persisted in the Great Valley throughout the Civil War, farmers in the region were able to grow and then transport surpluses of meat and corn to market. Recent scholarship has challenged the concept of East Tennessee's isolation and has shown that the region, along with other parts of Appalachia, quickly shifted to commercial agriculture after settlement and continued to function as a part of the market economy. All sorts of people—corn and hog farmers, drovers, those who fed the hogs and sheltered the drovers, and the town and country merchants—participated in the trade loop. Indeed, the region was so sufficiently integrated into the Southern market that, as shall be seen, trade connections influenced political choices when the sectional crisis erupted in 1861.[14]

Integration into the market economy, however, did not mean that all East Tennessee farmers were well off. Despite the widely accepted view of historians (and many contemporary visitors) that most farmers lived comfortably and land ownership was relatively common, East Tennessee's economy was much more complex, with greater disparity of wealth than previously accepted.[15] While there were few plantations in the valley and the majority of East Tennesseans were able to obtain the basic necessities of life, recent scholarship has revealed that there were still great differences between the material resources of households able to produce for the market and those restricted to a subsistence life-style. For instance, Robert Tracy McKenzie has found that the percentage of landless households in upper East Tennessee was far greater than previously calculated by historians such as Frank Owsley, who argued that the majority of farmers before the war owned their own land.[16] Indeed, Paul Salstrom contends that economic conditions on the eve of the Civil War were deteriorating so badly that southern Appalachia was entering into the first stages of a demographic crisis, as population growth dangerously exceeded the supply of arable farm land.[17]

Slave ownership was even less widespread than land ownership. A hog and corn economy fostered little need for black labor. This is vividly illustrated by the fact that, in 1860, only two counties—Jefferson and Knox—could boast that more than 6 percent of its citizens were slaveholders. Of those East Tennesseans who owned slaves, 85 percent held less than ten. Only one man in 1860 could claim possession of more than one hundred bondsmen.[18] Slaveholding density was also quite low. Chase C. Mooney discovered that the ratio of slave to whites was about one to twelve, and in some counties the figures dropped to about one slave for every sixty whites.[19]

Small slaveholding patterns were indicative of the relatively few slaves as a percentage of the valley's overall population. On the eve of the Civil War, less than 10 percent of the region's population was slave. In the eight largest slaveholding counties (Greene, Hamilton, Hawkins, Jefferson, Cocke, Knox, McMinn, and Roane), slaves comprised 10.9 percent of the population; their numbers had increased only slightly since 1790, when they were 8.6 percent of the inhabitants.[20] Indeed, one historian argues that the number of slaves as a proportion of the population reached its zenith quite early, around 1810.[21]

Notwithstanding the fact that the majority of East Tennesseans were nonslaveholders, relatively large numbers of bondsmen resided in the region's cities and towns. Although the majority of the region's few slaves were distributed throughout the rural districts, there were many blacks in the cities. In fact, a larger proportion of urban dwellers than country people were slaves. In most of East Tennessee's largest urban areas, slaves comprised as much as one-quarter of the population, and in some cases, more than one-third. In 1850, for example, 22.4 percent of the inhabitants of Knoxville, 24.4 percent of Maryville, and 30.0 percent of Kingston were slaves, in counties that were only 11.6, 8.7, and 12.7 percent slave, respectively. Similarly, by 1860 the percentage of slaves residing in Athens had reached 35.0, although this represented only 11 percent of the total slaves in McMinn County. This pattern was nearly identical to those in other parts of Appalachia, especially western North Carolina, where, although the "peculiar institution" was agriculturally focused, many slaves were held by the professional and business classes located in the cities and towns.[22]

As demand for hogs and grain continued strong during the first half of the nineteenth century, an increasing number of East Tennesseans searched for a better way to meet that requirement by linking the rich farmlands of their region with outside markets. Not surprisingly, these East Tennessee boosters turned to the newly developed railroad as the one internal improvement that would bring greater economic prosperity to their region. In their estimation, the railroad would offer the best means by which to overcome the difficulty which geography had placed on transportation routes out of the valley. The attitude of Robert Y. Hayne was typical of the optimism felt by many. A South Carolinian and Charleston resident, Hayne vigorously lobbied in East Tennessee for rail connection between his state and city and the bread basket of the Great Valley. In a speech before a convention of railroad promoters in Knoxville, Hayne declared that the benefits of the "iron horse" were such that "trade, in all its branches, will be doubled, and the demand for labor, and all the productions of industry, so increased so as to give a new face to the whole country."[23] His words fell on receptive ears. For many ambitious East Tennesseans, the railroad would become the means by which to elevate both their region's and their own social and economic positions by forging a link with what they considered to be their natural economic and social allies in the southern Atlantic states.

Chief among the advocates of railroad trade with the lower South was Dr. J. G. M. Ramsey of Knoxville, who was, according to historian Stanley Folmsbee, the "first in East Tennessee to envision the possibilities of rail communication with the Atlantic seaboard."[24] One of the few men in the region to whom the term "original secessionist" can be applied, no one more than Ramsey was so clearly associated in public imagination with the campaign to bring railroads to the valley. As early as 1828, Ramsey was beginning to advocate publicly that the railroad, not the river, eventually would be the major artery for the trade of East Tennessee. River communication, he argued, could never hope to provide the region with the same benefits as "land communication with Charleston and Augusta," cities where there would be less competition from the produce of the West than in New Orleans.[25]

J. G. M. Ramsey (c. 1850), leader of the economic reform of the pre–Civil War years and the region's most outspoken secessionist. Courtesy of McClung Historical Collection, Knoxville.

Inspired by Ramsey's dream of an Atlantic connection, leaders of lower East Tennessee began laying plans to unite with a railroad under construction in Georgia, which was to run from Augusta to the Tennessee River and then on to Memphis. Despite several false starts and near bankruptcy, the East Tennessee and Georgia Railroad, as the new line was christened, was completed by the summer of 1855.[26] In June of that year, the first train ever to enter Knoxville rolled into town amid crowds of rejoicing citizens. "We vividly realized," reported one observer, "that a new era for Knoxville had arrived."[27] The city, and indeed all of lower East Tennessee, finally possessed a reliable and inexpensive connection with the markets of the Atlantic seaboard.

Simultaneous with the organization of the East Tennessee and Georgia in the late 1840s, interest in railroads spread to upper East Tennessee as well. Following conventions held in Rogersville, Jonesboro, and Greeneville, the state legislature granted a charter of incorporation to the East Tennessee and Virginia Railroad Company in January 1848. Ground was broken in the spring of 1851; and a little over seven years later, the last spike was driven.[28] At that moment, an uninterrupted route existed between New York and Atlanta, with lines going on to Pensacola, Augusta, Charleston, and Montgomery. At a time of increasing sectional conflict, the newly completed railroad was perceived by many as the instrument by which the Union would be preserved. In language strangely reminiscent of Henry Clay's "American System," one East Tennessean optimistically boasted that "the completion of this route is not merely the union of Knoxville and Bristol, but the binding together of the North and South with a bond indissoluble."[29] The irony of it all was that the railroad ultimately unleashed forces completely counter to the hopes of its promoters, forces that would divide, rather than unite, the people of East Tennessee.

As the railroad began to make its way into the valley, a major change occurred in the region's farming economy. Now that the Atlantic seaboard, including markets and ports in the cities of Virginia, Georgia, and South Carolina, was more easily accessible, agriculture in East Tennessee witnessed the development of a new cash crop. By the middle of the 1850s, valley farmers were beginning to move away from raising their traditional staples of corn and hogs and toward the planting of wheat, a cereal that had been grown for years in small quantities but which now, because of the railroad, would become one of the chief money crops of East Tennessee. The coming of the railroad marked the shift from a largely self-sufficient agricultural economy that produced surpluses for the market to a more commercialized form of farming.

During the last decade of the antebellum period, the Great Valley experienced a wheat boom. Across the region, production of the grain rose on average a staggering 384 percent between 1850 and 1860. In contrast, corn production grew only a little over 6 percent, while hog raising actually dropped by nearly 25 percent. Although corn still outstripped wheat in terms of total number of bushels grown (12,929,163 to 2,339,497), much of the corn raised was intended for home consumption, to be eaten by man and beast, while wheat found its way onto the export market. To accommodate this new demand, East Tennessee farmers had to bring more land under cultivation, increasing their improved acreage on average by nearly 25 percent, although total farm size only rose on average by about 4 percent. Also reflective of rising wheat demand was the welcomed change in the value of farms, which increased by a healthy 193 percent between 1850 and 1860.[30]

The boom was felt almost immediately. Even before completion of the East Tennessee and Georgia, farmers, but especially the townspeople who handled the shipment of the grain, were experiencing the blessings of the "iron horse." The *Rogersville Times*, obviously in anticipation of the opening of the road in its community, reported that the people of Cleveland and Charleston in lower East Tennessee were already seeing the "good effects of Railroad advantages." "Instead of drawing off their wheat and oats as they formerly have done at this season of the year," the paper enthused, "they are disposing of both at wholesale—and at very fair prices."[31] Soon the coastal cities of Georgia and South Carolina, as well as rail centers in Piedmont Georgia, began to receive East Tennessee wheat and flour. "Charleston and Savannah are beginning to regard our wheat crop, as an item of importance," declared the *Knoxville Register* in 1857. The editor went on to detail the vast quantity of Tennessee wheat expected to be shipped to South Carolina.[32] The Virginia cities of Petersburg, Lynchburg, and Richmond, as well as Charleston, South Carolina, were common destinations for the wheat crop of upper East Tennessee, while that grown around and below Knoxville found its way to such places as Macon, Augusta, Columbus, Atlanta, Savannah, New Orleans, and Charleston. Commission merchants from these points advertised extensively in East Tennessee newspapers seeking wheat and flour. Indicative of the great demand for the grain, merchants in Atlanta and Augusta announced that they were devoting themselves exclusively to purchasing wheat and flour during 1857.[33]

If cotton was king in the Deep South and West Tennessee, then wheat wore the crown in the Tennessee Valley. Other traditional products, such as butter, corn, and hogs, were still in demand, but wheat was by far the most sought-after commodity. Whereas pork and corn had dominated market reports prior to 1850, after that time wheat joined them at the center of regional business concern. "Wheat is now almost the only staple we have, and either the raw material or flour is the only article we have to send to market," claimed the *Knoxville Southern Citizen.* "It is true we send forward much bacon, feathers, and stock, but receipts from these are by no means large."[34] East Tennessee wheat became such an important staple that, by 1858, it commanded a premium on the New York market.[35] "For the past month, the transactions, for the single article of wheat, have been exceedingly heavy," reported the *Knoxville Register* during the late summer of 1855. "Immense amounts have been sold here, and for *cash,* thus giving a reality and vitality to the trade, not before felt for many years. Following this our merchants may expect an unusually active business."[36] The editors of the *Knoxville Southern Citizen* related that orders for flour from factors in New York, Charleston, and Augusta had been so great during the second week of March 1858 that they were "beyond their [the Knoxville Mills Company] capacity to supply." Knoxville flour was so good, the paper boasted, that it commanded "fuller prices than that from any other mills in the country."[37]

Production of wheat and flour only increased as demand during the 1850s remained at an all-time high. Indeed, so much wheat was grown that some feared the price would be driven down. The editors of one East Tennessee newspaper remarked that "we have never seen or heard tell of as much wheat being raised in this part of the country." In Blount County, farmers were carried away with a sort of wheat fever. During a one-week period in August 1857, twenty to thirty wagons a day were depositing their cargo of grain at the county seat of Maryville, and large quantities were also being hauled to the Holston (present-day Tennessee) River town of Louisville. "The depots on the Rail Road are crowded," reported the *Maryville East Tennessean,* "the cars not being able to ship it [wheat] as fast as it is deposited."[38] During the twelve-month period ending October 31, 1858, 3,117,211 pounds of wheat and 834,384 pounds of flour, accounting for over four-fifths of all outgoing freight, were shipped from the town of Jonesboro alone. Indicative of the large quantities of grain and flour being shipped southward, 5,784,061 bushels of wheat, 350,917 barrels of flour, and 719,026 sacks of flour were sent from Chattanooga down the Western and Atlantic Railroad into Georgia between 1852 and 1859, the peak years of the wheat boom. Even hogs were being loaded onto rail cars for shipment southward, rather than being sent by the traditional method of driving.[39]

Another reason for wheat's popularity stemmed from the relative ease with which it could be raised. Planting was a simple affair. Fields were cleared and plowed and the seed was then scattered and covered with a harrow during the fall months. Little, if any, manure was used in the process. Almost no cultivation was required after planting, and farmers could usually enjoy a relatively long "laying by" time during which they could attend to other chores. The grain was allowed to mature during the winter and harvested the following summer, usually in June. Despite the fact that the reaper and threshing machine were available to farmers as early as the 1830s, few were used, largely because the uneven valley surfaces and steep hillsides limited their use to only the flat bottom land lying immediately adjacent to rivers. As a result, harvesting was generally accomplished in the same manner that it had been for generations, with a sickle, scythe, or cradle. The seed would then be threshed by flailing or trampling it beneath the feet of cattle or horses. The average yield was from seven to nine bushels an acre, although some of the more fertile counties in upper East Tennessee could get almost fifteen per acre.[40]

One side effect of expanded wheat production in East Tennessee was a concomitant rise in the region's slave population. Notwithstanding the fact that wheat growing required only minimal cultivation, its explosive appearance on the agricultural scene apparently required an expanded labor force to keep up with demand. Across the region the total number of slaves rose almost 21 percent between 1850 and 1860, while slaves as a proportion of the total population increased on average about 18 percent. The change was most dramatic in those counties experiencing the greatest upswing in wheat production—Meigs, Monroe, Polk, Rhea, and Sullivan—where the total number of slaves shot up over 30 percent. Growth in the slave community outpaced even that of whites. Total number of whites increased on average throughout the counties of East Tennessee about 14 percent; but as a proportion of the total population, whites actually declined about 1 percent.[41]

While the railroad facilitated the export of produce from East Tennessee, it also encouraged importation of hundreds of visitors from the Deep South. A region that previously had seemed remote and cut off from the mainstream of Southern society now appeared much closer to many Southerners. "Let the Southern planter and his 'delicate lady,' desirous of escaping from the exhaling of the miasma . . . no longer regard the pure

East Tennessee atmosphere . . . as unattainable," encouraged the *Knoxville Register*.[42] As evidence of Knoxville's new importance in the business world, the annual Southern Commercial Convention was held in that city in August 1857. The avowed purpose of the meeting was to discuss how the Southern states could more easily cooperate in matters of trade and agriculture; although given the number of prominent Southern nationalists, such as J. D. B. DeBow, in attendance, some East Tennessee critics claimed that the convention was nothing more than an opportunity to hatch a secessionist plot. Whatever the real agenda of the meeting might have been, it did present several East Tennesseans, including future Confederate congressman William H. Sneed of Knoxville, who served as vice president of the body, with an opportunity to acquaint themselves with other Southerners, especially those whose political philosophy leaned decidedly toward secession.[43]

Tourism also offered a chance to interact personally with men and women of the Deep South, and, in some cases, even led to the union of families from the two regions. The mild summer climate and beautiful mountain scenery beckoned planters from Georgia and Alabama to visit East Tennessee. There were many watering holes scattered about the region. Chattanooga entrepreneur and nascent secessionist James A. Whiteside opened a hotel on Lookout Mountain in June 1857. The four-story building was complete with cottages for the servants who accompanied the guests, most of whom were from the plantation districts. Other leading hotels included the Ocoee House in Cleveland, Red and White Sulphur Springs near Rogersville, and Allegheny Springs in Blount County, all of which opened in the 1850s.[44]

But no resort enjoyed the prominence or popularity of Montvale Springs in Blount County. The resort's proprietors, H. P. Redding and his successor, Sterling Lanier (grandfather of renowned Southern poet Sidney), were both Georgians who developed Montvale and then advertised its comforts and wonders extensively in newspapers throughout the southern Atlantic and Gulf states.[45] Once rail communication was established with Georgia, Montvale began to bustle. The *Maryville East Tennessean* gleefully reported during the summer of 1857 that the Springs were "'all the go' now-a-days. Passengers go through this place by *fifties*." The editor, James Z. Swan, who in five years would command a company of Confederate infantry from Blount County, optimistically added, "There is already a crowd at that noted watering place and if visitors continue to gather in a few weeks as fast as the past few, they will be crowded." Among the influential vacationers there was S. A. Atkinson, editor of the *Augusta (Ga.) Dispatch*, who, according to Swan, "expressed himself much pleased with the appearance of [the] village and the surrounding countryside."[46] In fact, one visitor noted that by the late 1850s, Georgians predominated among Montvale's numerous Deep South guests.[47]

Such a heavy preponderance of outsiders prompted some enterprising young men to venture up to the Springs to meet the daughters of wealthy Low Country planters in hopes of improving their social status. A prime example was William Gibbs McAdoo, Knoxville lawyer and Southern nationalist, who met and successfully courted at Montvale in 1856 a "beautiful widow" from St. Mary's, Georgia, Mary Faith Floyd, the daughter of Gen. Charles Rinaldo Floyd and granddaughter of Gen. John B. Floyd, War of 1812 hero and renowned Indian fighter. Through their marriage, McAdoo gained thousands of acres of prime Georgia plantation land and hundreds of slaves, to boot. No doubt because of his wife's connection with that state, McAdoo in 1861 moved his family to the Georgia state capital of Milledgeville, where he assisted Governor Joseph E. Brown in organizing the Georgia militia.[48]

Beyond building the tourist industry in East Tennessee, the railroad sparked

William Gibbs McAdoo and Mary Faith Floyd in the early 1850s. Their courtship and eventual marriage illustrated the union of Deep South families with those of the Tennessee Valley as a result of the economic ties created by the railroad. Courtesy of the Georgia Historical Society, Savannah.

a growth in cities and towns that was unparalleled in the region's history. Towns were the center of support for the railroad. Townspeople were the road's most vocal promoters and subscribed most of its stock. Its completion ushered in a new era of prosperity. What in most cases had been little more than villages in 1850, ten years later had doubled, and even tripled, in size. The most notable example of this expansion was Knoxville. The 1860 census reveals that, after its connection to the railroad, Knoxville's population began to soar. Between 1850 and 1860, the city grew from 2,076 to 5,300, an increase of 155.3 percent.[49] With five large commission mercantile firms and twelve dry-goods dealers in operation in 1860, it became the major distribution and merchandising center for the region.[50] Chattanooga, which began as a mere village of several hundred in the late 1830s, had grown so rapidly after the railroad reached the town that, by 1856, it had exceeded the size of the county seat of Harrison and required its own court to handle business matters.[51] Other towns along the rail line, including Cleveland and Charleston, experienced similar patterns of growth.[52]

The railroad even created new towns. The need for convenient points along the route for collection and shipment of farm produce sparked development up and down the valley. Both Bristol, in Sullivan County, and Morristown, built near the juncture of Jefferson, Hawkins, and Grainger Counties, sprang up during construction of the East Tennessee and Virginia Railroad. Despite their late starts, they quickly outgrew many neighboring villages which had been bypassed by the road. Morristown's development was particularly rapid, the railroad transforming it from a mere crossroads in 1850 to a town of five hundred on the eve of the war. "It is concluded that we have the most desirable location in all East Tennessee for a town of unlimited size," boasted the *Morristown Intelligencer* on the day the East Tennessee and Virginia was completed. "The shipments to and from this point are such as to recommend the speedy building of a more sizeable, substantial, and more respectable Depot. We often find our smoke-house Depot insufficient to contain half the articles put off, and consequently the yard is unavoidably occupied in lieu of such Depot deficiencies."[53]

Sweetwater, located in Monroe County, was typical of these new railroad towns. Built as a depot for the county seat of Madisonville, which was nine miles away from the track, Sweetwater quickly eclipsed its parent community. By the time construction on the road reached the infant town around April 1852, streets and lots were already laid off and a depot, which during harvest season would contain thousands of bushels of wheat, was nearing completion. Nearby merchants and businessmen were attracted by Sweetwater's prospects for success, and soon their shops and storehouses lined main street. Other commission merchants, such as future Confederate general John C. Vaughn, erected hotels to accommodate the railroad's numerous travelers. During the summer months, wagons from the surrounding countryside converged on the town to deposit farm products and to carry away groceries and manufactured goods. One resident remembered that "wagon trade at that time was phenomenal." Farmers would queue up in their vehicles and wait an entire day, or more, before unloading their produce. Lines were sometimes so long that a special campground had to be cleared for those who were forced to spend the night. On some evenings it was not unusual to see twenty or thirty wagons parked within the enclosure. Traffic was so heavy that at times the railroad was incapable of providing enough cars to ship the grain immediately, so it had to be stored until sufficient transportation was available.[54]

The greatest beneficiaries of this new trade were the town merchants. Although raising wheat put some cash into the hands of local farmers, most needed manufactured goods or groceries, not money, and they were willing to barter their grain and other foodstuffs for those items they could not grow or make themselves. Moreover, few, if any, sold their produce directly to consumers. The vast majority required the services of a middleman, a role that was performed by store operators and commission merchants. In some important ways, valley merchants served that same function for farmers that cotton factors served for planters of the Deep South.

The store actually became a marketing agent for the farmers' crops. Lewis Atherton, in his study of Southern merchants before the Civil War, argues that in the upper South, there existed a rural economy where cash was scarce and produce was marketed by trade between merchants and farmers. Competition at times was so fierce that, rather than wait for produce to reach the towns, merchants would often intercept farmers coming in from the rural districts laden with produce for sale. Store operators would offer salt, molasses, and other basic necessities in exchange for wheat and corn. They would then travel to the Deep South, sell the produce acquired from farmers, and purchase the dry goods and manufactured goods with which to restock their shelves, thereby continuing the cycle. In Knoxville, for instance, the Bank of Charleston authorized its East Tennessee agent, future Confederate colonel and Democratic politico William M. Churchwell, to make cash advances to valley merchants on produce collected and shipped southward.[55] Atherton describes one highland merchant who traveled about every six weeks to the Low Country selling farm produce and replenishing his store inventory. Atlanta became a major center for wholesale dry goods distribution. Merchants would travel to the city to purchase dry and manufactured goods imported from the North for resale in their retail operations. Extensive advertising in East Tennessee newspapers by hotel owners in Savannah also suggests that it, too, was a common Georgia destination for valley merchants. Some East Tennessee storekeepers even engaged in driving cattle and hogs overland to market. Livestock was bartered for groceries and the animals maintained on the merchant's farm. When a sufficient number had been obtained by this process, they were either sold or headed southward on a drive. Because merchants were usually better acquainted

Future Confederate general John C. Vaughn in the 1850s, when he was a Sweetwater merchant. Courtesy of Thomas County Historical Society, Thomasville, Georgia.

with current market prices, many farmers found this to be a more efficient method to dispose of their surplus meat.[56]

In this manner, great quantities of wheat and other foodstuffs were transported to market. In fact, Atherton contends that this system proved to be "the most stable of various marketing schemes to collect farm crops to export to outside markets."[57] In some instances volume was so great that a few merchants were engaged full time in supplying nothing but the produce of the Great Valley to commission agents in neighboring states. For instance, the Welcker family of Kingston in Roane County assembled produce collected by smaller storekeepers from local farmers and then shipped it for resale in their extensive retail outlet in Talladega, Alabama. The Lenoirs, also of Roane County, conducted a similar sort of operation in addition to their textile mill, which used imported Georgia cotton for spinning into thread and other items.[58] In Meigs County, Decatur merchant Newton J. Lillard attempted to obtain an appointment as a purchasing agent for a Georgia firm. "My situation is two miles from the river and fourteen from the railroad in a settlement where a great deal of surplus wheat is growing," Lillard informed R. H. Patton in Augusta. "You please write & see whether they will make me an agent . . . there is no person buying as an agent in this place." Lillard's books reveal that he was bartering dry and manufactured goods purchased in Charleston, Augusta, and Atlanta for wheat grown in East Tennessee.[59] So much produce was available for market that in Knoxville soon-to-be secessionists William G. Swan and Joseph A. Mabry devised an idea to facilitate its collection. The two generously offered land for the construction of a market house, which the city built in 1853 as a central location for farmers to trade and sell their surpluses to the town's merchants.[60]

As their economy became increasingly interdependent with that of Virginia and the lower South, many sections of East Tennessee began to enjoy an economic prosperity that had not been seen in half a century. Production for the market increased the bartering power of some farmers, put cash in the hands of others (the increase in the number of slaves suggests that there was cash to invest in that form of property), and enhanced the economic status of commission merchants, storekeepers, and the lawyers who handled their legal affairs. Under the headline "New Era in East Tennessee!" a Maryville merchant proclaimed in the pages of the *East Tennessean* that the railroad had brought real buying power to the people of the valley. It had "placed within the reach of every industrious man the means to buy what he wants," he declared, "with the certainty of being able to pay for it."[61] The *Knoxville Register* was equally optimistic. "As we stood last week and saw the swift passenger train dart up to our very city . . . we vividly realized that a new era for Knoxville had arrived," asserted the editor. "Business men at a distance whose eyes have been tempted hither . . . let them no longer delay their coming."[62]

The influx of wealth that the railroad brought to the valley accelerated a trend toward the concentration of merchant and professional classes in the region's cities and towns. Access to markets heretofore less easily reached, and the new money that could be made by exploiting these markets, lured ambitious young men into the business arena. In a land of predominantly small farms, the hustle and bustle of the rail stops and county seats offered the upwardly mobile, such as Knoxville merchant Samuel House, a chance to enhance their social and economic status. Writing to his father attempting to lure him into moving from Georgia to Knoxville, House reported that society in the East Tennessee city was good and, most important, that money could be easily made. "Most all here are parvenues," he disclosed not long after his arrival in 1859. "Money is the standard by which everything is weighed," a prospect that convinced the elder House to bring his entire family permanently from Marietta.[63]

Conditions in Roane County were typical. Among the oldest of counties, Roane had enjoyed an economy as healthy as any in the region. Bounded along its entire eastern border by the Tennessee River, the county was penetrated by the railroad during the late 1850s. In 1860, Roane boasted of four towns and villages of varying sizes and importance. Two of these—Kingston and Post Oak Springs—were situated along major river and road transportation routes. The other two—Loudon and Lenoir's Station—were relatively new railroad hamlets, although Loudon had for sometime flourished as a river port as well. The most significant of these places was the county seat of Kingston, a picturesque, old eighteenth-century town nestled in a bend near the confluence of the Clinch and Tennessee Rivers, with Loudon coming in a close second.[64] Census figures reveal that the county's business-professional middle class was heavily concentrated in these four urban centers. In fact, 87 percent of the merchants, 62 percent of the physicians, and all of the lawyers resided there. In contrast, only a little over 13 percent of farmers lived in a town or village.[65]

The situation in nearby Blount County was remarkably similar. Although it lay outside the railroad's route, the county was traversed along its northern boundary by the Holston River, and connection with the rail line lay just across the numerous ferries which reached over into Knox County. Five towns and villages dotted the countryside: Maryville, Louisville, Friendsville, Unitia, and Morganton. Of these, Maryville, the county seat, and Louisville, a port town on the Holston, were the most important. Even though its population was smaller, Louisville, its shore lined with steamboat landings, merchants' shops, and warehouses, actually overshadowed Maryville as an economic center.[66] As in Roane County, Blount's businessmen and professionals gravitated to the towns. The vast majority of merchants (87 percent), physicians (64 percent), and lawyers (100 percent), were urbanites. Barely 12 percent of those who claimed agriculture as an occupation lived alongside them.[67]

Invariably, economic interdependency also forged closer ties between valley townsfolk, especially merchants and lawyers, and their clients and business partners in the Deep South and Virginia. "The great desideratum has been an outlet to the Southern Market," asserted the *Knoxville Register* the day the trains first rolled into town. "That has been attained." The editor went on to predict that now "a new era, will, before a great while dawn upon us," and that "a great change will be brought upon us in our business and social relations."[68] The business-professional classes of East Tennessee were bound to the commission merchants in Augusta, Richmond, Savannah, and Charleston with a common economic interest that transcended the physical distances between them. Through the long-established economic connections that the railroad firmly cemented, the townspeople of the valley came to have a stake in the continuance of the trade in foodstuffs that linked them to Virginia and the neighboring states to the south.

On a return trip from Montgomery in the winter of 1857, one enthusiastic Chattanoogan reported in the local newspaper that the merchants of the Alabama capital had "a looking-forth eye to the trade and produce of Tennessee." The business community in that city hoped that East Tennesseans would remember that Montgomery was a good place to sell produce and to buy groceries. The Alabamians, he closed, sent this sentiment to the merchants of East Tennessee: "May closer business ties bind more strongly together the two States, and lead largely to promote their mutual prosperity."[69]

The events of 1861 would put those ties to the test.

They Made Me a Rebel

The telegram had just flashed news of the bombardment. Fort Sumter had been fired on by Confederate forces, and James Whiteside was elated. The Chattanooga entrepreneur and railroad promoter had long advocated secession, and now the moment for Tennessee to choose sides had finally arrived. The attack called for a celebration. Whiteside stepped out from his hotel atop Lookout Mountain and walked to a nearby school, where he persuaded the headmaster to allow the young students to accompany him back to the yard of his resort. There, on the brow of the mountain, Whiteside had two barrels of coal tar ignited. The giant bonfire illuminated the spring night, filling the air with its pungent odor. With Whiteside's hotel lit for all of Chattanooga to see, the school boys delivered speeches on the virtues of secession and the girls sang "hastily improvised songs." Tennessee was going out of the Union.[1]

For secessionists like Whiteside, the firing on Fort Sumter and Lincoln's subsequent call for seventy-five thousand volunteers to put down the "rebellion" had occurred none too soon. Ever since the president's election in November 1860, this small but vocal minority of Southern nationalists had advocated that the residents of the Great Valley join their fellow Southerners in protesting the election results by leaving the Union. Most believed that separation not only would, but should, come. As early as 1858, arch-secessionist J. G. M. Ramsey had considered dissolution of the Union as unavoidable. "We are destined to a separation," he confided to a South Carolina friend three years before Sumter. "Sooner or later it must take place. It is inevitable."[2] Ramsey, echoing the arguments of fire-eating extremists like William L. Yancey and Robert Barnwell Rhett, proclaimed that Southern and Northern society had grown incompatible and should divorce one another. Assured that the South was right to consider its institutions and liberties threatened by an increasingly hostile North, secessionists welcomed separation. "I often feel that the South ought to secede," complained future Confederate soldier R. P. Fickle of Sullivan County six months prior to Lincoln's election, "and let the fools of the north see that they must be the greatest sufferers."[3]

Some of East Tennessee's college students were especially vocal advocates of secession. At schools all over the valley, young East Tennesseans petulantly argued in favor of separation. At Washington College outside of Jonesboro, Henry M. Doak was called on by his classmates to lead the secession side of a public debate held on campus in the fall of 1860. Doak, the great-grandson of Samuel Doak, the first resident minister in Tennessee, declared that "slavery was the school in which the lower orders of all countries had learned the way to liberty and a higher life" and avowed himself for secession from the North. The college president, although himself a proslavery advocate, was opposed to disunion and, as Doak put it, persuaded him to "suppress" his ideas.[4] During the same time, Robert M. Rhea delivered at Maryville College one of Yancey's speeches calling for the establishment of a Southern Confederacy. The defiant act so enraged Rhea's professor that the young man was saved from expulsion only by the timely intervention of the college president, "whose sympathies were decidedly Southern." Rhea and his fellow students, among whom was Joseph T. McReynolds, future major of the Thirty-seventh Tennessee Infantry, formed a military company and drilled in the evenings after school.[5] F. K. Berry of Sweetwater boldly gave an address advocating secession at the January 1861 Hiwasee College "Literary Society Celebration." Apparently his remarks met with his classmates' approbation, for twelve of the fifteen members of the college's two literary societies enlisted in the Rebel army during the first year of the war.[6] Although most of the faculty at Tusculum College in Greene County were "ardent Union men," according to one secessionist pupil, "most of the students . . . espoused the cause of the South, and much friction resulted." A number of young scholars, including J. A. Biggs and Charles F. Henley, dropped out and rushed to join the Southern ranks as the secession crisis erupted.[7]

Lincoln's election further emboldened valley secessionists. With their candidate John C. Breckinridge defeated at the polls, Democrats especially became more vocal. "Some Brecks here are for going out of the Union," rejoiced William Gibbs McAdoo from Knoxville. The day after the election, some jokester tied an old tin bucket with a slip of paper inscribed "Going out of the Union" to a dog's tail. The animal "went out rattling along Gay Street quite to the amusement of the crowd." McAdoo hoped that "the vicarious secession" of the dog would "answer all the purposes of his friends and 'Save the Union.'"[8] When Henry M. Doak arrived in town in the fall of 1860, he found the secession flag already floating over Gay Street from a tall pole. The proseparation element was "easily in control," despite threats from the Unionist majority. A secessionist infantry company, the "Knoxville Guards," was drilling on the streets daily[9]. The situation was similar in Rogersville. "I think that the secession and disunion party have gained strength with us during the last ten days," reported one Hawkins County Unionist. "Last summer and fall," he ruefully observed, "we had no secession men among us. Now every village Breckinridge democrat you meet is a secessionist." He charged that their party leaders had become "clamorous secessionists" who intended to make separation the central issue in the next election.[10] While Kyle's observation may be somewhat exaggerated, it is interesting to note his association of secessionist sympathy with townsfolk or, as he styled them, "village democrats." One resident of Monroe County informed Andrew Johnson that "so many of our Citizens are under a state of excitement and talk about *Secession and revolution* as an ordinary matter and apparently without one thought to the ultimate Consequences."[11] Johnson's son related to his father that even in their home town of Greeneville a "Palmetto flag was hoisted on the streets one day by some irresponsible boys but it was soon forced down."[12] In Sullivan County, secessionists such as W. P. Hunt asked if East Tennesseans were "to tamely submit and be driven to a level with the negro or shall we take the Constitution in our own hands and take care of ourselves?"[13]

The answer for some was simple. Ramsey declared, "It is time for separation." Years later he wrote that his "allegiance has always been . . . first to my native Tennessee and second and through her to the United States." Secession was necessary, because, in his opinion, the North "had violated the constitution."[14] *"We are a divided people,"* proclaimed another Knoxville proponent of secession. *"The last link is broken."* Peace and unanimity were impossible, he argued, so long as "this dangerous *leprosy* of *Abolitionism*" was allowed to stand.[15] At least one secessionist could not wait for Tennessee to leave the Union. William Gibbs McAdoo supported the cotton states in their stand against Lincoln's presidency, confiding to his diary, "I go with them, make common cause with them, fight for them to the last drop of my blood." Frustrated by Tennessee's indecision, McAdoo symbolically seceded from the state during the last days of 1860 and relocated in Georgia, his wife's home. "I am a Georgian," he proclaimed. "I came to Georgia to go with her at once out of the union, and to take part in her destinies for weal or for woe."[16] Ramsey also was growing restive. "'Tennessee, you see, is conservative and tardy," he complained, "but when her time comes will secede too." The state's reluctance he blamed on its politicians, who were more concerned with self-advancement than principle. "Her leaders though cannot resist the seduction of Lincoln's patronage," he lamented.[17]

Some of those leaders found little charm in Lincoln's election. In Knoxville, two federal government officials decided that the moment had arrived to sever their ties with Washington. C. W. Charlton resigned as postmaster in February 1861 because, as he explained, he could not "consent to accept office at the hands of Abraham Lincoln." Claiming to be "a Southern rights man and ardently devoted to movements of the Southern cause," Charlton openly professed that he "would infinitely prefer sinking with them [the cotton states] to enjoying the emoluments of office under Black Republican rule."[18] U.S. District Attorney John Crozier Ramsey, eldest son of J. G. M., agreed with Charlton. In tendering his resignation, Ramsey, who was destined to become one of the most hated Rebels in East Tennessee, explained that "being a native of the South," he could not "hold office under one whose policy is to deprive my section of the country of its constitutional rights, and violate the equality of the States."[19]

Such sympathies were not confined to Knoxville. Indeed, throughout East Tennessee, federal employees, especially those in the postal service, were suspected of disloyalty to the new administration. Their secessionist sympathy is not surprising, since Democrats had dominated the White House for nearly a decade. The patronage dispensed by grateful Democratic presidents to those seeking federal offices in the region placed the postal routes of East Tennessee in the hands of secessionists. A Unionist in Blount County requested a copy of Andrew Johnson's antisecession speech, but suggested that it be sent to the post office in Knoxville because "the P.Ms. at this place [Louisville] and Maryville are Vile Disunionists and suppress such Docs. as those you sent to them to destribute."[20] The postmaster at Cedar Creek in Greene County was described as "a damned secession traitor" who "ought by all means be turned out."[21] Cleveland postmaster Thomas W. Johnson, a Buchanan appointee, was referred to as "a red hot disunionist" by a Bradley County Tory.[22] From Rogersville, Andrew Johnson learned that his "old friend" Andrew R. Edmonds, who had served as postmaster since 1853 "has gone off . . . on *secession* and I think dont expect to continue as Post Master," while William H. Crouch, postmaster of Jonesboro, who was characterized as "a *disunionist* of the deepest *dye*," resigned shortly after Lincoln's inauguration.[23] The *Athens Post* reported that future Confederate general John C. Vaughn was "removed from the post office at Sweetwater . . . [because] he is too strong a democrat for Lincoln."[24]

News of Lincoln's election triggered a series of public meetings calling for a state convention to decide what course Tennessee would take now that a "Black Republican" would soon occupy the White House. In Knoxville, a meeting of moderate Unionists, such as law partners John M. Baxter and John M. Fleming and future Confederate colonel John J. Reese, was held in early December to call on the governor to push for a convention. "It is no longer a question of Union or Disunion," the attendees maintained. "The Union is, we may say, already dissolved. It is only for Tennessee to determine whether she will connect herself with a Southern or Northern Confederacy." Later that same month, another meeting was held at the Knox County courthouse. Led by a committee composed of the town's leading secessionists, including William H. Sneed, William A. Branner, J. G. M. Ramsey, William C. Kain, William G. Swan, and John H. Crozier, the assemblage, on the same day that South Carolina seceded, adopted a resolution favoring a convention. It declared that "the preservation of the Union . . . is the object nearest the heart of the people of Tennessee, but when the Union becomes subversive of these ends, its existence is no longer desirable to them." Those in attendance proclaimed their support for the cotton states, and opposed "any coercive measures towards any of said states."[25] On December 31, Maryville secessionists, including John E. Toole, Samuel Pride, and J. G. Wallace, convened a similar meeting at the Blount County courthouse to present a list of grievances against Lincoln and the Republican Party and to clamor for a convention of the slaveholding states. The following day, secessionists in nearby Louisville expressed their desire for a state convention and resolved that "if a majority of the Southern States dissolve their connection with the Federal Government and form a Southern Confederacy, we are for Tennessee going with the South at all hazards and to the last extremity."[26] Citizens in Meigs County were not content to wait on the constitutional process and simply adopted an ordinance of secession in late January.[27]

In response to such pressure in East Tennessee and around the state, the legislature in mid-January complied with a request from Governor Isham G. Harris for a February referendum on whether Tennessee should hold a convention to consider secession. The legislature also authorized the selection of delegates, so that another election would not be necessary, should the convention be approved. Immediately valley secessionists launched a campaign to convince the people of their section to vote in favor of the convention and to embrace separation from the Union.[28] Although he declined nomination as a delegate from Monroe County, John C. Vaughn warned his fellow East Tennesseans that "the cry of Union for the sake of Union, at this time in his opinion, was treason to Republican liberty."[29] In announcing his candidacy as a delegate, William H. Sneed of Knoxville railed against the abolitionists and asserted that "there is no hope but under the hammer and shield of our own state cooperating with the South."[30] "The only question for Tennessee to decide," averred a Monroe County disunionist, "is whether she will go with the South or still remain as the tail end of a Northern confederacy." He assured those who might have any doubts that "Old Monroe is all right" on the issue of separation.

Pro-Confederate newspapers in the region joined in agitating for support of the convention. Typical was the position assumed by the secessionist *Chattanooga Advertiser,* which began running a series of editorials calculated to persuade the unconvinced that unification with the newly formed Confederacy was the only recourse left to East Tennesseans. Under the title "Tennessee Not a Border State," the paper's editors argued that the Volunteer state was a part of the Deep South. "It is a misnomer to call Tennessee a border state," the paper declared. "All of her surroundings are Southern and slaveholding, and if she fails to unite with the South, she will present an example of degrading servility to Black Republican domination." In another column, the editors, perhaps fearing that the mass of voters would not be persuaded by simple appeals to Southern unity, raised the specter of racial equality. East Tennesseans, they argued, should not "be placed on the broad platform of social and political equality with the kinky head." The state's salvation, they averred, "depends on her uniting with her Southern sisters."[31] The *Knoxville Register* also called for Southern unity and white solidarity. At the same time that Parson Brownlow was telling East Tennesseans that they had no interests in common with the cotton states, the *Register* was arguing that "it is the duty and interest of Tennessee to go with the South." The paper's editor, George W. Bradfield, charged that "Lincoln repudiates all distinction on account of color. . . . According to his doctrine the *Negro* is as good as the White man." Bradfield urged his readers not to vote for candidates who were in favor of "coercion and civil war" but to "go for the South and against coercion and Negro equality." He proclaimed optimistically that "secession is a fixed fact."[32]

Upper East Tennessee also had its share of secessionist journals. Indeed, so many newspapers in the area advocated secession that the *Jonesboro Express* was compelled to admit that it was "the only political paper published in the first Congressional District that opposes the made scheme of the disunionists."[33] The *Bristol News,* which was under the editorship of J. Austin Sperry before he took over the helm of the *Knoxville Register* in March 1861 and transformed it into the mouthpiece for the secessionists (and later for the Confederate government) of East Tennessee, was particularly outspoken. Another paper enlisted in the fight for separation was the *Jonesboro Union,* which came out strongly in support of Landon Carter Haynes, an avowed disunionist candidate, as a delegate to the convention. The *Union's* editor, A. G. Graham, saw little hope in fighting to preserve the Union. "Those who are engaged in this weak-minded business," he insisted, "might as well be singing psalms to a dead horse."[34]

Such posturing was intended for consumption not only by the large number of Unionist voters but also by those defenders of Southern rights who still did not believe that the crisis had arisen which justified splitting the nation. The advocates of immediate secession faced stiff opposition from such hard-line Unionists as William G. Brownlow and Andrew Johnson; and they also had to persuade those who believed in the constitutionality of secession that the hour had arrived for action. This latter group, known as "conditional Unionists," represented the vast majority of those who eventually sided with the Confederacy. In his recent study of Unionism in the upper South, Daniel Crofts describes these people as "reluctant Confederates"—that is, Rebels who attempted to avert war and were forced by events to choose sides with the South. Clinging to the hope that the new president would not use force to coerce the seceded states back into the Union, they were part of an upper South Unionist coalition that worked for a compromise to hold the country together.[35]

But unlike unconditional Unionists, such as Brownlow and Johnson, who supported the Union at any cost, conditional Unionists placed qualifications on their commitment to national unity. Basically, they fell into two broad, sometimes overlapping, categories. On one hand were those whom Crofts terms as "anticoercionists," who would oppose secession only so long as Lincoln did not make a military strike against the South.[36] "For myself," confided one resident of Jefferson County, "much as I am for union—I pray God there be no shedding of blood. Let that happen and the severance is perpetual."[37] The wife of ultra-Unionist Horace Maynard angrily expressed to one Northerner that "any attempt at coercion will be madness & wickedness. Every man in the South is a soldier; & even the negroes would fight as they did in the Revolutionary [War]."[38] At a meeting at New Market in Jefferson County, Southern rights advocates resolved that should the Federal government "attempt to put into practice the odious doctrine, that the negro and the white man are equal in all respects, that we will resist with all the powers which nature and nature's God has placed in our hands." They added that "we are opposed to the use of force by any power, to coerce the free people of any of the Seceding States."[39] Apparently Democrats recognized the sensitivity concerning Northern aggression and used the issue to drum up support for secession. Following an impassioned plea to Congress to accept the Crittenden Compromise, T. A. R. Nelson was advised by a friend, "I am glad in your speech you have said nothing of the right of coertion—sentiment is very divided on that question—Democracy having done all the development—oppose coertion." Peck added that "Tennessee [is] so far right but let the North continue her course and she will join the South—the feeling even in E. Tenn. is at present that way, nothing but a desire to know the course of Lincoln."[40]

Joining with the anticoercionists in the conditional Unionist crowd were the "extended ultimatumists," those who would stay in the Union so long as there existed a reasonable hope for compromise. In other words, they would place demands on the new Lincoln government, seeking security for the South and its institutions; if these were not met, they would advocate a peaceful separation.[41] For example, in late November the editors of the *Greeneville Democrat* calmly asserted that "our convictions are . . . opposed to anything like present [immediate] secession." They favored instead calling a convention of slave states to draft a bill of rights, which, should it be rejected by the North, would be a signal for secession. Echoing the arguments of the anticoercionists, the paper drew the sword, claiming that "secession is a right belonging to the States of which it will be wrong to deprive them by coercion," adding that, "in our opinion that right is very clear."[42] A group of Monroe Countians, at a meeting in Madisonville, declared that if Washington failed to protect the South's constitutional rights, "we are then ready to join our Southern sisters in a disruption of the Federal Government as the best means left us to vindicate our honor and preserve our rights."[43] In a similar vein the *Athens Post* argued that "the North must be made to feel her dependence on the South—and must be made to feel that the South is a unit and will demand her just Constitutional rights. . . . Otherwise we can see nothing else but that the Union is lost."[44] A Greeneville Democrat informed T. A. R. Nelson that the people of East Tennessee desired "redress by all honorable means in the union and under the Constitution of their fathers and to the last extremity"; only then, he concluded, "if nothing avail, [should there be] an honorable and gallant withdrawal of the whole South . . . from the vile contact of New

England. As John Letcher of Virginia says—'to slough them off.'"[45] At least one conditional Unionist suggested that not the South, but the North, should be forced into separation. "The South ought to meet in convention and in a respectful manner demand her rights," he urged, "and if not granted then let the whole South move together and take possession of the Capitol as belonging to us."[46]

Returns from the special election in February 1861, calling for a state convention, reveal that most East Tennesseans were still willing to compromise. Slightly less than 20 percent of voters in the region favored a convention, and proconvention advocates carried only two counties—Sullivan and Meigs—both traditional Democrat strongholds. More significant, secessionist delegates to the convention suffered an overwhelming defeat at the hands of their Unionist opponents. For instance, in Blount County, Unionist John F. Henry swamped secessionist William S. Prater by a vote of 1,762 to 234. In Hancock County secession candidates Samuel Powel and Reuben Arnold together garnered less than 200 votes, while their opponents received nearly 1,500. The Union candidate in Roane County won by 1,684 to 68; his counterpart in Jefferson County garnered 2,000 more votes than the secession delegate. Similar defeats were experienced in Grainger, Greene, Hawkins, and Cocke Counties, where Unionist candidates won handily by a margin of seven to one.[47]

The results in East Tennessee were in stark contrast to those in the middle and western sections of the state, where 48 and 74 percent, respectively, of the voters cast ballots for a convention. In fact, East Tennesseans played the decisive role in defeating the convention movement. Nearly 50 percent of the almost seventy thousand statewide votes against calling a convention were cast in East Tennessee.[48] Southern rights advocates were painfully aware that their section had handed Unionists a stunning victory. "One of our Gay street merchants remarked upon our streets this week," reported the *Whig*, "that 'this,' meaning Knoxville, 'is a d——d Abolition hole,' and as far as South of our river, it was a *puke* of an abolition hole, or words to that effect."[49] When a Nashville reporter wrote back from Greeneville that "the people of this country were for the Union 'without an if,'" he struck a sensitive spot for one East Tennessee secessionist. "Being unwilling to lay under such a slander," the outraged Greeneville disunionist complained to the editor of the Nashville *Union and American*, "and believing it to be true to our town, myself, and my friends, I beg leave to contradict any such statements as it is too vile a slander to rest under."[50] A Knoxvillian informed Andrew Johnson that secessionists were "furious with rage at the result of the election on the 9th" and were accusing Union men of being "submissionists."[51] Although Parson Brownlow hailed the results as a sure sign that Tennessee was firmly in the Union, some Unionists sensed that, for secessionists, the February defeat was only a temporary setback. "The disunionists are defeated, but they will work more unceasing to accomplish their design than Ever," warned a Bradley County Unionist. "They have Entered the wedge and will continue to strike untill the Maul is wrested from their hands."[52] Another Unionist expressed similar fears. "Gov. Harris, & Landon C. Haynes, are nowhere," he crowed. "Haynes, openly avowed secession here not long since. They both are dead as hell, and buried, and upon their backs is written 'No resurrection—' However, if Tennessee, secedes hereafter," he added ominously, "they may be resurrected."[53]

Fortunately for them, secessionists did not have long to wait for the "resurrection." Within a matter of weeks, they had recovered from their defeat in February and were once again agitating for separation. During the two months between the convention vote and the firing on Sumter, future Confederate officers John B. McLin and Reuben Arnold and future Confederate senator Landon Carter Haynes were canvassing upper East Tennessee, boldly speaking in favor of disunion. On one occasion in early April, all three participated in a Democratic states' rights meeting held in Blountville. Along with Sullivan County secessionists and soon-to-be Rebel officers James P. Snapp and George R. McClellan, Haynes and Arnold urged the crowd in "a very eloquent speech" to insist that Lincoln meet the South's demands in a "reasonable time" or accept the separation of the North and South as "perpetual."[54] Secessionist campaigning was so strong in Sullivan County, that one alarmed Unionist there alerted Andrew Johnson that "there is more Secession element in Sullivan than in a majority of Counties in East Tennessee." He went on to complain that "[the secessionists] are endeavoring to revive the old party lines between Whig & Democrat, and branding those who disagree with them and stand by the Union as *Black* Republicans."[55] In Bledsoe County a local separationist made a speech the day Fort Sumter was attacked in which he urged East Tennesseans to unite with the Confederacy or they would become "*choppers* of wood and *haulers* of water to the Black Republican States!"[56]

But it was Lincoln's call for volunteers in the wake of the bombardment on Sumter that truly revived secessionists' hopes of getting East Tennessee out of the Union. With the threat of coercion now a reality, conditional Unionists quickly abandoned their former position. "I feel reluctantly compelled to say," lamented one newly minted Rebel, "that I am forced to the conclusion . . . that there remains no longer any hope of preserving the Union & we can do no good by persisting longer in our efforts to save the Union, but may possibly do much harm by dividing & distracting our people at a time when we should have entire & cordial unanimity of feeling." He advised that, "our government is gone & our next duty is to our state & people."[57] Some seemed stunned by reports of Lincoln's decision. "Most of us hardly knew where to turn," remembered Confederate Col. W. W. Stringfield. There was a feeling that the president's response was too heavy-handed. "He should have called congress together instead of 75,000 troops," Stringfield insisted. Like most conditional Unionists, Stringfield was an old Whig who had cautioned his fellow East Tennesseans to be moderate during the days before Sumter. And like so many Whigs, Stringfield had alienated many Democrats before the war, but found himself in their camp once the shooting began. "While opposed to secession, I was also opposed to every phase of Lincolnism," he would recollect later in life, "and when Lincoln called for 75,000 troops, I rushed the other way and soon volunteered into the Southern army."[58]

Others were also ready to fight. "The Boarder States *will never join hand in hand* with the *Diabolical corruptions* of Black Republicanism," howled one enraged secessionist. "Before they will respond to Lincoln's call for 75,000 troops to coerce and whip the South they will *Cecede* in *solid columns.*"[59] One college student informed a relative that he would no longer wait on Tennessee to make up its mind: "I have 'seceded' from the university and expect to 'secede' from the state tomorrow." Although unsure what he would do next, he was certain that "while the Confederate states strive to maintain the position they have assumed I expect to back them; *provided* I live that long."[60] The *Athens Post* contended that it was immaterial who fired the first shot; what mattered was that Lincoln and his party had betrayed Southern Unionists. "Action is longer unavoidable," the *Post* vowed, remarking that the "State is solemnly pledged by its Legislature, and by the People . . . to resist coercion, to the death if necessary."[61]

In the excitement of the moment, Unionist resolve began to crumble. In Sullivan County, Democrats were whipping up the war spirit, causing some Unionists to reverse their course. "Every possible effort will be made to prejudice them against you," a local Unionist warned T. A. R. Nelson a week after Sumter.[62] That same day, East Tennessee Democratic leader Landon Carter Haynes learned that the secession banner was afloat in Jonesboro. "We have a Confederate flag upon the Union office," reported Haynes's correspondent. "I feel that our cause is fast rising," he optimistically added.[63]

Southern flags were also going up in other towns. The day after Lincoln's call for volunteers, an invitation went around to all the young ladies in Madisonville to help make a flag, which was quickly completed and flown from the courthouse. Others illuminated their homes in a general celebration.[64] The president's belligerency had transformed the Monroe County seat into a hotbed of separationism. "All, to a man, are for immediate secession," enthused one Madisonville merchant. "The Southern flag is on our C. H. every day, and no other flag is thrown to the breeze here." He boasted that "there is not one Union man in this town."[65] In Hawkins County, "a large and respectable portion of the citizens of the vicinity" resolved that "Tennessee should take immediate steps to dissolve all connection with the Lincoln government and attach herself to her sister Southern States."[66] The sentiment was similar in Meigs County. "So far as we can learn," the *Athens Post* reported, "the people of Meigs are unanimous in their determination to resist the policy of the Lincoln administration to 'overrun, seize, hold, and possess' the South." At Charleston in Bradley County, citizens publicly vowed resistance to Lincoln, boldly stating, "We hereby declare the Union dissolved."[67]

On May 6, the state legislature in Nashville passed an ordinance withdrawing Tennessee from the Union and declaring the state sovereign once again. In a rare observance of democratic principles among the seceding states, the legislature further resolved that a declaration of independence be submitted to the people for ratification on June 8.[68] Voting to support the state's separation from the Union were four senators and seven members of the house from East Tennessee, including William M. Bayless of Washington County, S. T. Bicknell of Blount, Phillip Critz of Hawkins, and Richard R. Harris of Bradley County. Many of these political leaders were destined to serve the new Confederacy in one capacity or another.[69] At the close of the session, the legislators returned home to drum up support for the separation ordinance in the June referendum, and, in many cases, to face the wrath of their angry constituents.[70]

Passage of the secession ordinance triggered a new round of celebrations and saber rattling in East Tennessee's towns. In Bristol, there was "great rejoicing" at news of the legislature's action, and the town was illuminated in honor of the occasion, prompting the *Nashville Union and American* to predict accurately that "Sullivan County will give a unanimous vote for the ordinance on 8th of June."[71] In Knoxville, former Unionists publicly disavowed their love for the United States and declared that if Tennessee were invaded, they would shoulder their "musket[s] to resist the invaders."[72]

A meeting was held in Jonesboro, calling for a convention in Nashville "to advocate the cause of State Rights, and to resist the encroachment of Black Republicanism in its unauthorized crusade upon slavery and the rights of the South." Alarmed by Lincoln's call for troops for the purpose of "holding them [the seceded states] in subjection and governing them by military force instead of the 'consent of the governed,'" the assembled citizens passed a resolution supporting Governor Isham G. Harris's stand against the president and declared that "we are for Tennessee taking a stand now and forever with her sister States of the South" in order to maintain their shared rights "'at all hazards and to the last extremity.'"[73] Maryvillians gathered at the Blount County courthouse pledging their support for secession and their opposition to Lincoln. When James A. McKamy, a young merchant who would rise to lieutenant colonel in the Rebel army, pleaded during the meeting for volunteers to defend the South, "quite a number of persons responded to the call," according to the *Athens Post.*[74]

Despite the celebrations and the tough talk, secessionists in East Tennessee knew they had a fight on their hands. If the returns of the February election were any indication of the sentiment in their region, they would have to bring all of their persuasive skills to bear in order to thwart the campaign of the unconditional Unionists, who were sparing no effort to defeat the ordinance of separation and to mobilize East Tennesseans against the Confederacy. Already, hard-liners such as Parson Brownlow were attacking the action of the legislature through the press. Respected Unionist political leaders such as Democrat Andrew Johnson and Whigs T. A. R. Nelson, Horace Maynard, and John Baxter were taking to the stump in a bipartisan denunciation of the ordinance, pleading against any alliance with the Confederacy. Numerous pro-Union rallies and meetings were held in nearly every county. The most important of these rallies took place in Knoxville on May 30–31, 1861, attacking secessionists and calling for a separate East Tennessee state.[75]

Undaunted by the task before them, prosecession newspapers immediately launched a campaign aimed at countering the Unionist arguments. "We repeat, let us acquiesce in the decision of the majority of our citizens," implored the *Chattanooga Gazette.* Pledging that "the last drop of our hearts' blood shall be a ready defense to our sense of right," the paper pleaded for unity in the valley. "We have heard it said that the people of East Tennessee would rebel against an ordinance dissolving our connection with the Federal Government. We deny any such charge of disloyalty. . . . We repeat, let us have no dissension at home."[76] In a similar vein, the *Athens Post* claimed that Blount County

Unionists were "waking up" and "declaring themselves opposed to Mr. Lincoln's coercion policy." The editor asked his readers, "Will not our Union friends see the great necessity of coming out from under them [the repressive policies of Lincoln], and give us a united South against a united North?"[77] Appeals for solidarity were coupled with fears over racial equality. In a vain effort to frighten the Union-supporting yeomanry into voting for separation, the *Cleveland Banner* entreated East Tennesseans to cast their ballots for secession "so that we may be independent of a government that would crush our institutions and make us the equal of the negro."[78] Other secessionists papers played on the region's traditional spirit of independence. Reminding its readers that the legislature had placed ratification in their hands, the *Knoxville Register* urged voters to place on their ballots the words "SEPARATION. REPRESENTATION." "But," the paper continued in language calculated to shame its opponents, "if you are dead to all the influences surrounding you demanding the emancipation of the South . . . you must place on your ticket NO SEPARATION. NO REPRESENTATION." As a way of further discrediting the Unionists, secessionist newspapers began once again referring to their opponents as "submissionists," suggesting that Unionists lacked the intestinal fortitude to stand up to Lincoln and his tyrannical policies.[79]

Secessionists coupled their media campaign with a stump speaking program. Realizing that success depended on winning the support of the Whig majority, secession leaders invited prominent Middle Tennessee Whig Party officials to conduct a tour of the valley. Among the speakers were men of statewide prominence, such as state representative Gustavus Henry and former Mississippi governor Henry S. Foote. They traveled together and separately, sometimes covering the same ground twice, one after another. Moreover, the speakers were all former Unionists, men who had supported Tennessean John Bell in his unsuccessful bid for the presidency and who had fought for compromise until after Sumter. Undoubtedly, secessionists hoped that the sight of such prominent Whigs publicly recanting their earlier Unionism would win converts to the cause of separation.[80]

The speaking blitz began in mid-May. It was particularly aimed at towns like Clinton, Tazewell, Maynardville, and Sevierville, which were located in heavily Unionist and traditionally Whig districts. The speakers set out, as one Unionist derisively phrased it, to "enlighten" the people of East Tennessee on "the glories of secession & rebellion."[81] In Roane County, W. T. Avery from Memphis and former East Tennessee state representative Jacob F. Foute, now of Memphis, addressed a crowd of about two hundred. Avery "was listened to with marked attention," while Foute called on his old East Tennessee friends "to stand by their brothers in the West." The newspapers reported that the crowd, which was mostly Unionist, "treated the speakers with great courtesy," but gave no indication if any minds were changed.[82] John F. House, a Montgomery County representative and Bell elector, delivered in Rogersville "a most impressive speech" to what the *Knoxville Register* called "a respectable audience." The *Register* noted that House's listeners were "very calm and listened to the whole speech with profound interest."[83] Union men gathered in Maryville to hear Foote urge them to embrace separation. The crowd adopted by acclamation a resolution endorsing the vote in the legislature by Representative Bicknell in favor of the ordinance.[84] Gustavus Henry finished his canvass of the region with speeches in Athens and Chattanooga. The *Nashville Republican Banner* hailed Henry's campaign as a success, and described the people of East Tennessee as "gallantly declaring themselves for resistance and preparing for the conflict. We doubt not they will speedily become entirely and heartily united."[85]

Such boasting was premature, to say the least. Despite claims to the contrary, there is little evidence that the speakers swayed many minds. Although newspapers proclaimed that the Whig leaders influenced East Tennesseans "to renounce their submission to the Northern yoke," the reality, as the June vote revealed, was that few were persuaded.[86] Turning out and listening attentively to public figures could not be confused with accepting their ideas. "Union men will not leave their farms to hear *Secessionists*," Brownlow bellowed, "when they know that but one side of the question is to be heard."[87] Indeed, some Unionists were skeptical of what they perceived as the speakers' eleventh-hour conversion. When Foote and House spoke in Cleveland, for example, the crowd, according to one Unionist, was unimpressed. While they had claimed last year that secession leaders "ought to be hung and would be hung," complained ultra-Unionist John C. Gaut, "now they come as *latter day saints* from Nashville to tell us that this same treason and rebellion is a most glorious thing in the eyes of God, and exceedingly well pleasing to Isham G. Harris, John Bell & Co. at Nashville." "In short," he concluded, "I tell you that Foote, House, Henry & Haynes have not changed a single man that I know of."[88] Certainly, Gaut's observations were colored by his uncompromising Unionism; but since both Bradley County and Cleveland rejected secessionism by wide margins, he must not have been too far off the mark.

As the date for ratification of the secession ordinance neared, secessionists became more desperate in their appeal. In a last-ditch effort to sway the com-

mon folk, they played on their fellow Southerners' sense of chivalry. Predicting the evils that Lincoln's armies would wreak on the South, one secessionist
urged the women of East Tennessee to go to their male relatives and "place
your hand on their shoulders or your arms about their necks and plead with
them to go on the 8th of June and cast their suffrage for SEPARATION AND REP-
RESENTATION, and rescue your liberties from the hands of the enemy." Identifying herself as "A Tennessee Woman," a writer to the *Knoxville Register* challenged the men of East Tennessee to meet bravely the coming conflict. "Gird
on you armor, husbands and brothers, fathers and sons," she demanded,
"'Separation and Representation' your watchword, not that you love the
Union less but that you love your country more."[89]

The election results confirmed the secessionists' worst fears. Regionwide,
only about 30 percent of the nearly fifty thousand votes cast was in favor
of ratifying the secession ordinance. While secessionists carried the day
in Middle and West Tennessee, they were successful in only six counties
in the East: Meigs (64 percent), Monroe (57 percent), Polk (70 percent),
Rhea (64 percent), Sequatchie (61 percent), and Sullivan (72 percent). There
were large proseparation minorities in several counties, including Hamilton
(41 percent), Marion (41 percent), Washington (42 percent), and McMinn
(44 percent), but only in McMinn did they even come close to upsetting
the Unionist majority. In some counties, such as Scott, Morgan, and Sevier,
secession totals were embarrassingly low. Results in Sevier were particularly galling to secessionists, where a mere 4 percent of the electorate voted
for separation.[90]

Despite a crushing defeat in the region, some Rebels were satisfied. They
may not have won at home, but they picked up more support than initially
anticipated. Moreover, regardless of events in East Tennessee, the state was
leaving the Union. "The vote in Middle and West Tennessee is almost a
unit and the secession vote in East Tennessee is larger than expected," rejoiced David M. Key of Chattanooga. "We are in the South, and long live
the South I say."[91] The *Knoxville Register* took great pains to point out the
fact that although the decision in Knox County was for the Union, the
majority voting against secession had declined by nearly one thousand votes
since the February election.[92] Claims like this, however, were only a measure of how badly the separationists had been beaten.

The reasons for secessionist failure are varied. In part, proseparation
forces were defeated because they lacked a central figure or spokesman
around whom to rally. Unlike western North Carolina, where Democrat
senator Thomas L. Clingman emerged to champion the cause of states'

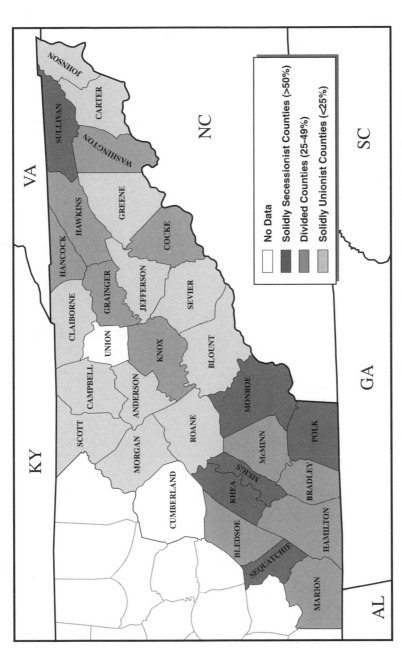

The Vote for Ratification of the Secession Ordinance in East Tennessee, June 8, 1861. Map by Deborah Cahill.

rights and Southern independence, East Tennessee never developed a secessionist leader talented enough to challenge the Unionist argument effectively.[93] Indeed, Rebel leadership suffered from its own mediocre political ability. O. P. Temple boasted that "in the contest of 1861 the
overwhelming weight of talent among the leaders in East Tennessee was
on the side of the Union."[94] The men who would eventually control
Confederate East Tennessee are conspicuously absent from any list of the
region's antebellum political leadership. With the notable exception of
Landon Carter Haynes, all of them were relative unknowns before 1861.

Although they were not incapable, men such as William H. Sneed and
John H. Crozier were no match for the vituperation of Andrew Johnson,
the demagoguery of Parson Brownlow, or the eloquence of T. A. R.
Nelson. Even the silver-tongued Haynes was ineffective against such a team.
The Unionists had a special knack for reaching the common people. They
were able to play upon the fear of planter domination and political revolution that so gripped the small farmers of the region. Secessionist David
M. Key perceptibly observed that Johnson and Nelson were able to make
"our backwoods yeomanry think that the Southern Confederacy is about
to try to 'douce' them, take away all their liberties and elect a king to rule
over them and grind them into powder."[95] Secessionists proved incapable
of fashioning and delivering a message that could appeal to the people,
thereby dooming their movement to failure. The electorate simply did not
share the separationists' fears that Lincoln posed a threat sufficient enough
to warrant the dissolution of the Union. Nor were secessionists capable
of overcoming the Unionist argument that East Tennessee had little, if
anything, in common with the South that justified revolution. From the
beginning J. G. M. Ramsey had sensed that the majority of East Tennesseans would never support separation and thought it folly to submit the
secession ordinance to the people for ratification. He urged Harris simply
to "declare by proclamation Tennessee absolved from all allegiance to that
[the U.S.] government" and allow the electorate to vote for nothing more
than representatives to the Confederate congress.[96]

The fact that most secession leaders were Democrats must have further
hampered their ability to convince a largely Whig electorate to embrace separation. Most East Tennessee Whigs nourished a bitter hatred for the Democratic Party. The antagonism between Parson Brownlow and Andrew Johnson
was typical of the enmity that existed between the two parties. Because they
tended to view their antebellum opponents as disunionists, cooperation between Whigs and Jacksonians was nearly impossible.[97] Even the apparent bi-

partisan unity of Middle Tennessee Whigs and East Tennessee Democrats did little to lure East Tennessee Whigs to the secessionist cause.

Only in the towns did secessionists realize any genuine gains. Even there, however, their success was by no means unqualified. The majority of villages and urban areas, especially those lying along the railroad, voted in favor of separation, but there were notable exceptions. The region's two largest cities, Knoxville and Chattanooga, reported secession majorities of 68 and 89 percent, respectively; in Sullivan County, the rail towns of Bristol and Union (present-day Bluff City) to a man voted for the ordinance. In Meigs County, Decatur supported secession, as did Sweetwater in Monroe County. Yet in Roane County only the village of Post Oak Springs favored ratification; Kingston, Lenoir, and Loudon all gave large majorities to the Unionists. Similarly, in Blount County secessionists carried Maryville while narrowly losing in the Holston River port town of Louisville. Although places such as Charleston and Calhoun voted nearly 100 percent for secession, only a few miles away the Bradley County seat of Cleveland cast a majority of its ballots against secession.[98]

Differences of opinion between city and country and even between one town and another vividly illustrate the fractured nature of nineteenth-century politics in the Great Valley. East Tennesseans tended to vote as a community rather than as individuals, a process which in 1861 often pitted one precinct or "beat" within a county against another. Even in the larger towns, schisms based along voting districts over the issue of disunion nearly lost the election for secessionists. For instance, Knoxville, the home of such archsecessionists as J. G. M. Ramsey and William G. McAdoo and the vocal anti-Union newspaper the *Register*, clearly was divided in its sentiment. The city was partitioned into three voting districts: Court House, Market House, and East Knoxville, which legally was still a separate town in 1861 even though its returns were combined with Knoxville's. Court House cast most of its vote against ratifying the ordinance, while Market House was nearly equally divided, a slight majority favoring separation. Only in East Knoxville, outside of the city proper, did secessionists succeed convincingly. Voters there cast 99 percent of their ballots for separation, giving pro-Confederate forces the edge they needed to carry the city. If the returns from East Knoxville are deducted from the total, as technically they should be, then Knoxville rejected secession.[99]

One striking feature of the six secession counties is that in 1860 John C. Breckinridge, candidate for the Southern wing of the Democratic Party, easily carried all of them. In fact, all six had been traditionally loyal to the Democratic Party in a region dominated by Whigs throughout the antebellum years. Conversely, the strongest center of Union support was concentrated in the old Second District, a group of counties located in the central portion of the valley, where Democrats made their poorest showing before the war. This is not to say, however, that there exists a high degree of predictability based on party affiliation. As table 1 reveals, there were other traditionally Democratic counties, such as Hawkins, Hancock, and Washington, that, although they possessed large proseparation minorities, rejected secession. All three had heavily favored Breckinridge in 1860 (50, 60.1, and 56.4 percent, respectively) but showed considerably less enthusiasm for separation in 1861 (38.3, 30.7, and 41.4 percent, respectively). Another notable example is Greene County, which not only was one of the most heavily and consistently Jacksonian in the valley but also one of the most ardently Unionist. The citizens of Greene County had thrown their support to Breckinridge in 1860 by over 65 percent, but they had just as overwhelmingly rejected secession eight months later, voting 78 percent against the separation ordinance.[100]

Table 1

Votes for Breckinridge and Secession in Traditionally Democratic East Tennessee Counties

County	Breckinridge (%)	Secession (%)
Bradley	43.0	26.8
Claiborne	53.5	16.7
Greene	65.4	21.7
Hancock	60.1	30.7
Hawkins	50.0	38.3
McMinn	46.5	44.1
Meigs	68.6	64.3
Monroe	53.2	58.6
Morgan	50.5	5.7
Polk	64.3	69.9
Rhea	55.2	64.1
Sullivan	71.4	71.7
Washington	56.4	41.4
Region	44.4	31.0

Note: The vote for Breckinridge was in November 1860, and the vote for secession in June 1861.
Source: From Mary Emily Robertson Campbell, *The Attitude of Tennesseans Toward the Union, 1847–1861* (New York, 1961).

Nor is there a clear connection between slaveholding and secessionist sympathy. On average, only about 10 percent of the population of the secession counties was slave, compared to 8 percent of the Union counties. The two counties with the highest percentages of slaves in the region—Bledsoe (15.5 percent) and McMinn (14.1 percent)—both opposed secession. In fact, the two most heavily proseparation counties, Sullivan and Polk, had slave populations of 7.9 and 4.9 percent, respectively, far below that in such Union strongholds as Jefferson (12 percent) and Roane (13 percent). Polk's paltry slave population is comparable to that of Sevier (5.9 percent) and Johnson (4.6 percent), two counties of unquestionable Unionist sympathies.[101]

What the statistical evidence reveals is that the June vote was indicative of larger forces at work in antebellum East Tennessee. A comparative analysis of the prosecession counties with the antiseparation counties suggests a connection between rising levels of wealth and secessionist sympathy in the rural districts which was similar to that in the towns. In almost every category, the secession counties experienced faster rates of growth between 1850 and 1860, the decade of railroad construction, than those rejecting ratification of the secession ordinance. Indeed, in a number of the Unionist counties not only was growth considerably slower but also in some cases there were actually declines in many economic indicators. This contrast in levels of economic expansion probably influenced the self-perception of individual East Tennesseans and oriented voters either toward or against unification with the new Southern Confederacy.

While there may have been little difference between Union and secession counties in terms of slaveholding, the rate of slavery's growth in the latter was considerably greater than that of the former. In table 2 it can be seen that in the counties where the vote was 50 percent or greater for secession, the total number of slaves increased by over 30 percent between 1850 and 1860; while in those counties with a secession vote of 25 to 49 percent, slavery increased by nearly 24 percent during the same period.[102] By way of contrast, the slave population increased only a little over 20 percent in those counties where secession polled less than 25 percent of the vote. As a proportion of the total population, slaves once again grew at a much faster rate (29 percent) in the secession counties than in the moderately Unionist (16 percent) and heavily Unionist (3 percent) counties.

Conversely, the pattern of white population growth is exactly the reversal of that for slaves. In this instance, the total number of whites grew by only 12 percent in the secession counties, nearly 10 percent in those counties with divided loyalties, and almost 20 percent in the solidly Union-

Table 2
Slave and White Populations in East Tennessee Counties, 1850–1860, by Secession Vote

	SLAVE POPULATION		WHITE POPULATION	
	Increase (Decrease) as Percentage of slaves	Increase (Decrease) as Percentage of Total Population	Increase (Decrease) as Percentage of whites	Increase (Decrease) as Percentage of Total Population
Secession Vote				
>49%[a]	30.5	29.0	12.6	(2.5)
25–49%[b]	23.9	16.0	9.8	(0.2)
<25%[c]	21.6	3.0	19.6	1.0
Region[d]	24.2	17.7	14.4	(0.6)

Notes: [a]No. of counties = 5.
[b]No. of counties = 11.
[c]No. of counties = 12.
[d]Total no. of counties = 28.
Source: Seventh and Eighth Censuses of the United States, 1850 and 1860.

ist counties. Whites actually declined as a proportion of the total population in the secession counties (−2.5 percent), stood still in the intermediate counties (−0.2 percent), but increased slightly in the strongly antiseparation counties (1.0 percent).

Thus, at first glance, a greater increase in whites in the Unionist counties appears to reflect a healthy, even vibrant, economy. Yet when compared with changes occurring in farm sizes and crop production, an entirely different picture emerges. As table 3 displays, while the number of farms in the separationist counties was declining (−4.3 percent), it was on the increase in those counties voting less than 25 percent for secession (8.2 percent). Conversely, farm size in the secessionist counties was on the increase during the ten years prior to the war (8.5 percent) but was shrinking in the heavily Unionist areas (−6.2 percent). These averages obscure the fact that the situation in some Unionist counties was degenerating into an economic and demographic crisis. For example, in Sevier and Jefferson Counties total farm size dropped 31 and 46 percent, respectively, while in Blount it spiraled downward at an alarming rate of 65 percent. A recent study by Paul Salstrom graphically illustrates the declining standard of living and the resultant demographic crisis facing Appalachia as a whole on the eve of the Civil War, as food production declined and population rapidly increased.[103] Furthermore, the value of farm land in the secession counties rose by a staggering 350 percent, more than twice as rapidly as it did in the moderately and solidly Unionist counties, only widening the economic division between them.

Changes in agricultural output also demonstrate a diverging economic path for Union and secession counties. The most dramatic change in crop production between 1850 and 1860 occurred in wheat. As table 4 indicates, both voting categories experienced a dramatic rise in wheat growing (almost 385 percent across the board), although secession counties edged slightly ahead of the others in raising this grain. New demand for wheat prompted a slight shift away from the region's traditional corn crop in the secession counties (−2.1 percent), while production of corn remained at a constant level in the divided counties (−0.6 percent) and actually rose (10.4 percent) in those counties where secession was least popular. Livestock production also reveals a contrast, albeit less significant, between pro- and antiseparation counties. Both hog and cattle raising declined (down 24.4 and 4.2 percent, respectively) on secessionist farms, while on farms in heavily Unionist regions, hog raising fell less precipitously (−20.2) and cattle raising actually went up (12.5 percent).

These figures suggest several possibilities. First, with less emphasis on raising livestock and a smaller overall population, the secession counties needed less corn and hogs for domestic consumption. Second, there is the likelihood that counties favoring separation were profiting more from wheat production than other counties and, as a result, were taking more land out of corn and livestock production, or a combination of both. Increases in wheat production, farm size, and number of slaves, accompanied by concomitant declines in population and in traditional corn and livestock raising, indicate that secessionist farmers were in a better position to shift away from producing export crops that could also be consumed at home toward a more profitable crop like wheat that was intended primarily for the market. As the value of their land and personal wealth increased, so did their hopes for the future. They had every reason to feel optimistic about their regional and personal future and to join the townsfolk of the valley in favoring political and economic unification with the new Confederacy.

Conversely, Unionist counties, especially those most solidly rejecting ratification of the secession ordinance, had little about which to feel optimistic. They were witnessing an alarmingly brisk expansion in their white population, while the size of farms continued to shrink. They also showed fewer signs of surrendering their attachment to hogs and corn and embracing wheat

Table 3

Change in Farms in East Tennessee Counties, 1850–1860, by Secession Vote

	Percentage Increase (Decrease) in Value of Farms	Percentage Increase (Decrease) in Number of Farms	Percentage Increase (Decrease) in Average Farm Size
Secession Vote			
>49%[a]	345.5	(4.3)	8.5
25–49%[b]	140.4	(13.6)	37.8
<25%[c]	177.8	8.2	(6.2)
Region[d]	193.0	2.0	3.5

Notes: [a]No. of counties = 5.
[b]No. of counties = 11.
[c]No. of counties = 12.
[d]Total No. of counties = 28.
Source: Seventh and Eighth Censuses of the United States, 1850 and 1860.

Table 4

Agricultural Production in East Tennessee Counties, 1850–1860, by Secession Vote

	Increase (Decrease) in Wheat Production	Increase (Decrease) in Cattle Production	Increase (Decrease) in Corn Production	Increase (Decrease) in Hog Production
Secession Vote				
>49%[a]	389.8	(2.1)	(24.4)	(4.2)
25–49%[b]	388.2	(0.6)	(24.3)	(8.3)
<25%[c]	376.9	10.4	(20.2)	12.5
Region[d]	383.7	6.1	(23.7)	1.2

[a]No. of counties = 5.
[b]No. of counties = 11.
[c]No. of counties = 12.
[d]Total no. of counties = 28.
Source: Seventh and Eighth Census of the United States, 1850 and 1860.

production. They could ill afford to do so. With farm acreage contracting and people multiplying, there was more demand than ever to produce more food for home consumption on less land. And as food production in Unionist counties declined, the residents of these counties faced a growing demographic crisis that would only accelerate when the war swept through the region. Indeed, as Paul Salstrom has recently demonstrated, per capita food production fell in some categories by more than a half in the mountain South between 1840 and 1880, the year in which industrialization began in Appalachia. The resultant drop in living standards not only led to the region's dependency and loss of self-sufficiency during the postwar years but also would have added fuel to the sense of decline and resentment detected among Unionists by historians Charles Bryan and John Inscoe.[104]

But what scholars perceive today may not have been so apparent in 1861. Unfortunately, few secessionists left any written record that they understood the connection between their rising economic fortunes and their loyalty to the South. Most had clung to the Union while there was hope, fearing the repercussions that separation and war would bring yet unable to resist standing with their neighbors in Virginia and Georgia when Lincoln forced them to act. A few months after the June ratification vote, W. R. Smith of Newport penned a letter to his old friend T. A. R. Nelson. Smith was disappointed that the former congressman was denouncing his colleagues as traitors for not supporting the Union. "I am very sorry you have allowed yourself to form such conclusions with regard to your friends," lamented Smith. He explained to Nelson that they had not been false to their government but were "rebel[ling] against what they believed to be an unconstitutional, unnecessary & iniquitous course on the part of Lincoln & Seward." Like most East Tennessee Confederates, Smith did not want secession, but the new president and his advisors left him little choice. "They accomplished," he averred, "what all the secessionists of the South could not do—they made me a rebel."[105]

The Social Origins of East
Tennessee's Confederate Leadership

More than sixty years ago, Samuel Cole Williams, a distinguished attorney and amateur historian, wrote that "the leaders in favor of the Confederacy in East Tennessee anterior to and during the war have been neglected—in sharp contrast with those who favored the Union cause." He
encouraged historians to investigate the region's Rebel leadership, indicat-
ing that "the field is one of promise to the researcher."[1] Despite Williams's
urging, no one has accepted the challenge.[2] As a consequence, East
Tennessee's Civil War experience continues to be interpreted in terms of
the region's Unionists and their stand against the wave of secessionist sentiment that swept across the South in 1861. In the work of most historians, East Tennessee typically is portrayed as a land of small, independent
subsistence farmers, as rugged as the mountains in which they lived, who
stubbornly and courageously resisted all attempts to drag them into a
southern Confederacy dominated by aristocratic, slaveholding cotton planters. Secessionists, when mentioned at all, are perceived as differing little
in background and motivation from their fellow travelers in the Deep South
and generally are cast as insignificant players who operated on the periph-
ery rather than at the center of events, so weak and so few that they ex-
erted little or no control over the destiny of their region.[3]

But the saga of East Tennessee's Unionists, no matter how intriguing
it may be, is only half the story. The long obsession with Southerners who
spurned secession has caused most writers to ignore certain important
trends and people in the antebellum history of East Tennessee. In the
process there has developed a myopic, if not distorted, view of the region.
By attempting to explode the old myths of solidarity in Southern society
on the eve of the Civil War, historians have created new myths of Unionist solidarity in Appalachia. Indeed, among historians, interest in Unionists has been so pervasive that the general public has little, if any, notion
that East Tennessee possessed a large, vocal, and determined Confederate

minority in 1861.[4] If ever there is to be a broader understanding of the forces which gave rise to the internecine struggle which erupted in East Tennessee during the summer of 1861, the gauntlet Williams flung down must be taken up, and the inquiry expanded to include all segments of the region's population, including those who adhered to the Confederate cause.

What, then, were the roots of secessionist sympathy in East Tennessee? First of all, contemporaries argued that anti-Unionism in the region was an urban/town phenomenon. They recognized that such sentiment emanated from the cities and villages that dotted the Tennessee Valley floor. "Outside the towns and railroad lines," observed Oliver P. Temple, a leading East Tennessee Unionist, "with the exception of two or three counties, the country became a unit, a solid compact body, in favor of the Union."[5] Prior to the February 1861 vote calling a convention to consider secession in Tennessee, the *Knoxville Whig* commented that "when we go out of the town [Knoxville] into the country, Secessionists are as scarce as *hens' teeth*. The honest yeomanry of the country hate secessionists, hate their doctrines, and will tell them at the ballot box . . . what they think of them."[6] Later, reporting the returns from the June 8 secession referendum in Tennessee, the *Whig* noted, "we have only partial returns from the election and these are along railroad and wires, where there has been a stream of secession fire for months. When the mountain counties come in, the returns will be more favorable to the Union ticket."[7] The *Whig's* fiery editor, William G. "Parson" Brownlow, considered the connection between businessmen and separation "the secret spring" of secession. "Merchants, Railroads and others largely indebted to the North are the most clamorous for Secession," he observed shortly after Sumter. "Wherever a merchant is found largely indebted to the North . . . they are throwing up their hats for Jeff Davis."[8] Historian James B. Campbell echoed these early observations, declaring that "supporters of the Confederacy in East Tennessee were . . . living in or near the towns."[9] Voting returns confirm that nearly every town along major transportation routes—rivers, roads, and railroads—favored separation from the Union.[10]

East Tennessee Confederate sympathizers also have been characterized as men and women of wealth and station, the largest of slaveholders, who easily found common cause with planters outside the region. "As a rule," asserted Thomas W. Humes, a prominent Knoxville Unionist, "secessionists and the disaffected toward the newly chosen government in Washington were more numerous in East Tennessee among the rich and persons of best social position, and were greatly outnumbered among the middle and poorer classes."[11] James Campbell agreed with Humes's evaluation, noting that secessionists "were of the wealthy and aristocratic classes," while Unionists "came from the yeomanry of the rural and mountain regions." In fact, Campbell boldly asserted that "the war in East Tennessee assumed the character of a class struggle between smallholders and the plantation owners in the towns."[12] More recently, Willene B. Clark, in a similar vein, claims that "the larger landowners—the gentry—were the most likely to side with the Confederacy, for they felt more akin to the plantation South than did the subsistence farmers."[13]

Are these traditional assumptions about East Tennessee secessionists valid? Were those who assumed Confederate leadership in the region during the early months of the war indeed "aristocratic" townsmen? Unfortunately, research on Rebel leadership in the region to a large extent has been hampered by the lack of readily accessible biographical data from which to create an appropriate group profile. Unlike Unionists, who met in conventions at Knoxville and Greeneville in the summer of 1861, Confederate sympathizers held no mass meetings during the course of the secession crisis. So, while it has been possible in the past to identify and examine the backgrounds of those leaders who supported the Union by studying the delegates to the various antiseparation gatherings, it has been much more difficult to make a similar analysis of secessionists.[14]

For example, in his study of the Civil War in East Tennessee, Charles Bryan examined the delegates to the Union convention held in Knoxville in May 1861. Out of the nearly five hundred men in attendance at this meeting, Bryan selected a random sample of forty-six (10 percent of the convention) and then used the 1860 manuscript census to gather evidence concerning the characteristics of these delegates. His study revealed that a solid majority (65 percent) was involved in agriculture as an occupation. These forty-six individuals generally were older men; thirty-four (73 percent) were forty years of age or older. In addition, Bryan discovered that although most of the convention's leadership consisted of relatively prosperous men, such as Connally F. Trigg, O. P. Temple, and John Baxter, most of the participants were by no means wealthy: over 60 percent held real and personal property valued at less than five thousand dollars. Bryan's investigation also revealed that nineteen (41 percent) of the sampled delegates were slaveholders, but the vast majority of these were small holders. Of those who owned slaves, 83 percent owned fewer than ten, and 61 percent fewer than five. Overall, the convention was made up of old Whigs, although several prominent Democrats attended, including the former governor, U.S. senator Andrew Johnson.

Bryan argued that Unionists were strongly influenced by their age and background. Most of the delegates, he declared, had "witnessed the gradual decline of their section in state affairs during the past two or three decades." They had developed a distinct distrust of Middle and West Tennessee, regions they perceived as being dominated by men of wealth, large slaveholdings, and the Democratic Party. They also nourished a growing sense of resentment toward Nashville, which they believed had fallen under the control of the plantation districts. Bryan argued that this sense of isolation and loss of influence greatly accounted for East Tennessee's stand against the secessionist wave that swept across the rest of the state after President Lincoln's call for troops to suppress the "rebellion."[15]

While the secessionists held no conventions, a comparative analysis of East Tennessee's "separationist" leadership is possible by examining the military men who served as either field or line officers in the Confederate army during the early months of the conflict.[16] As a number of recent studies have demonstrated, Civil War units, particularly those from the South, tended to replicate local personal loyalties and to reflect in their command structure local political and social relationships. For example, in his analysis of wartime Orange County, North Carolina, Robert Kenzer found that Confederate enlistment was based on "neighborhood patterns," meaning the members of each company were usually residents of the same community. Volunteers selected for command men to whom they normally looked for leadership, because they were determined "to reproduce existing local loyalties as a means of accommodating themselves to the uncertain experiences ahead." Similarly, Martin Crawford contends that in Ashe County, North Carolina (just across the mountains from East Tennessee), there was an insistence by volunteers upon "familiar authority" when it came to selecting leaders. As in Orange County, the volunteer companies raised in Ashe were composed of members from the same neighborhoods and were "direct extensions of the community itself, communities away from home." As a consequence, volunteers re-created local allegiances "through the jealously guarded prerogative of choosing company officers."[17]

The sample upon which this study is based, therefore, consists of those officers—colonels, majors, and captains—who commanded the volunteer regiments, battalions, and companies which were tendered to the Confederate government from East Tennessee during the first year of the war. Since they were elected by the troops they commanded, rather than appointed by the authorities in Richmond, these officers, it safely may be argued, occupied positions of leadership in their towns or communities—roles that made them the logical and natural choice to command their fellow citizens in the field. This was even more the case when, as will be shown, few of these men possessed previous military experience and none could be classified as "professional" soldiers. All of this strongly suggests that their selection for command stemmed from varying degrees of leadership as civilians, making them more comparable to the Union political leaders than one initially might suspect. It should be added that, because they were the very first to enlist for the war, these officers likely were the most enthusiastic to embrace the Southern effort for independence and, therefore, truly represent the secessionist element in East Tennessee society.

During 1861, eighty Confederate cavalry, infantry, and artillery companies were raised in East Tennessee. Assuming each company matched the roughly one hundred men required for acceptance into Confederate service, then approximately eight thousand troops volunteered from the region during the first year of the war. These units hailed from twenty-three different counties, nineteen of which are located in what is known as the Great, or Tennessee, Valley. Bounded on the east by the Smoky Mountains and on the west by the Cumberland range, the Great Valley is in fact a series of ridges and small valleys which traverse the entire length of the region on roughly a northeast-southwest axis from the Virginia border to the Georgia state line. One company was formed on the Cumberland Plateau, and the remaining three companies were organized in nearby Sequatchie Valley, a parallel geographical formation separated from the larger Tennessee Valley by a high, craggy wall known as Walden's Ridge.[18]

Of the 108 officers who commanded East Tennessee Confederate military units during 1861, 100 could be located in the 1860 manuscript census. Of that number, 79 percent dwelled in a town or city. Moreover, 93 percent lived on or near a major transportation route, that is, within a town or post office district through which the route passed. A majority (56 percent) lived along either the East Tennessee and Georgia or the East Tennessee and Virginia railroads. Twenty percent resided along a major road, turnpike, or stage route, while another 14 percent lived in proximity to a navigable river.[19] These statistics confirm the strong urban/town connection detected by other historians. They also suggest the important role that communication and trade connections to areas outside East Tennessee may have played in influencing secessionist sympathy. Particularly significant is the fact that more than half of East Tennessee's volunteer officers lived close to the railroad, which, more than any other internal improvement of the antebellum period, linked the region with markets in both the lower South and Virginia.[20]

That commercial ties to areas outside the Great Valley may have been an important factor in the decision to support secession also is suggested by an examination of the occupations of the Confederate military leaders. As table 5 indicates, while the livelihood most commonly named by these men in the 1860 census was farming (38 percent), a majority (62 percent) came from the commercial and professional ranks, with a quarter (25 percent) directly engaged in mercantile or related businesses as their primary source of income.[21] In this manner, secessionists markedly differed from their Unionist counterparts, of whom, according to Bryan's study, only about one-third (35 percent) appear to have been associated with business and the professions. As secessionists vied with each other for rank and prestige in the newly formed Rebel army, town-based merchants and lawyers quickly emerged as the region's most ardent Confederates. Indeed, the two men who became the only Confederate generals from East Tennessee, Alfred E. Jackson of Jonesboro and John C. Vaughn of Sweetwater, in 1860 were prosperous merchants.[22]

Even those Southern commanders who gave farming as their occupation often pursued several business ventures in addition to working the land. It was not uncommon for entrepreneurs to invest in a variety of money-making projects, such as Dandridge resident William D. Fain, who gave as his occupation "farmer, merchant, & manufacturer," despite the fact that census enumerators were instructed to list only one occupation per respondent. Such also was true of William T. Gass of Rhea County. Although listed as a farmer, Gass owned a carding factory and a grist and saw mill, practiced law, and even dabbled in iron and coal mining prior to the war. Similarly, Sterling T. Turner

Table 5
Prewar Occupation of Selected East Tennessee Confederate Leaders

Occupation	N
Business	
Merchants	25
Railroad related	2
Professional	
Lawyers	22
Doctors	5
Law students	4
Civil servants	2
Teachers	1
Engineers	1
Farmers	38

Note: Total *N* = 100.
Source: Eighth Census of Tennessee Population Schedules for Various Counties.

farmed near the Roane County town of Wrightsville, but he also found time among his many chores to serve as director of the Athens branch of the Bank of Tennessee. "Farmer" Jacob Hamilton of Hawkins County was also a merchant and hotel owner.[23] Other notable examples are Benjamin Welcker of Roane County and James W. Gillespie of Rhea County. Although he listed himself as a farmer, Welcker's family ran an extensive merchandising operation in North Alabama; while Gillespie, who referred to himself as a physician, was apparently a shrewd businessman who operated a very lucrative mercantile establishment in the county seat of Washington and on the side traded in livestock.[24]

Since census enumerators were instructed to list only one occupation per respondent, individuals were forced to select one source of income over another. Why so many of the sample would have been hesitant to consider themselves merchants or businessmen is not easy to discern. Certainly the prevailing republican ideology of the mid-nineteenth century, which prized the sturdy, independent yeoman farmer, may have led many to value their agricultural pursuits above all others. It is also true that, in a society that subscribed to what Clement Eaton refers to as "the ideal of the country gentleman," Southern merchants lacked prestige, ranking far below agriculturalists and professionals in the estimation of the community. Perhaps, too, a greater proportion of their income was derived from farming, which caused them to classify themselves as farmers. John Inscoe found that, across the mountains in western North Carolina, landholding and farming alone were not "viable options for accruing wealth," so most affluent western Carolinians were merchants, bankers, lawyers, doctors, or some combination, just like their neighbors in East Tennessee. Furthermore, as historian Lewis Atherton notes, it was not uncommon for farmers to move in and out of merchandising throughout the antebellum period. The changes in the Great Valley's economy during the decade prior to 1860 may have prompted some to open a mercantile operation as a second source of income. Not only did these so-called farmers begin to move away from diversified agriculture to the raising of more grain crops, but also many may have sought to take advantage of the increased wealth that the railroad was bringing to the region by expanding into new areas of enterprise. Overall, they may have considered themselves still farmers, while in reality, they had become much more.[25]

One might add that a careful comparison of the military and census records reveals that many of junior officers, first and second lieutenants, who often superseded in command those in the sample, also were recruited from town-based business and professional classes. Although not included in the sample, they, too, provided leadership, frequently assisted captains in raising companies for Confederate service, and were elected to their posts by the men they commanded. Such was true of 2d Lt. Jacob Alexander, Forty-third Tennessee Infantry, a twenty-one-year-old merchant from Dandridge who later raised and commanded a company in the Sixty-second Infantry Regiment; 1st Lt. Chesley Jarnigan, Thirty-seventh Tennessee Infantry, a twenty-eight-year-old merchant from Rutledge who rose to company command before his death at Chickamauga in September 1863; 1st Lt. Samuel Toole, Third Tennessee Infantry, a twenty-one-year-old law student from Maryville, scion of one of the oldest and largest mercantile and railroad-boosting families in the region, who was quickly promoted to the rank of lieutenant colonel; 1st Lt. David K. Byers, Nineteenth Tennessee Infantry, a twenty-year-old merchant's clerk from Jonesboro; and 1st Lt. Simeon D. Reynolds, adjutant of the Twenty-ninth Tennessee Infantry, a thirty-five-year-old hotel keeper from the railroad and river port town of Loudon, later major of the Sixty-second Regiment.[26]

What about the connection between slavery and secessionist leadership? Despite the traditional assertion that East Tennessee's Confederate leaders were drawn from the planter class, none of the officers in this study can be classified as "planters." As the leaders of a revolutionary movement committed to preserving the slave system, they were an unusually slave-poor lot. Among the group, the average number of slaves owned was about three per officer. A majority (57 percent) did not own any slaves at all. This figure closely compares to the 59 percent Unionists in Bryan's sample who held no slaves. Among those Confederates who owned slaves, 79 percent held fewer than ten, nearly matching the 83 percent of Unionists in the same category. Even the largest slave owner, Chattanooga resident C. C. Spiller, who held fifteen slaves, does not qualify as a planter by most accepted standards. Nonslaveholders predominated among central East Tennesseans, where twenty-one of the thirty-one officers (68 percent) owned no slaves; in upper and lower East Tennessee, slaveholders and nonslaveholders were almost evenly divided, with nonslaveholders in a slight majority.[27]

An examination of slaveholding patterns in East Tennessee in 1860 sheds additional light on the social origins of the region's Rebel military leadership. In all, seventeen counties were represented by the forty-three officers who owned slaves; some were the larger slaveholding counties in the region, including Bledsoe, Roane, and Jefferson. The mean average holding among slave owners in these seventeen counties was 5.5 slaves per owner, while the mean holding among those officers owning slaves was 5.6 bondsmen.[20]

At first blush, these figures seem to suggest that slaveholding among the sample was fairly typical of that found throughout the Great Valley. They also seem to indicate that, of those members of the sample who held slaves, most came from the ranks of the middling, rather than from the larger, slaveholding class. However, the fact that slaveholding patterns among secessionist leaders were similar to that of their Unionist counterparts, coupled with other data about age and wealth, indicates a greater attachment to slavery by the Confederates. Given their relative youth and greater wealth (which will be demonstrated below), secessionists appear more wedded to the institution of slavery than Unionists. Because they were younger and already owned as many slaves as the older men, one could conclude that slavery was an important factor in their decision to support secession. Secessionists may not have been planters in the strictest sense of the word, but they did have more of a stake in the slave system than their antagonists.

But notable examples of planter opposition to their state's separation from the Union makes it difficult to forge a certain link between slavery and secession in East Tennessee. Indeed, some of the most powerful slaveholders in the Great Valley fought against secession. For instance, W. C. Kyle, one of the leaders of the Knoxville convention, held fifty-two slaves, making him the largest planter in Hawkins County and one of the twelve largest in the Valley.[29] In East Tennessee, Unionism found favor not only with the poorer and nonslaveholding classes, as traditionally has been asserted, but also among the wealthiest of planters. O. P. Temple admitted as much when he wrote that "the largest as well as the third largest slaveholders in Knox County were Union men." He explained that this was not unusual, because "there were many of that class who never yielded to that delusion [secession]."[30] Slavery may have been a factor in the decision to secede, but not all planters saw Lincoln's election or the firing on Sumter as a threat to the "peculiar institution."

Of course, economics was not the only reason for favoring secession. Another significant characteristic of East Tennessee's Confederate leaders that would have tilted them toward separation was their relative youth. In 1860, the average age of those included in the sample was 35.2 years. Seventy-four members of the group were between 20 and 40 years of age, while only six were above the age of 50. The oldest officer was Robert W. McClary of Polk County, who went into the field at age 67. The youngest was A. Kyle Blevins of Hawkins County, who was elected captain at the tender age of 19. In contrast to the Union delegates in Bryan's study,

73 percent of whom were 40 years of age or older, only 28 percent of the Confederates fell into this category.[31]

A major problem when dealing with age is the fact that one would expect soldiers to be younger than political leaders. This would be especially true if the sample included officers from later in the war, once battlefield attrition, the rigors of campaigning, and incompetence all had taken their toll on the early-war commanders. By 1863, captains and field officers were usually men who had come up through the ranks and had superseded their considerably older 1861 counterparts. It is precisely for this reason that, in the hope of achieving a more accurate comparison, the sample was limited to military leaders commissioned during the first year of the war, rather than the entire wartime officer corps.

Simply comparing Union and Confederate officers does not overcome the problem. Indeed, any comparative analysis of military leaders presents difficulties of its own. Most Union regiments from East Tennessee were not raised until 1862–64, at a time during the war when younger men were selected for command; and those few raised in 1861 were organized outside Confederate lines in Kentucky by men who would have needed youth to withstand the arduous journey over the mountains. Any attempt, then, to compare mid- to late-war Federal officers with early-war Confederates would produce questionable results. Only a comparison of 1861 Confederate leaders with 1861 Union leaders, even if one is military and the other political, can yield useful data.

Notwithstanding these difficulties, it appears that East Tennessee's Rebel leaders were younger than their Unionist counterparts. This raises the possibility of a generational difference or "gap," whereby attitudes toward separation were influenced by age and the time period during which these men reached maturity, not to mention the natural rebelliousness of youth. Indeed, the plausibility of a generational theory is even more likely, given the fact that many of the leaders of the Knoxville convention, including such luminaries as T. A. R. Nelson, Thomas Arnold, W. C. Kyle, Seth J. W. Lucky, and Frederick Heiskell, had sons who served in the Confederate army or government.[32]

This East Tennessee pattern of secessionist fervor based on age fits a similar trend across the South in general. In two recent studies, Gary Gallagher and Peter Carmichael argue that attitudes among Southerners toward secession and an independent Confederate nation were influenced by age. Young men who came to maturity during the 1850s, Gallagher and Carmichael contend, were more vocal in their support for secession and exhibited a stronger sense of

Southern nationalism than did their fathers. Having grown up during a period of intense sectional discord and in a "highly charged atmosphere that emphasized southern distinctiveness," they felt less attachment to the Union and saw war and secession as welcome inevitabilities, freeing their region from what they perceived as materialistic, ungodly Yankees and their assault on slavery and Christian civilization.[33]

Further evidence suggesting a generational gap can be found in the fact that sometimes fathers and sons even faced each other on the battlefield. For example, James M. Henry, a captain in the Federal army and a Unionist from Blount County, had a son who was also a captain, but in the Rebel army.[34] The most celebrated incident where father and son were under arms but on opposing sides was that of the Clift clan of Hamilton County. The elder Clift, a wealthy and prominent Unionist, rose to the rank of colonel in the Federal cavalry. No doubt to the old man's consternation, both his sons fought as officers under the Southern banner.[35]

Rebel leaders appear to not only have been younger than their antisecessionist neighbors but also wealthier. While over 60 percent of the delegates to the Knoxville convention sampled by Bryan held real and personal property valued at less than five thousand dollars, only 40 percent of the separationists fell into this category. These figures seem even more remarkable when it is remembered that many of the Confederates, because of their relative youth, still were living at home when the war began or were just launching their careers, and consequently, had only begun to accumulate wealth. The fact that secessionists were younger and controlled more property than their Unionist counterparts is significant, since in other parts of the country and the South, wealthier men also tended to be older men.[36]

Eight officers in the sample possessed wealth in real and personal property valued at over $30,000. Leading the pack was merchant-farmer Benjamin F. Welcker of Kingston, the richest man in the sample, whose net worth was valued by the census taker at $57,000. Welcker's personal property amounted to $25,000, but included only eleven slaves. At thirty years of age, James C. Bradford of Jefferson County held $19,000 in real and $17,000 in personal property; but, surprisingly, none of it was invested in slaves. Similarly, thirty-eight-year-old Cleveland resident William L. Brown claimed $14,000 in real and $18,000 in personal property but owned no slaves, although he named farming as his occupation. Rhea County merchant Warner E. Colville was worth $36,000, of which $29,000 was in personal property. Yet Colville owned only five slaves, the total value of which, even if they were all prime field hands, would have been no more than $5,000.[37]

Benjamin F. Welcker, c. 1862, wearing the uniform of a lieutenant colonel. A merchant in Kingston when the war began, Welcker was typical of East Tennessee's secessionist leadership. Courtesy of Knoxville Chapter No. 89, United Daughters of the Confederacy.

Total real property held by the one hundred Confederate officers was approximately $475,000, while total personal property amounted to roughly $510,000. While it is likely that those engaged in farming purchased more slaves in response to the boom in wheat trade, individual holdings were still small. Since most officers had little money tied up in slaves, this disparity between real and personal property, while not great, probably resulted from emphasis

on investment in store stock, such as clothing, dry goods, hardware, and groceries. A larger sum of personal property also indicates something about secessionists' attitudes toward wealth. Given their small average slaveholdings, it
is possible that greater levels of personal property reflect a conscious effort
on the part of these townsfolk to acquire life's "creature comforts"—larger
homes, elegant furniture, fine clothes, jewelry, and carriages, perhaps even railroad stocks and bonds—rather than land and slaves, the twin investments
usually associated with the planter class. Inasmuch as East Tennessee was not
a significant slaveholding region (slaves composed only about 10 percent of
the total population in 1860), these professionals and businessmen invested in
tangible goods rather than in slaves. While it cannot be determined with any
certitude, it does appear that this "conspicuous consumption" on the part of
secessionists indicates an effort to use their wealth in a way that would reflect
their rising status in an Appalachian society that placed limited emphasis on
slaveholding as an economic system or as a symbol of affluence.

The statistical evidence gleaned from the 1860 manuscript census suggests that Confederate military leadership in East Tennessee came not from
the old elite families, as earlier writers intimated, but instead sprang from
a rising commercial-professional middle class that was emerging as the
region became even more firmly integrated into the market economy. Of
course, a few of these men were descended from the region's gentry, for a
quick glance at the roster will disclose names like McClung, Powel, Cocke,
and Brazelton, all associated with the early settlers of East Tennessee.
However, an examination of the list will also show many more families—
such as Brock, Holland, Hankins, Coulter, Legg, Lynch, Turner, and Dill—
who were outside the traditional mainstream of power. The 1850s was a
period of change in the economy of East Tennessee. Farmers continued
to raise their traditional commercial products of hogs and corn but also
began to shift dramatically toward the production of wheat for markets
outside the Great Valley. The railroad facilitated this trade and continued
a trend already established through land and river communication by linking even more strongly the region's towns and cities to markets in such places
as Georgia, eastern Virginia, and South Carolina (states which either took
an early lead in breaking up the Union or were later solidly Confederate),
bringing a new era of prosperity to the region. Apart from the planter class
itself, Rebel leaders in the Tennessee highlands were primarily young farmers, merchants, and lawyers who resided in towns and villages along major
transportation and communication routes. The evidence strongly suggests
that economic interdependency forged closer ties between East Tennessee

townsfolk, especially merchants and lawyers, and their clients and business partners in the Deep South and Virginia, and as a consequence oriented them toward the Confederacy. By actively participating in and directing the new trade in wheat, as well as the long-established trade in grain and hogs, they may have forged strong economic and even social ties with commission agents and merchants in other parts of the South. With East Tennessee firmly integrated within the Southern economy, the beneficiaries of the wheat boom and railroad lines took up the sword to sustain the prosperity that access to Southern markets had brought to their region.[38]

Contact of East Tennessee merchants and businessmen with other Southerners would have also contributed to anti-Unionist attitudes. Periodically, merchants were forced to take extended trips outside East Tennessee, either to sell produce obtained from farmers or to purchase the supplies needed to restock their depleted store shelves. Usually their travels took them to places such as Atlanta, Augusta, Savannah, and Charleston. There, frequent personal interaction with Southern businessmen and planters would have offered East Tennessee entrepreneurs an opportunity to see and understand the world beyond their own borders. Discussing the issues of the day, sharing common concerns and fears, walking the streets of these cities all would have exposed Great Valley merchants to the South and its people and perhaps would have oriented these East Tennesseans toward a more "Southern" perspective.[39]

Of course, a few exceptions to these generalizations existed. Several prominent Knoxville merchants, such as James Hervey Cowan, David Deaderick, and Perez Dickinson, remained loyal to the Union throughout the secession crisis. Significantly, however, all three men were over fifty years of age and had established their businesses over thirty to forty years prior to the war. In the case of Dickinson, his Massachusetts origins probably influenced his sympathies. But Deaderick and Cowan had younger relatives who sided with the South. Deaderick's four sons enlisted in the Confederate army over their father's objections, while Cowan's son-in-law, Charles McClung Alexander, served as major of the Fifty-ninth Tennessee Infantry until his death in December 1862.[40]

Yet another factor that may have shaped the attitudes and allegiances of Tennessee Valley secessionists toward their fellow Southerners were ties to the Democratic Party. Of the thirty-five members included in the sample who held political office or gained some political experience prior to 1861, thirty were identified with a party organization. Out of that group, the overwhelming majority (twenty-four) were Democrats; the balance (six) were Whigs. This

breakdown presents a reverse image of the political affiliation of Bryan's Unionists, among whom old Whigs far outnumbered Democrats. Unlike Unionists, separationists would have felt less resentment toward a Tennessee state
capital dominated by Democrats; nor would they have experienced alienation
from the states of a Deep South controlled by them. Moreover, several East
Tennessee Democrats who turned secessionist had held important positions
within the state party organization. This was true of Samuel Powel, a thirty-
eight-year-old attorney from Rogersville, who held the prestigious office of
attorney general when the war began; and of thirty-six-year-old Sweetwater
merchant John C. Vaughn, who was a delegate to the Democratic National
Convention in Charleston in 1860. Considering the intensity of party loyalty
in Jacksonian America, East Tennessee Democrats could be expected to identify with others of their own political persuasion. It should be no surprise, then,
that, with a few notable exceptions, such as Andrew Johnson, they closed ranks
behind Democratic Gov. Isham G. Harris after Lincoln's call for troops.[41]

Given their position, occupations, party affiliation, and relative youth,
it is very likely that these officers held a view of their region which differed significantly from that held by Unionists. Profitable and stable commercial and political ties to areas beyond the mountains seem to have translated into an optimistic view of East Tennessee as a region "on the rise"
economically, if not politically, and increasingly integrated with the rest
of the South. Unlike Unionists, whom both Charles Bryan and John Inscoe
have suggested saw the Great Valley as a region in decline, many secessionists viewed Southern independence not only as a way to defend the South's
racial and economic system, but also as a way to continue their efforts to
bring economic prosperity to their region. Pleased with the progress that
improved transportation routes had brought to East Tennessee and faced
with the possibility of their Deep South and Virginia markets might be
closed off if their area remained in the Union, secessionists believed that
separation was a gamble worth taking. As part of a new generation of
emerging wealth, secessionists represented a small but powerful minority
who resented the drag which the older men, with their grudge against
Nashville and the more prosperous sections of Tennessee, had placed, like
a great albatross, around the neck of the economic and political fortunes
of their region. Secession and war gave them the opportunity to wrest
control of the Valley's future away from their less forward-looking elders.
Thus while Unionists talked of preserving the nation or of forming an
association of upper South and mountain states, free from the tyranny of

the planter class, secessionists set their sights upon economic and political unification with the Confederacy.[42]

This optimistic view of East Tennessee was best articulated by J. Austin Sperry, editor of the *Knoxville Register* and a rabid disunionist. In an editorial penned over a year after the war began, Sperry presented the secessionists' grievances against the Union leaders, while offering the hope that separation would translate into economic prosperity for the Great Valley. Sperry blamed the Unionists—men such as Andrew Johnson, Parson Brownlow, and Horace Maynard, who had been the leaders of East Tennessee prior to the war—for using the media to attack one another for mere political gain, rather than using it as a means of attracting investment capital to the region. "It is not strange that the attractive scenery of our mountains was neglected by Southern tourists, nor that Southern enterprise made no investment in our mining districts," he lamented. "The press, and thence the politics, and the character of the leading men of East Tennessee have materially affected the fortunes of the country and retarded its advancement in all the elements of wealth, intelligence, and prosperity." But now that the Tennessee Valley was united with the Confederacy and "freed from the presence of these dangerous men," Sperry predicted that mines, schools, and resorts would spring up across the country. "Our people shall be envied," he boasted, "and East Tennessee shall become the Paradise of the South."[43]

Socioeconomic and political bonds with other Southerners also helped to shape regional self-image in another way, too. The evidence suggests that Rebel military leaders saw East Tennessee as more "Southern" and themselves more as "Southerners" than did their opponents, who tended to perceive Southern society and its institutions as brutish and corrupt.[44] Whereas Unionists rarely, if ever, referred to themselves as Southerners or to East Tennessee as a part of the South, Confederates frequently applied those cultural and geographical terms in describing themselves and their region. In the process of becoming a part of the Southern community, young merchants and professionals came to identify more with Georgians, South Carolinians, and Virginians who held similar goals and aspirations than they did with their fellow highlanders. When Confederate treasury agent J. G. M. Ramsey declared that antebellum East Tennessee "was essentially an Atlantic country," by which he meant South Carolina and Georgia, he betrayed a perception of himself and his region as a part of the culture and economy of the Deep South.[45] Seeing himself as a

Southerner and deploring his native state's slowness in responding to Lincoln's election, Ramsey's friend William Gibbs McAdoo removed himself and his family to Georgia in early 1861, declaring that "if they [the cotton states] will go . . . I go with them, make common cause with them, fight for them to the last drop of my blood."[46] Similarly, Sam Houston Hynds, an officer in the Third Tennessee Infantry, perceived himself first as a Southerner and only secondly as an East Tennessean. "I see it stated that E. Tenn is trying to disconnect herself from the middle and west, if she does, then Farewell to E. Tennessee," he declared. "I love her people and her mountains, but if her people can be lead off by such unprincipaled men as Johnson and Co. I can no longer look upon her soil as a fit place for me to stand."[47] Such language would have sounded strange coming from the mouth of Parson Brownlow, Andrew Johnson, or Horace Maynard.

A closer examination of the personal life of one member of the group, John M. Lillard, sheds additional light on the "making" of an East Tennessee secessionist. One month shy of his thirty-fourth birthday when Fort Sumter was fired upon, Lillard, known to contemporaries as "a leader of east Tennessee Confederates," was born in that part of Rhea County which later became Meigs. After having seen action in Mexico as a noncommissioned officer, he returned home determined to make his fortune. He began to invest heavily in copper mining in Polk County and to acquire small tracts of real estate, a trend which he continued throughout the 1850s. A dual practice in law and medicine, coupled with a keen interest in politics, led to his election in 1853 as a Democrat to the lower house of the Tennessee General Assembly, where he served one term. During his tenure, Lillard focused most of his energy on projects which would enhance his own farming, mining, and other business interests, such as the East Tennessee and Georgia Railroad. He tried, for example, to obtain state funding for a branch line to connect Meigs County with Chattanooga, a growing city which he hoped would eventually become the hub of a major transportation network connecting river and rail traffic in the lower valley.

Along with his younger brother Newton, a merchant through whom much of Meigs County's wheat crop found its way to Georgia and himself a future Confederate officer, John Lillard became a leading citizen of Decatur, the county seat of Meigs. His 1858 tax evaluation reflects his rising economic status: seventy acres of land ($800 value), four town lots ($100 value), copper shares ($625 value), one slave ($800 value), and one piano ($300 value), for a total value of $2,625. When war came, there was little doubt in his mind which way he would go. His reflections on seces-

John M. Lillard, c. 1862. From *Confederate Veteran.*

sion to a friend in North Carolina betrayed his perception of himself not as an East Tennessean but as a Southerner. "I think," he declared, "that if the whole south had done so [secede] at first, war would have been avoided." But with Lincoln's call for troops, that was now an impossibility, he lamented. "It is fight or submit," he insisted, "and we know what all true southerners will do in that event." Lillard organized one of the first companies raised in Meigs County and was quickly elected colonel of the Twenty-sixth Tennessee Infantry.[48]

What factors led to the selection of men such as Lillard for command? One obvious qualification, military experience, seems to have played a minor role in the decision. As table 6 illustrates, only twenty-one of the sample were found to have possessed any prewar knowledge of the art of warfare. Of that figure, combat experience in Mexico predominated, with twelve having served in one of several regiments raised in East Tennessee during that conflict. Three were graduates of, or had attended, military academies (Virginia Military Institute or West Point), while an additional five had seen service as militia officers. One member's sole military qualification was that he was a veteran of the Cherokee War (of removal) of the 1830s.[49]

A more important factor was prewar government service. As noted earlier, approximately one-third (35 percent) had held public office prior to 1861 and were able to parlay their political experience into a commission in the army. Table 7 shows that nearly an equal number had served on both the state and county level. Fourteen had served at least one term in the state legislature, while about as many had held some county office, such as a sheriff or court clerk. Two members of the sample had held a federal office or appointment—John H. Hannah, who was postmaster of Benton; and William M. Churchwell, who was in the U.S. House of Representatives when the war began.[50]

Given the fact that nine of the fifty-two men who possessed some military or political background could lay claim to both, only 43 percent of the sample had some recognizable prewar leadership experience. Why the remaining 57 percent were selected to command is not clear from their collective resume. Only wealth and their professional occupations—factors which Martin Crawford argues were prerequisites for leadership among the volunteer companies raised in the North Carolina mountains[51]—set them apart from the average East Tennessean and could have influenced

Table 6
Prewar Military Experience of Selected East Tennessee Confederate Leaders

Military Experience	N
Mexican War	12
Military academy	3[a]
Militia officer	5[b]
Cherokee War (1830s)	1

Notes: Total $N = 21$.
[a] Includes one cadet who resigned prior to graduation.
[b] Does not include those officers appointed after April 1861 but prior to the June secession referendum.
Source: See chap. 3, n. 48.

Table 7
Prewar Political Experience of Selected East Tennessee Confederate Leaders

Political Experience	N
State legislature	14
County office	
Sheriff	5
County clerk	4
Trustee	2
Clerk and master	1
Judge	1
Justice of the peace	1
Register	1
Other	
U.S. Congress	1
Postmaster	1
Presidential elector	1
City council	1
Census enumerator	1
Attorney-general	1

Note: Total $N = 35$.
Source: See chap. 3, n. 49.

their fellow citizens to elevate them to positions of leadership in the army. The average property holding among the group was far greater than the regional average; and the fact that many of them owned any slaves at all placed them in a higher social and economic position than most East Tennesseans.

But if the reasons for their selection to command are uncertain, one thing is quite clear: the majority of East Tennessee's leading secessionists were men who, despite their wealth, lacked either the power or the talent to control political affairs on either the state or local level. Only in the four counties of Polk (where all six company commanders were involved in politics), Sullivan (where half of the six line and field officers were political figures), Meigs (where three out of five of the sample held office), and Rhea (where half of the six military leaders were also prewar politicos) does it appear that secessionists even approached anything akin to real political power at the grass-roots level. Not surprisingly, these four counties reported the largest secession majorities of any in the region: 72, 70, 64.3, and 64.1 percent, respectively.[32] Indeed, nearly half of those in the

Table 8

Comparison of Selected East Tennessee Unionist and Secessionist Leaders, by Category

Category	Secessionists (%)	Unionists (%)
Occupation		
Agriculture	38	65
Merchant-professional	62	35
Wealth		
Estates worth		
$5,000 or more	60	40
Age		
40 years or older	28	73
Slaveholding		
Slaveholders	43	41
Less than 10 slaves	79	83

Note: Total $N = 146$.

sample who held office (sixteen out of thirty-five) were politicians from five counties favoring secession. In stark contrast, none of the three officers from heavily Unionist Greene County (which included the two sons of Union leader Thomas Arnold) and none of the six from staunchly loyal Bradley County appear to have held any position of authority. Stated in another way, outside of a few counties, secessionists did not control the reins of political power in June 1861, as the vote on separation so vividly attests, and they were able to persuade only a minority of their fellow citizens to follow them into war.

Of course, there were those who possessed political power in counties where Unionists predominated. Samuel Powel, for instance, both served in the legislature as a Democrat and, as previously mentioned, was state attorney general when the war began. Powel was from Hawkins County, one of several where, even though they lost, secessionists made a good showing. Likewise, James G. Rose, a twenty-five-year-old merchant from Sneedville who represented Hancock County as a Democrat in the General Assembly, also hailed from a county with a large minority favoring separation.[53]

But such were the exception. In general, although they occupied an economically powerful position, the influence of secessionists diminished once out of the cities and towns that dotted the Valley floor. Outside of a few counties, they were unable to control most of the rural voters of the region and were incapable of translating their growing economic power into any real political muscle. As table 8 illustrates, secessionist leaders were mirror opposites of their Unionist opponents in nearly every attribute, with the significant exception of slaveholding. In terms of occupation, wealth, political party affiliation, and age, disunionists did not fit the profile of the traditional East Tennessee leader. Deriving their strength from their commercial and business ventures rather than from agriculture and Whiggery, this young, rising middle class was unable to command the allegiance of a majority of East Tennessee's yeomanry. This failure exposed a rift between the cosmopolitan advocates of change and the defenders of the old local order—a rift which, in many ways, portended the savagery and bitterness to come.

East Tennesseans Are Willing to Fight

At 4:30 on the morning of April 12, 1861, a signal gun in the Confederate batteries at Charleston, South Carolina, fired a shot which triggered the bombardment of Fort Sumter. Among the Rebel artillerists shelling the fort that day was a young East Tennessee secessionist, John Crawford Vaughn. That an East Tennessean would be in Charleston firing the first shots of the Civil War would have seemed strange to many in 1861, and even more so to historians over a century later. For Vaughn, however, committed as he was to Southern independence, his presence there that day was not only normal, it was necessary.

Vaughn's stand with his fellow Southerners against Federal authority was significant, for it revealed his sense of unity with the Deep South in its struggle to create a new nation. What he experienced that April morning with the South Carolina volunteers apparently convinced him that not only he personally but also his native East Tennessee must be brought into the conflict, now that war was inevitable. As soon as the guns in Charleston Harbor fell silent, he dashed home and raised the first company from Monroe County to be offered to the Confederate government. Within only a few weeks, Vaughn would be elected colonel of the Third Tennessee Infantry, PACS (Provisional Army Confederate States), the first Confederate regiment raised in the region and the third regiment from Tennessee accepted into Confederate service.[1]

Vaughn was not alone in his rush to arms. In the wake of Sumter's fall and Lincoln's call for troops, East Tennessee volunteers began to flock to the Confederate banner. Even before their state officially left the Union, young men such as Vaughn hastily organized military units to meet the expected Northern invasion. In towns and villages across the region, the spectacle of raw troops mobilizing for war was a common sight that spring. A company composed of Maryville College students, many of whom were destined for leadership roles in the emerging Southern army, drilled nightly on the green in Maryville. The unit never made it to the front, however, because the students all left to join other commands when the school closed late that April.[2] To the north in Jonesboro, a company of young Rebels paraded through the town and listened attentively to saber-rattling speeches at the Washington County Court House, each soldier bearing upon the left breast of his uniform the motto Resistance.[3] In neighboring Sullivan County, volunteer companies arrived in the county seat of Blountville clad in all sorts of uniforms and carrying a variety of weapons, "looking like anything else than soldiers," remembered one eyewitness. The most striking feature about the raw recruits was their flags, each bearing its own motto or device such as, "Come, boys, let's meet them," "Don't tread on us," "Let us alone," and other "high spirited legends."[4]

In fact, there was so much competition for recruits, and hence a commission in the new army, that aspiring officers devised ingenious ways to lure volunteers. For example, Stephen M. Cocke formed his company in Morristown with the assistance of a brass band. Cocke and the band started at one of end Main Street and marched toward the other, the band blaring patriotic tunes and men yelling and falling in behind as they moved down the street. By the time Cocke and his musicians reached the end of Main, the captain had his quota of recruits.[5] Another would-be commander held a barbecue and cannon firing in Hawkins County to stir enlistment in the Rebel army. The festive occasion was complete with speeches by such secessionist luminaries as Landon C. Haynes and Felix Zollicoffer, who urged the crowd to rally to their country's defense.[6] Benton, county seat of Polk County, was the scene of a torchlight parade, with the volunteers in the front, women in the center, and men and boys in the rear. "The procession being formed," enthused one participant, "the torches burning and every door and window brightly illuminated with candles we marched through the different streets of town, and being but a few days after the state of Virginia had withdrawn from the old Union, the procession marched to the tune of 'Old Virginia.'" From doorways and windows girls tossed bouquets of flowers at the soldiers as they trod by on their way to the public square. Around eleven o'clock, with two new companies ready to go to the front, the excited, and no doubt tired, revelers were dismissed after listening to the obligatory secession speeches on the courthouse lawn.[7]

Even in the heavily Unionist counties, Confederate leaders attempted to entice recruits into the emerging Southern army. From Greeneville, one Rebel reported to Confederate officials that "the prospect of success is flattering three companies in this county being nearly completed."[8] Reuben Arnold, son of prominent Unionist Thomas Arnold, and H. G. Robinson, former editor of the *Greeneville Democrat*, received commissions as colonel and lieutenant colonel, respectively, and were busily enlisting young Greenevillians in order to offer a regiment for state service.[9] One of J. G. M. Ramsey's sons ventured up to Jacksboro in ultra-Unionist Campbell County, where according to his father he "bearded the lion in his den." The younger Ramsey courageously planted a Confederate flag on the courthouse lawn and proceeded to urge "the young men of the mountain country" to follow him back to Knoxville and enlist. While he spoke, a small band of "bullies" tried to intimidate Ramsey, but he calmly finished his speech and, to his father's surprise, made it back home with several volunteers in tow.[10]

These and other recruiting efforts were so successful that by late May over twenty companies from across the Great Valley had arrived in Knoxville and were encamped just outside of town at the fair grounds. The city quickly became the major staging point for units raised in the region. The *Register* kept the local citizenry up to date on the status of troop arrivals, one day reporting that a company from McMinn and Jefferson had just taken up quarters in the city and that three more from Washington, Polk, and Rhea were soon to follow.[11] A unit raised in Jonesboro, led by West Point dropout Zadock Willet, particularly caught the paper's attention, the editor describing Willet's command as "a full company and of the true East Tennessee mettle."[12] Captain Hannah's company from Polk County marched into town to the beat of a very special drum—one that had seen service in the Revolutionary War and which, according to its owners, had beat in the charge on Yorktown eighty years earlier. It had been carefully preserved, and, reported the *Nashville Republican Banner*, "the Polk boys say it shall be beat again at the charge on Washington." The paper cheered the men and their instrument on to battle, crying "victory again, say we, to the drum and the gallant fellows who follow it in its second mission for Independence."[13]

Of all the communities in East Tennessee, the towns responded the most enthusiastically to the call for volunteers. As in western North Carolina, where enlistment was greatest in urban districts, the vast majority of recruits to the Southern cause during the early stages of the war were drawn from the region's towns and villages.[14] Companies bearing nicknames like the Blountville Guards, Knoxville Grays, Decatur Guards, and Greeneville Guards filled out the ranks of the first regiments organized during the summer of 1861. Typical was the Nineteenth Tennessee Infantry. Organized on June 11 of units encamped at Knoxville, nine of its ten companies were composed of townsfolk hailing from Chattanooga, Rogersville, Knoxville, Blountville, and Jonesboro. Other regiments, like the Twenty-sixth and Twenty-ninth Infantry, were similarly constructed.[15]

What motivated young East Tennesseans to enlist in 1861? How did their motivations differ from that of the region's Rebel leadership? A number of possibilities exist. Bell Wiley in his monumental work on the common soldier of the Confederacy contended that Southerners volunteered out of a desire for adventure and because of community pressure to go and fight. Gerald Linderman has identified courage as another factor prompting enlistment. The notion of courage—"heroic action undertaken without fear"—served as "the goad and guide of men in battle," according to Linderman, the ideal which compelled Civil War soldiers to rush to arms in 1861. And most recently, Reid Mitchell has argued that Southerners were compelled to join up by a combination of factors that were all interrelated. Confederates, he contends, perceived themselves as struggling ultimately for freedom, in much the same way as their grandfathers had fought against the British for political independence. Some were moved by racism and fear of slave insurrection, while others saw the South as a land of economic opportunity or a separate culture that was worth fighting to maintain. Still others were motivated by simple hatred of Yankees. All of these formed a "reasonably coherent ideology," in that no one factor could be divorced from the other. Economic opportunity and the notion of a distinct separate culture rested upon the cornerstone of slavery which the Yankee threatened to destroy. The destruction of slavery would ruin the South's prosperity and raise the specter of racial equality, all of which fed a loathing for the Northern soldier.[16]

Nearly all of these motivations can be detected among the young men who swelled the ranks of the new military units in East Tennessee. Not surprisingly, these recruits were filled with the patriotism and war fervor typical of other Southern volunteers. "East Tennesseans are ready and willing to fight," crowed one Rebel soldier, predicting that "they will prove it when the time comes."[17] Similarly, Lt. Richard M. Saffell was confident that the men from the Great Valley would be heard from in the coming conflict. "I have no fears," he boasted to his brother-in-law, "but that the 3rd East Ten. Regiment, which is the 26th Ten., will do their duty & if placed in where the chance affords, will distinguish themselves."[18] Another member of the Twenty-sixth, Hannibal Paine, also believed that his regiment was destined for glory. "When organized we will have one of the finest Regiments that has ever went from East Tennessee," Paine confidently predicted, "and should oppertunity offer upon the battlefield, I think we will win for ourselves undying laurels, and gain a glory and renown equal to any secured by Tennessee's sons, or the sons of the South."[19] "At all events we will conquer," asserted another Confederate, "and then we will have one of the proudest and best governments in the known world."[20]

Richard M. Saffell, c. 1861. A Knox County farmer who spent much of the 1850s clerking with merchants in Atlanta, Saffell was killed near the end of the war at Bentonville, leading the Twenty-sixth Tennessee Infantry. His body was never recovered. Courtesy of Special Collections Department, University of Tennessee Libraries, Knoxville.

Defending the valley from invasion by Federal troops, coupled with sheer hatred for Yankees, seems to have compelled many to enter the army. "I shall have no opportunity to come home soon," complained Capt. George P. Faw of the Twenty-ninth Tennessee to his family, "as it is generally understood that the enemy is coming in large force to make their way into our valleys in East Tennessee and our business is to keep them out."[21] One volunteer declared that he and his comrades were fighting for "the reclamation of our own country, our Sunny South—the land where blooms a waste of flowers from the base pollution, usurpation, and tyranny of Abraham Lincoln, and its restoration to a state of peace, liberty, and independence."[22] Some, such as James Scruggs of the Fifty-ninth Tennessee, interpreted their defense of home and family as a part of their revolutionary heritage. "When I think of the foe taking the bounty and beauty of the South," confided Scruggs, "I seem to hear the Spirit of '76 thundering along the At[lantic] coast To Arms! To Arms! Southerners, or your liberties are gone!"[23] And as the guardians of their homes and families, Rebel soldiers perceived themselves as morally superior to the opponents. "We fight for principles," proclaimed Samuel H. Hynds, a member of the Third Tennessee in Virginia, "the Federal troops fight for want of employment." This sense of self-righteousness gave rise to utter contempt for the Yankees. "I hate our enemy more and cannot return to Tennessee satisfied unless I feel confident I have honorably rid our land of at least five," Hynds seethed, "but that won't pay the South for sending me here."[24]

Although Reid Mitchell contends that most Confederates were motivated by either a desire to defend slavery or by a fear of racial equality, East Tennesseans seemed to have been little concerned over the issue of white supremacy. In only one instance was preservation of the peculiar institution cited as a reason for enlisting. Following the murder of four whites in Hawkins County by two slaves in May 1861, a secessionist woman wrote her brother, "I hope the Lord will blaze the armies of the South. There is some excitement yet about the negro insurrection, but none of the impudent have been punished at all. . . . Bachman has quit school and says he will volunteer if his two brothers get home from New York to take care of the farm."[25] Such attitudes were rare, however, in a region of few slaves, where blacks constituted less than 10 percent of the total population in 1860. In this respect, East Tennesseans were similar to other Southern troops from the western theater who, Larry Daniel has found, exhibited little, if any, apprehension over slavery as a motivation for enlistment.[26]

Also missing from the qualitative evidence is any mention of economic factors as a reason for fighting for the Confederacy. While the leadership class was probably motivated by a desire to continue the prosperity that better trade connections with the South were bringing to East Tennessee and, thus, to protect their Southern markets, their followers apparently were less directly influenced by the new wealth. On the other hand, as the company nicknames suggest, many of these young men were townsfolk who would have enjoyed the benefits that the railroad offered the region, even if the connection was not readily apparent to them. Their rising expectations as urban and village dwellers would have set them apart from many of the more rural people in the region who either failed to enlist or who joined the Union army.

More commonly, East Tennesseans were motivated by community pressure to join the army. Family, friends, and society at large questioned the courage, and hence the manhood, of any who failed to respond to the call of duty. Unionist Thomas Humes suggested that many who enlisted in the Southern ranks did so only out of fear of "the reproach of their communities for want of the right affection and just conduct, or worse still, to be called 'Scalawags' and 'Lincolnites.'"[27] Following Gov. Isham G. Harris's 1862 proclamation calling out the militia, one recent recruit commented that "those who are able and do not go now are not worthy of the respect of the ladies and soldiers. Madisonville has done very well but there are a few more who ought by all means to go."[28] Community pressure was also used to steady men already in the ranks. "I don't want to hear of one of the Meigs boys a Being shot in the back tho I am not afraid of that," an East Tennessee father admonished his soldier sons.[29] The *Chattanooga Gazette and Advertizer* reported that the Ladies Relief Society of Chattanooga had blankets to give to the troops after the battle of Mill Springs but added that the women "desire us to say, however, that the blankets will not be handed out *indiscriminately,* and that as many of the 'boys' as *run* in the late encounter with the Yankees will go blanketless."[30] Such expectations led one soldier to confess, "I couldn't stay in town long enough now, when all the boys have gone to fight . . . and to be sneered at and called one of the flat-footed Milish, by those who are not able to go to the wars." "No," he concluded, "I couldn't stand that."[31]

Not all volunteers were so certain of their commitment. Some reached a decision to enlist only after a measure of soul searching. While ultimately loyal to their state and to the South, they found drawing the sword against the old Union difficult, even if Lincoln was threatening them with what they perceived as subjugation. "I am now a Volunteer in the Southern army," confided Samuel Lyle of Dandridge to his cousin nearly a year after Sumter. "I did hope this matter could be settled without me having anything to do in the affair at all, but it seems as if I was mistaken in the matter."[32] A similar attitude was voiced by James A. Caldwell of Madisonville. "You wish to know which I would fight for, if I should be called out, the North or the South," Caldwell replied to a female relative (who no doubt wondered why he was not in the army). "I will just say that I don't wish to fight either," he confessed. But if forced to choose sides, "although I hate to leave the Union, but there is no Union now, I will of course fight for my native South," he finally admitted. Notice Caldwell's choice of words. Only if he were "called out" would he fight. Caldwell's hesitancy was not imaginary; it would be almost ten months, under threat of conscription, before he finally decided to go into the army.[33] His ambivalence, and that of others like him, would resurface as repeated defeat on the battlefield softened their resolve to continue the fight.

The number of Confederate troops raised in East Tennessee is difficult to determine with any exactness. Estimates vary according to the method of calculation. In a recent study of white Union troops from Tennessee, Peter Wallenstein figured that as many as 48,800 men from East Tennessee, or 36 percent of the total Confederate troops from the state, entered the Southern army. Wallenstein's estimate, which is based on a much broader definition of the region than is traditionally (and legally) accepted, is probably double the actual number. Defining East Tennessee as those counties with white populations above 70 percent, Wallenstein includes all of the highland rim area of the state, counties usually associated with Middle Tennessee, as a part of the eastern grand division. If estimates are made solely on the basis of the thirty-three counties historically a part of East Tennessee, then it is necessary to arrive at a much lower figure. From those counties, 15 regiments, 7 battalions, and 6 batteries of artillery were raised for Confederate service during the course of the war. Normally, regiments were made up of 10 companies, battalions of 5 (on average), and each battery was considered a single company. Therefore, according to these calculations, 191 companies from East Tennessee were organized during the war. If we assume that a regulation company was composed of 100 men (and many Confederate units were notorious for never reaching regulation strength), then no more than 20,000 East Tennesseans voluntarily entered the Rebel ranks. This figure does not include the approximately 5,000 conscripts who were enrolled and assigned to the army from camps of instruction after passage of the April 1862 conscription law. Even if we include those men and others from the Great Valley who enlisted in regiments from neighboring states, as a few did, then no more than 25,000 East Tennesseans (or 13.4 percent of the 186,652 officers and men from Tennessee who, according to *Tennesseans in the Civil War,* fought in the Rebel ranks) could have served in the Southern army. Significantly, this figure of 13.4 percent corresponds better than Wallenstein's 36 percent with East Tennessee's secession vote, which comprised only about 14 percent of the statewide total favoring separation.[34]

When Governor Harris began to organize Tennessee's defensive forces following Sumter, he divided the state into three military departments roughly corresponding to the three grand divisions—East, Middle, and West. Harris appointed Richard Caswell of Knoxville as brigadier general in the new Provisional Army of Tennessee and assigned him to command the East Tennessee Brigade. Other East Tennesseans appointed to important positions were Richard G. Fain of Rogersville as commissary general, S. T. Bicknell of Maryville as assistant quartermaster general, and John P. McCown of Sevierville as commander of the state artillery. Caswell was charged with organizing regiments from the independent companies raised in the valley. To assist Caswell in this difficult task, Harris named Maj. David M. Key of Chattanooga and former state representative James W. Gillespie of Rhea County as assistant adjutant general and assistant inspector general, respectively, and assigned them to Caswell's staff. Together, the trio organized the First, Second, and Third East Tennessee Infantry Regiments (later redesignated the Third Provisional, Nineteenth, and Twenty-sixth Tennessee Infantry Regiments, respectively) from the companies stationed in Knoxville. The cavalry companies were formed into temporary battalion-sized units or were allowed to continue independent operation until such time as a sufficient number had been raised to organize a regiment. These commands were turned over to Confederate authorities in June when the state officially joined the Richmond government.[35]

During the remainder of the summer, recruitment slowed but then picked up again in the fall. When Harris issued a call for twenty thousand more volunteers that autumn, Key and Gillespie, their work for the state completed, raised the Fifth East Tennessee Regiment (Forty-third Tennessee Infantry) and tendered it for Confederate service. Caswell's nomination as brigadier general was never confirmed by the Confederate Congress, and he retired to his farm in east Knox County.[36] Throughout the rest of the year, volunteers continued to enlist (though not as eagerly as they had in the spring) so that by the end of 1861, six regiments of infantry, three battalions of cavalry, and two batteries of artillery were either in or ready to take the field, with several additional regiments nearing completion of their organization.[37]

While on paper the East Tennessee troops may have looked ready to fight, they lacked one essential ingredient to perfect their organization and to turn them into an effective fighting force—weapons. Throughout the first year of the war, Caswell and his successors found it nearly impossible to procure the small arms, especially muskets and rifles, necessary to arm the volunteers properly. Although the Third Tennessee under the command of Col. John C. Vaughn apparently obtained arms shortly after arriving in Virginia (Vaughn's was the only Tennessee unit to participate actively in the first battle of Manassas), few other regiments were so fortunate.[38] For instance, in May 1861, a number of newly arrived companies in Knoxville were sworn into the state's service and then marched into town expecting to receive a shipment of muskets and rifles from Chattanooga. The disappointed recruits returned to camp empty handed, because the promised arms did not arrive.[39]

As volunteers continued to enlist, the government found itself even more hard pressed to arm its troops. More and more weaponless men began to crowd into the camps around Knoxville, embarrassing Confederate officials in the region. Brig. Gen. William H. Carroll in command at Knoxville claimed that he had on hand about four thousand men who "could be brought immediately into the field if I could only supply them with arms." As it was, he grumbled, "out of my entire force, I could not muster more than 300 men efficiently armed."[40] An ordnance officer reported to Carroll in December that two hundred rifles which Carroll had sent to the shops to be fitted for bayonets were unfit for duty, and some of them, the officer declared, were "entirely worthless."[41] Carroll complained bitterly to Richmond and informed Secretary of War Judah P. Benjamin that, because no weapons could be had from the government, he had collected two thousand "ordinary country rifles" with which to arm his brigade of East Tennesseans and placed them in armories in Memphis, Nashville, and Murfreesboro to have them altered for field service. None of these was ever repaired. Instead Carroll received from Memphis about four hundred old flintlocks, which he considered "almost worthless." No doubt these were castoffs from West Tennessee regiments which had obtained newer models.[42]

Despite Carroll's clamoring, the situation showed little sign of improving. A weapons' inspection of the Thirty-seventh Tennessee in December revealed that half of the regiment's arms were "wholly unserviceable and most of the remainder unfit for service." The regiment's marching orders were counter-manded and the men sent back to camp.[43] As late as January 1862, the Forty-third Tennessee was still confined to camp in Knoxville, because the men were unarmed.[44] By spring, conditions had changed little. Just before the battle of Shiloh, for example, a Middle Tennessee regiment offered the Thirty-seventh its old flintlocks, which it had recently replaced with modern weapons. "Rather an improvement on nothing, or what we have, some of the flintlocks accepted," noted a member of the Thirty-seventh in his diary.[45] In Morristown, the Fifty-ninth Tennessee did not receive weapons until late May 1862, nearly a year af-ter the state had seceded.[46]

The difficulty experienced in securing arms was symptomatic of a larger problem confronting East Tennessee Confederates, one which reached all the way to the capital in Richmond. Throughout the Confederacy there existed a growing suspicion toward all East Tennesseans that worked to the disadvantage of those loyal to the Confederate government. Either because of the region's known Unionist sympathies or because of the tra-ditional rivalry between the divisions of the state, Middle and West Ten-nesseans and Southerners in general tended to distrust and even dislike Confederate troops from the Great Valley. "It was the habit of certain persons in 1861 and for years afterwards," remembered Thomas W. Humes, "to speak contemptuously of East Tennessee because of its devotion to the Union."[47] The diehard Unionism of their neighbors made East Ten-nessee Confederates guilty of treason by association in the minds of many Southerners. "To hail from East Tennessee was a reproach in the South," lamented Col. W. P. Bishop of the Twenty-ninth Tennessee. Once while troops were marching through Georgia, a woman asked a member of the Twenty-ninth "if he was not ashamed to own that he was an East Tennes-sean." The soldier emphatically replied that he was not. "I am proud that I belong to that much abused country," he asserted, "and I think that if one Confederate soldier is entitled to more credit than another, the greater praise is due those who came into the Southern army under difficulties such as we had to contend with."[48]

Indeed, most East Tennessee soldiers believed that they deserved not scorn but special credit for defying their region's Union majority and enlisting in the Southern army. Abraham Fulkerson of the Sixty-third Tennessee de-clared that "many times it required a heroic effort to do what was believed to be right; hence it cost something to be a soldier." He reasoned that "on this account the East Tennessee soldiers are entitled to much more credit than those living where sentiment was undivided," an obvious jab at Middle and

West Tennesseans.[49] Lt. Bird G. Manard of Ashby's Second Tennessee Cavalry conceded that few East Tennesseans entered the Southern ranks, "but this did not lessen the ardor of enlistment," especially when "public sentiment was against them."[50] Another valley Rebel argued, "Secession in East Tennessee, unlike every other section of the South, was not the primrose way to office, emolument and distinction; on the contrary, it was the direct road to political, social and pecuniary ruin." He resentfully observed that "no other people in the South have made such a sacrifice."[51] A member of the Twenty-ninth Tennessee declared that "the men who had the nerve to stem the popular current and enter the army in the face of all opposition" were motivated by a sense of duty and patriotism "that needed only the opportunity to develop them into first-class soldiers."[52]

The constant pounding they received at the hands of their fellow Confederates made East Tennessee Rebels defensive and resentful. "You middle and west Tennesseeans, living where there is not . . . any division of sentiment upon the justness of our cause, have never rightly comprehended the state of affairs, or the feelings of the people in East Tennessee," complained an East Tennessee officer to Governor Harris.[53] Responding to a charge leveled by the *Atlanta Intelligencer* that Greene and Sevier "stand out as the banner counties of toryism," the *Greeneville Banner* weakly replied that "out of 863 Southern men in Greene county [the number of secession votes cast in June 1861], she has furnished at least 500 volunteers to the Southern army."[54] In a similar vein, the *Greeneville Democrat,* apparently smarting from the same attack, fired back with much exaggeration that "for the benefit of our friends at a distance, we have the pleasure to say . . . that the idea of preserving the Union has become an obsolete idea with all men in upper East Tennessee."[55] The *Athens Post* defensively claimed that "East Tennessee, as much reviled as it is, has more troops in the Southern army in proportion to the Southern vote than any other part of the Confederacy. It cast 15,000 votes for the South, and has 17 regiments in the service."[56] A Knoxvillian, stung by accusations that Union sympathy was strong in his city, denied that his neighbors had abandoned their commitment to Southern independence: "I declare most emphatically, that no such state of affairs . . . exists here. The fact is, there is much apprehension existing abroad in regard to Knoxville and East Tennessee generally"—an apprehension he considered entirely misplaced.[57]

Fortunately for them, once the East Tennessee volunteers got a chance to "develop," they proved themselves loyal in the eyes of their fellow soldiers. "The Virginians swar that we have a regiment of the bravest men they ever saw from any State," bragged Benjamin F. Taylor of the Third Tennessee. "They give us the front when ever there is any fighting to do as they know we will not flinch."[58] At least one Marylander, McHenry Howard, agreed. Howard, whose First Maryland fought alongside the Third Tennessee at First Manassas, considered the "men of the Tennessee regiment" to be "good material for soldiers," even if they did have a fondness for whiskey.[59] Even a few civilians, like a group of ladies from Savannah, Georgia, concurred with this assessment of East Tennessee valor. With their own hands the women sewed a battle flag for the Twenty-ninth Tennessee and presented it during the summer of 1864 as the regiment fought to protect Atlanta from Federal capture.[60]

The toughest lot to convince, however, was the men from West and Middle Tennessee. When the Twenty-ninth was assigned to Brig. Gen. Preston Smith's brigade in the fall of 1862, it was the sole East Tennessee regiment in the brigade and, as such, had "more than one term of reproach applied to it." The general, however, welcomed the East Tennesseans and rode along the regiment's front, expressing his hope that "it would do its duty." He would not be disappointed. Shortly thereafter, in the battle of Murfreesboro, the regiment suffered nearly 35 percent casualties. This sacrifice endeared them to their fellow Tennesseans. The regiment's commander, Col. William P. Bishop, proudly remembered that "at the close of that memorable 31st of December any man in Cheatham's division was willing to take a Twenty-ninth man by the hand and call him comrade."[61] A similar tribute was paid to the East Tennesseans of the Thirty-seventh Tennessee Infantry of Bushrod Johnson's brigade. The brigade's four other regiments, all raised in Middle Tennessee, unanimously selected Maj. Joseph T. McReynolds of the Thirty-seventh as the most courageous officer from their command killed during the fight at Murfreesboro. As such, the twenty-three-year-old native of Blount County had his name inscribed on one of four guns captured from a Federal battery by Cleburne's division during the first day of battle.[62]

Despite such encomiums among soldiers, however, all was not well. Indeed, by late 1861 there were ominous signs that some East Tennesseans were already losing faith in Richmond's ability to win the war. Enlistment was slowing, and serious discipline problems were beginning to surface in some regiments already in the field. Between November 1861 and February 1862, only one regiment of infantry was organized in the valley, while sixteen were raised in Middle and West Tennessee during the same period.[63] "I am sorry to see the people in some portions of E. Tenn. so slow in volunteering," confessed Hannibal Paine of the Twenty-sixth Tennessee. "I think it speaks but poorly for their patriotism, when their own state is menaced with invasion, and their homes threatened with fire, sword, rapine, and plunder."[64] J. G. M. Ramsey suggested to President Davis that if Vaughn's regiment were returned to East Tennessee from Virginia, "it will excite (revive is not the word) the spirit of volunteering, which I am humiliated to say is very low."[65] The *Chattanooga Gazette and Advertiser* lashed out at the people of Knox County for failing to do more for the cause, accusing them of profiting from the war by selling food, clothing, and other supplies to the army at "exorbitant rates" while hesitating to sacrifice by going "into the ranks." The paper mistakenly claimed that "there has not been a single company made up in this County received into the Confederate service," observing that this was even more remarkable given the number of "original Secessionists" in Knoxville who had clamored the previous year for separation.[66] Even some already in the ranks were considering going home once their term of enlistment had expired. James Stakely, a member of the Fifty-ninth Tennessee, reported with disgust that his comrades were only slowly reenlisting for the mandated three-year term now that their twelve-months' service was ending. Fully half of the regiment's companies were at half strength, while in Company D, commanded by Capt. Reuben Giles, "none so far" had reentered the army. "Capt. Giles himself is not very strong on the 'three years' question, and consequently will not urge his men to reenlist," Stakely complained.[67]

Several factors contributed to the decline in enlistment during the winter of 1861–62. The tragic defeat in mid-January at Mill Springs in eastern Kentucky, where an army commanded by Felix Zollicoffer (which included several regiments of East Tennesseans) was routed, may have shaken the resolve of some not fully committed to the war effort. Zollicoffer, the darling of East Tennessee Rebels, was killed, and his men were driven back on Cumberland Gap, dangerously close to the Tennessee border. Probably more damaging to the government's efforts to encourage enlistment, however, were the famous bridge burnings of November 1861, in which Union saboteurs destroyed five railroad bridges, temporarily severing rail communication between East Tennessee and the rest of the Confederacy and spreading panic among the Confederates of the region.[68] With Unionists openly up in arms, it is possible that many who otherwise would have joined the Southern army decided to stay home and protect their families from attack. Unlike Middle and West Tennessee, where the only foe to fear was from without, East Tennessee Southern sympathizers had to confront enemies from without and within. Their homes surrounded by a hostile populous, with little or no support for their wives and children from the community once they were away, some men simply decided that it was not worth exposing their families to such dangers. L. B. Headerick, a militia officer from Greeneville, complained to Governor Harris that volunteers were unwilling to enter the army "if required to leave their wives and children to starve at the mercy of a far more relentless foe than any of Lincoln's thieves can be." Headerick tried to impress on Harris that the situation was "no fancy or imaginary picture, but . . . a stern reality."[69] Similarly, Albert G. Graham, editor of the pro-Confederate *Jonesboro Union,* advocated deporting Union leaders from East Tennessee as a way of encouraging Southern enlistment. "By removing the hostile element from our counties we have peace," he informed President Davis in early November, "and the Southern men can then enter the Army, because they know that their families are safe at home."[70]

With enlistment falling so far behind expectation, Rebel leaders stepped up their efforts to encourage young East Tennesseans to volunteer. In an appeal to county pride, the *Chattanooga Gazette and Advertiser* insisted that Hamilton County was "the Banner County" when it came to enlistment in East Tennessee, boasting that "Old Hamilton, with all her little dens of Lincolnism and dark corners of mid night ignorance has perhaps done more in the way of volunteers for the Southern cause than any other in the State." Hoping to stir similar sentiments in Sevier County, the *Gazette* decried the sobriquet "Little Massachusetts" that had been applied to Sevier County because of its intense Unionism. "'Old Sevier' is all right now," the editors protested, adding hopefully that "the scales have fallen from her eyes—and her boys are eager to participate in our glorious struggle for independence." In another column, the *Gazette* urged "every man in East Tennessee, who is capable of bearing arms, now shoulder his musket and prepare to meet the foe."[71] Not to be outdone, the *Athens Post* boasted "Old Monroe Ahead," claiming that the county had eleven companies in the service and that one hundred and fifty men from Madisonville had just joined up.[72] Crying, "To Arms East Tennesseans!" one Knoxvillian, echoing the call of the *Gazette,* pleaded with his neighbors "to awake to a full consciousness of their part . . . in the pending crisis," adding that "there is yet room for more *volunteers* from East Tennessee and they are invited to come forward and enroll themselves."[73]

When such pleas failed to generate a wave of voluntary enlistment, the government called out the region's militia units as a means of getting more men to the front. But even this order from the governor generated few new recruits. Despite encouragement from such loyal Confederates as "HJF" in Sweetwater, who in a letter to the *Cleveland Banner* argued that "it is everyman's duty who is subject to military duty to attend punctually and drill whether you know more than your officers or not," the response was disappointingly small.[74] "There has been but one Brigade reported [as] received at these Head Quarters," one militia officer informed his superiors. Out of four regiments subject to duty, only one thousand men, or a quarter of those expected, armed with a mere sixty muskets had turned out. Many people considered such a call equivalent to a draft and refused to participate, while "most of the loyal militia enlisted as volunteers" and were already in the army.[75] Militia major L. B. Headerick agreed. "I have just returned, cold and wet, from the Regimental muster ground," he complained to Governor Harris. "There I found, out of a regiment numbering over 1500 men subject to militia duty, 105 between the ages of 18 and 45 years—96 of those men were patrots or Southern men, 8 were 'Union men or tories.'" Those ninety-six composed "the strength of the Southern men left. . . . The others are now in the army of their country."[76] It was becoming increasingly clear that the Confederacy had received all of the "voluntary" help from East Tennessee that it was likely to realize.

Of course, all of this probably contributed to the East Tennessee soldiers' poor reputation. But as damaging as the conduct of lukewarm patriots may have been, nothing hurt their image in the eyes of the South more than the opinions of one man, Maj. Gen. E. Kirby Smith. Indeed, no understanding of the relationship between secessionists in East Tennessee and Richmond is possible without an examination of Smith's conduct as commander of the Department of East Tennessee. When Smith assumed command in March 1862, it marked the beginning of a strange relationship between the general and the people he came to lead that tainted the attitude of Richmond toward the Great Valley and hindered the war effort in the region. Although an outsider, Smith was the single most important Confederate in the valley during the spring and summer of 1862. As virtual military governor of the region, Smith played a pivotal role in developing the attitudes of the Confederate government toward the people he commanded. During his tenure, he advocated a policy that failed to distinguish between the loyal and the disloyal, painting for his superiors a picture of treason and disaffection which disheartened many secessionists and drove a wedge between the Davis administration and the Confederate element in East Tennessee. In short, Smith paved the way for the suspicion, oppression, and conscription that alienated Confederate East Tennesseans from their government in Richmond.

Born in Florida, Smith was a graduate of West Point who had spent his adult life in the military prior to resigning in 1861 to follow his native state out of the Union. His entire Confederate service before transfer to East Tennessee was in Virginia, where, coincidentally, he commanded a brigade which included Vaughn's Third Tennessee Infantry. While leading the East Tennesseans, Smith was badly wounded at First Manassas. Perhaps something unknown and ugly grew out of his contact with Vaughn and his men in Virginia that prejudiced him against East Tennessee even before his arrival there.[77] At any rate, Smith was appointed to replace Maj. Gen. George B. Crittenden, whose heavy drinking had only added to the department's problems after the death of Zollicoffer. Significantly, the Floridian was the first soldier to command in East Tennessee for an extended period of time who was not from the region or who did not have strong political and social ties to the people of the valley.[78]

Immediately upon arriving at his new headquarters in Knoxville, Smith began to fire off to Richmond discouraging reports about conditions in his department. "East Tennessee is an enemy's country," Smith declared in no uncertain terms to Adjutant General Samuel Cooper in early March.[79] "The people are against us, and ready to rise whenever an enemy's column makes an appearance," he warned. He cursed East Tennesseans as "an ignorant, primitive people completely in the hands of and under the guidance of their [Unionist] leaders."[80] In a broad, sweeping generalization, he informed Cooper that "the very troops raised here cannot always be depended upon." Many had gone into the service merely "to escape suspicion" and were "prepared to give information to the enemy, and ready to pass over to him when the opportunity offers." To counter this tendency toward treason, Smith pointedly asked if it would not be better to ship the East Tennesseans off to another part of the Confederacy, "where in a purer political atmosphere and removed from their present associations they can do little or no harm and may become loyal and good soldiers?"[81]

Thus after only days in the region, Smith believed he had found the solution to the government's problems. He attempted to convince Richmond that transferring East Tennessee troops to a safer environment was the only way to make them fight. Disclosing his contempt for the men under his command, he encouraged the government to remove local troops "and a draft might soon be made to which a population would respond." By sending them southward, "they would soon become loyal and effective soldiers."[82] As it was, Smith firmly believed his soldiers could not be relied on to perform even the simplest of military tasks, like picket duty. Moreover, he also suspected that even some of his officers were disloyal. Under such conditions, he explained, raising new regiments proved nearly impossible.[83]

Smith could find nothing redeeming in his new troops and he did all he could to poison Richmond against them. He grumbled that East Tennesseans preferred to sign up for twelve months' service, rather than enlist for the duration of the war, despite the fact that the government was no longer receiving twelve-month volunteers.[84] Apparently, it never occurred to him that, due to the unusual circumstances in his department, he should request a special dispensation authorizing him to accept these one-year enlistments. Instead, he simply rejected men who would not volunteer for an unspecified period of time and then condemned them as disloyal. As far as the militia were concerned, Smith whined to Cooper that they refused to assemble, which was not entirely true, "and even should they, they are not to be trusted," a comment not calculated to inspire Richmond's confidence in the region.[85] Cooper informed Smith that both President Davis and General Lee had been apprised of the situation in East Tennessee, particularly of the hostility of the people. Such a barrage of negativism could not have but taken effect in the minds of the Rebel high command.[86]

It would be unfair to argue that Smith had no provocation for leveling such damaging charges against East Tennessee's soldiery. The militia turnout was disappointingly low; desertions were reported in some units; military discipline may not have been as rigorous as Smith was accustomed to in Virginia. Conditions in the valley clearly were in a state of chaos after the disaster at Mill Springs. But Smith carried matters too far. He let his zeal for the Southern cause, or his unhappiness at a backwater assignment, blind him to the fact that East Tennessee was not Virginia. Because of the unique conditions existing in his department, East Tennesseans needed to be coaxed, rather than beaten, into the Southern army. He failed to appreciate the difficult circumstances confronting the Confederate population of his department and in the process allowed the disloyalty of some to obscure the commitment of others to the war effort.

A prime example of Smith's lack of appreciation for the complex conditions in his department occurred during the spring of 1862 when he had two regiments—the Thirty-sixth Tennessee Infantry and the First East Tennessee Cavalry—broken up and the men distributed to other commands, sent to the Deep South or discharged because he suspected them of disloyalty.[87] In the case of the Thirty-sixth, Smith was probably justified;

desertions in the unit were unusually high, even for an East Tennessee unit. The men of First Cavalry, however, did not deserve the shabby treatment they received. The whole affair erupted over a minor incident on March 13, 1862, in which two companies of the First were surprised and routed by thirteen hundred Federals at Jacksboro, Tennessee. In the fight, fifteen of the Rebels and their regimental colors were captured, but not until after the loss of about twenty killed and wounded. When he found out, Smith was furious. Ignoring evidence that the hapless cavalrymen put up a stiff resistance, Smith blasted their conduct. He accused the East Tennesseans of surrendering "without firing a gun," and, even more serious, of treason. "From what I have learned of the character of the troops from East Tennessee in our service, and of their strong Union proclivities," Smith reported, "I am satisfied that the capture near Jacksboro was the result of treachery."[88] Despite such serious (and unproven) accusations, two companies, no matter what their morale or loyalties, realistically could not have been expected to resist almost seven times their number. Moreover, the First had accumulated a fine record until this reversal in a lopsided fight. Yet none of this mattered to Smith, who ordered an inspection of the regiment, and indeed all of his cavalry, to determine "the degree of discipline and efficiency they have attained." In time, satisfied that nothing but treachery could have produced such results, Smith relieved the First's commanding officer and distributed the companies to other units.[89]

Smith also failed to draw any distinction between the loyal and the disloyal. Consistently, he made broad generalizations, lumping all East Tennesseans together in the same category. For instance, when five hundred Unionists were captured trying to reach Kentucky in April 1862, Smith consented to enlisting some who expressed a desire to join the Confederate army. He stipulated, however, that all so received would be required to serve in South Carolina, or anywhere, just so long as they did not return to East Tennessee. "Elsewhere they make good soldiers," he insisted.[90] Why they would have been more efficient defending someone else's home or more faithful in South Carolina to a government that trusted neither their patriotism nor their fighting ability, he never explained.

By the time Smith left in the late summer of 1862, he had irrevocably changed the nature of the war in East Tennessee. His open contempt for the people of the valley neither won their favor nor garnered many recruits for the Rebel army. Only two volunteer regiments of infantry and one battery of artillery had been organized during the five months between the end of December 1861, and the passage of the first Conscription Act late the following spring.[91] Smith, of course, cannot be entirely blamed for this. Perhaps, given the region's strong Unionist sentiment and the fear that some men had of leaving their homes unprotected, that was as much as reasonably could be expected. Still, it should be remembered that Smith had rejected all but those who would enlist "for the duration," and had broken up commands whose loyalty he questioned.

More insidious in its long-term impact was the manner in which the Floridian negatively influenced the Confederate government's attitude toward East Tennessee. He not only turned Davis and the army's high command against the people but also turned them against the soldiers, adding to an already uneasy feeling about the region. By casting doubt on the loyalty and efficiency of East Tennesseans in the ranks, Smith created an environment of mistrust that was, in many ways, a self-fulfilling prophecy. Most East Tennessee soldiers were loyal but somewhat parochial, and as events revealed, did not perform well when taken from their homes to fight in distant lands where they were abused and suspected. Smith's opinions would prompt Richmond to pursue conscription in the valley vigorously and then to order unwilling Tennessee "volunteers" to campaign in the Deep South. It was an unwise policy, one which proved the downfall of Confederate support in the region.

Thus, within the space of only a year, the nature of Confederate support in the Great Valley had changed dramatically. The enthusiasm of the war's early days had given way to hesitation, fear, and creeping ambivalence. Unable to inspire their fellow highlanders to greater sacrifice, the region's Rebel leadership had turned to a commander whose policies only worsened, rather than improved, the relationship between the people and their government. The willingness of East Tennesseans to fight, so evident in the heady days of the spring and summer of 1861, was seriously in question just twelve months later.

A *Damned* Stinking Cotton Oligarchy

John P. McCown was disgusted. The Sevierville native and West Point graduate had resigned his captain's commission in the Fourth U.S. Artillery in May 1861 and had entered the service of Tennessee as commander of the state's artillery corps under Isham G. Harris. Promoted to brigadier general the following October and major general six months later, McCown performed competently in the early battles of the western theater: Belmont, New Madrid, and the Kentucky campaign of 1862. Then, at Murfreesboro, Army of Tennessee commander Braxton Bragg had ordered McCown's division to launch the Confederate assault, an odd assignment given Bragg's dislike of the East Tennessean. Although the Rebel attack smashed the Federal right, Bragg ordered a retreat two days later—and began looking for scapegoats. He preferred charges against McCown, alleging disobedience of orders and charging that McCown was unfit for command. When a court-martial found him guilty, McCown declared that he would resign and go home to plant potatoes, railing that the Confederacy was nothing more than "a *damned* stinking cotton oligarchy . . . gotten up for the benefit of Isham G. Harris and Jeff Davis and their damned corrupt cliques."[1]

The growing indifference to Confederate success that McCown so bitterly articulated rapidly escalated during 1862–63 among the military population of East Tennessee. Although they were unable to leave the army and go home so easily, many soldiers of more humble rank shared McCown's frustration and dismay. Indeed, by the summer of 1863, East Tennesseans at all levels were simply losing the will to fight. The draft, the disaster at Vicksburg, poor leadership, and the abandonment of their homes to the Federal army all combined to erode confidence in Southern victory. Together, these factors worked to spread disaffection throughout the ranks, eventually disintegrating the East Tennessee soldier's already tenuous commitment to Confederate nationalism and Southern independence.

The first signs of creeping disaffection became manifest following passage of the Conscription Act of 1862 by the Confederate Congress on April 16. The first draft instituted in American history, it mandated that all white males between the ages of eighteen and thirty-five who were liable for military service would be subject to a draft. Those who were inducted or who were already in the army were obligated for three years service or less, if the war should end before the expiration of the term. The bill provided exemptions for certain enumerated job classifications considered necessary for the war effort. It also stipulated that men eligible for the draft could be excused from serving if they purchased a substitute to take their place at the front.[2]

Word that the government planned to pass a conscription law was initially well received among many in the Great Valley. Kirby Smith had led Richmond to believe that a draft would be acceptable to East Tennesseans, and a number of Confederates favored such an extreme measure as the only way to get men into the field.[3] For example, the *Cleveland Banner* had suspected weeks prior to the bill's passage that the government would be forced to enact a draft. "All persons between the ages of 18 and 45 may eventually be compelled to enlist for the war," the paper predicted in March, "even at the sacrifice of everything they hold dear on earth." The editors assured their readers, however, that "no patriot will hesitate to make this sacrifice, when necessary."[4] The *Knoxville Register* agreed. Considering a draft as necessary to enlarge the army, the paper commented that "the plan proposed strikes us as being the most equitable that could be adopted. . . . After passage of the law, all our citizens, between the ages designated, will be soldiers of the Confederacy. . . . This is eminately just and proper."[5] The *Athens Post* considered conscription inevitable, and admonished its readers that there was only "one sure way of avoiding a draft, and that is by volunteering."[6]

Reaction was similar when the proposal became law in April. Printing the act's entire text, the *Cleveland Banner* lambasted those who dared to criticize the idea of a draft: "Many of those who come under its provisions oppose it because, as they say, it is too closely approaching monarchy and despotism." Perceiving an ulterior motive in such objections, the editors suggested that "if we were them we would let some one who was not subject to the provisions of the law urge objections to it.[7]" One who was subject to it, T. W. White of the Sixty-third Tennessee Infantry, approved of the new law. White observed that "the law has broken into the arrangements of some very much, but if looked at the right way, it is the best law the Confederate Congress passed. If it had been done one year ago the war would have ended sooner."[8] Senator Landon Carter Haynes also declared himself in favor of the act. In an impromptu speech in Jonesboro in July,

Haynes argued that conscription would have a leveling influence on Confederate society. "He said he was for it as an absolute necessity," reported the *Bristol Southern Advocate.* "It puts all on the same footing—the kid gloved gentry out of the army as well as those within." Haynes assured the cheering crowd that conscription "will be a badge of immortal honor and a passport to fame in coming time."[9]

Such sentiments, however, were not shared by all. "In the minds of the people of East Tennessee," reported one Rebel officer in the valley to state officials, "there exists strong feeling never to be 'drafted.'" He predicted that conscription would yield few dependable troops, as most of those loyal to the Confederacy were already voluntarily in the ranks.[10] The *Athens Post* humorously speculated that because the law was aimed at young men, "it is thought that the demand for hair dye will rapidly diminish."[11] Even more revealing is the fact that enlistment, already agonizingly slow, completely dried up during the months following the bill's passage. No new regiments were formed during the six-month period between May and October 1862, when the government renewed enforcement.[12] Even President Davis's orders to suspend enrollment of conscripts in May did nothing to lure volunteers into the army.[13]

The less-than-enthusiastic response of the region's young men to the government's leniency raised the ire of more ardent Confederates. "Where are all the young Tennesseans?" angrily inquired one Chattanooga resident. "Are they waiting for other men to fight their battles . . . while they are pleasure taking at the different towns and watering-places of the country?"[14] The *Athens Post* carped that "the 25,000 men now stationed in East Tennessee to watch and keep in order the other 25,000 who *won't* volunteer, makes a loss to us of 50,000 efficient men."[15] Similar complaints emanated from the upper end of the valley. John C. Ramsey warned Knoxvillians "that the conscript law will soon be put in force in East Tennessee, and it is preferable to volunteer than to be conscripted."[16] In Greeneville, another irate Rebel, Reuben Arnold, informed his fellow citizens that "the time has arrived when every man capable of bearing arms should be in the field." Of all the Confederacy, Arnold declared, only East Tennessee had failed to furnish its quota of troops. This shame would haunt those seeking safety at home for the rest of their lives. "When the war ends all who have taken no part in it will go down to their graves with the stigma of *tories* and *cowards* sticking to their names," Arnold lashed out. "Volunteer while you have the chance."[17] His lecturing was to no avail. All across the region, recruiting officers had little to do that summer.

Convinced that firmness would garner more recruits than leniency, Richmond instructed Kirby Smith's successor, Brig. Gen. Samuel Jones, upon his arrival in September, to enforce conscription.[18] That same month Congress passed a new conscription act which raised the draft age to forty-five. Notice of enrollment of all subject to military duty appeared immediately in newspapers throughout the region.[19] Conscripts were promised that they would be furnished with "a blanket or other bed clothing," and that all examined and found in bad health would be discharged as unfit for service.[20]

Unlike in the spring, this time word that the government intended to renew drafting men into the service set off a flurry of volunteering. In fact, only days after his arrival, Jones wrote to Secretary of War George W. Randolph urging him to lift the conscription act until two regiments of volunteers which were then being raised could be mustered in. The thought of being drafted prompted not a few to reconsider enlisting. "From the most reliable information I can gather," Jones confided to Randolph, "I believe that a favorable change is coming over the minds and actions of the people of this section of the country." As evidence of this change of heart, Jones gleefully offered that "great numbers of people are preparing to volunteer in the army." He feared that if the regiments were rejected it would increase disloyal feeling, and if "they profess themselves desirous of volunteering and they are forced into the service as conscripts I should not regard them as reliable." The General optimistically concluded that "every man in East Tennessee whose services the Government needs may be brought into the service as volunteers," if only Richmond would see fit once again to suspend the draft.[21]

Confederate authorities, however, were unconvinced. By holding East Tennesseans' feet to the fire, Richmond was finally getting the response it wanted, and it made little sense to stop now. And yet, if new regiments were ready to be received, then it was illogical to break them up simply to comply with the terms of the new conscription act.[22] Therefore, instead of enrolling the volunteers as individual conscripts and distributing them to units already in the field, the War Department agreed to accept the newly formed regiments Jones spoke of under authority of a special law designed to circumvent the conscription act. Jones continued to pressure Randolph to suspend the draft, but to no avail.[23] The units raised prior to October 1 were the last ever organized in East Tennessee.

Officially designated the Sixtieth, Sixty-first, and Sixty-second Tennessee Infantry, the new regiments were composed of men from both upper and lower East Tennessee, with heavy concentrations of recruits from Sullivan and

Monroe, counties which had enthusiastically embraced secession.[24] Despite this fact, many of the men apparently volunteered under duress, with little enthusiasm, and only as a means of avoiding the stigma of conscription. "Though called 'volunteers,'" commented Brig. Gen. John S. Preston, Superintendent of the Bureau of Conscription, "their joining the service was compulsory and should be accredited to the energy exhibited in the enforcement of conscription." While undoubtedly some of these new recruits enlisted out of a sense of duty and commitment to Southern independence, Preston considered most to be motivated more by fear and shame. He argued that "these persons, for the most part, regarded it as disgraceful to be conscribed" and therefore "volunteered" so as not to be drafted.[25]

Most of the field and line officers of these new regiments had served in the early volunteer commands and had obtained commissions in the new units. Some had been privates, others lieutenants, and still others were company commanders who failed to win reelection when the army was reorganized in the spring of 1862. Many had combat experience, gained at places like Shiloh and Mill Springs. Several were veterans of First Manassas.[26] In fact, eighteen of the thirty captains (60 percent) possessed previous experience, and all but two of the field officers had served as junior officers in the early volunteer regiments.[27] For instance, Col. John A. Rowan of the Sixty-second began the war as captain of Company B, Fourth Cavalry Battalion, but was not reelected because of ill health.[28] Col. James G. Rose had raised Company D, Twenty-ninth Tennessee in 1861, but resigned to take command of the Sixty-first. Rose's lieutenant colonel, James P. Snapp, and his adjutant, James D. Thomas, previously fought as captains in the Nineteenth and Thirty-seventh Regiments, respectively.[29] Such a fortuitous arrangement provided these "conscript" regiments with experienced leadership, an attribute much needed, but surprisingly not always reliable in the difficult campaigns ahead.

The formation of the Sixtieth, the only one of these last regiments for which detailed organizational data exist, was probably representative of the other two. The regiment was composed exclusively of upper East Tennesseans. Half of the companies was raised in Washington County; Sullivan and Hawkins contributed two each, while Grainger and Cocke offered one each. The regiment initially presented eleven companies for muster, but Confederate authorities only accepted ten. Seven of the company commanders were veterans, and all of the field officers, except Col. John H. Crawford, had seen previous Confederate service. Both Nathan Gregg and James Alex Rhea, of Sullivan County, had served as lieutenants in the

Nineteenth Tennessee before accepting commissions as the Sixtieth's lieutenant colonel and major.[30] Crawford appears to have had nothing more
than a militia commission and the backing of prominent citizens in his
home county of Washington prior to taking command of the regiment
in October. In fact, as early as February 1862, the citizens of Washington
County had petitioned President Davis to commission Crawford to raise
a regiment in upper East Tennessee.[31]

When word spread that a new regiment was being raised in East Tennessee, Colonel Crawford was inundated with supplications requesting his
help in obtaining commissions. J. S. Shannon, an East Tennessean serving
with the Third Mississippi Infantry, found out that his friend, Crawford,
was putting a new command together and offered to come home and raise
a company for the colonel in exchange for Crawford's promise to reward
him with captain's bars.[32] Apparently, nothing ever came of Shannon's
proposal, for no further record of him can be found. More productive was
an application submitted by twenty-three-year-old Charles S. Newman for
the position of regimental adjutant. According to Newman, his creden-
tials included instruction at Virginia Military Institute and twelve months'
duty as drill master for the Sixty-third Tennessee. "I feel confident in saying," Newman boasted, "that I could be of no little service in preparing
the Regt. for active service." Crawford seems to have been impressed with
the young Virginian, and seeing the necessity for a good drill instructor,
he appointed Newman to the post.[33]

Recruiting began in September. Despite the enthusiasm of the officers,
many citizens were reluctant to commit themselves, forcing would-be company commanders to cultivate prospective soldiers if they were ever to reach
their quota. In Morristown, James C. Hodges found it particularly difficult
to induce men into the ranks. "There are as many as an entire company
about here who have the matter of joining my company under serious
consideration," he reported to Crawford. The problem, however, was that
none wanted to enlist if the draft was to be lifted. "Many of them are not
exactly satisfied that the Conscription law will be enforced here and they
desire to hold on till they learn definitely that it will be enforced." Hodges
suggested that if orders were published proclaiming the law's enforcement,
"I would fill my company within three days."[34] The situation differed little
in Cocke County. W. A. Wash spent several days just riding about the
countryside acquainting himself with the people and offering them the
opportunity to see him. He confided to Crawford that his "prospects for
getting a company are flattering," since "the volunteering spirit is very high

here just now." Wash was encouraged by the fact that "the people of the county seem to take an interest in helping me," which he attributed to "the fact that I am a stranger." Still, few had rallied to the colors.[35]

As a way of attracting recruits, enrolling officers promised that the new companies would be allowed to remain in East Tennessee. David K. Byers of Jonesboro assured all those who signed up that his unit was designed for local defense. "The Regiment will be subject only to the orders of the General commanding the Department of East Tennessee," he assured potential recruits, "and it is not likely that it will be ordered out of the Department. It is designed for home service."[36] Francis S. Blair declared to the citizens of Washington County that volunteers for his company "will not be liable to be taken out of the state."[37] This declaration must have appealed to men who were concerned about going to the front, leaving their families unprotected from Unionist guerrillas and draft dodgers.

Such tactics had the desired effect, for by October 1 the situation had decidedly improved. Samuel R. Gammon completed organizing his company, which he offered to Crawford with the observation, "I regard it as being one of the best that has been made in this [Hawkins] county."[38] Wash and Hodges both had nearly raised their quota, each expressing to Crawford their fear that the other would beat them in obtaining the required one hundred men.[39] Their apprehension proved groundless, however, because their companies were included in the final organization. On November 7 the Sixtieth Tennessee was officially mustered into Confederate service at Haynesville (present-day Johnson City) and immediately went to work preparing for duty.[40] Apparently, Newman proved an excellent drill master, for Company G won high praise from Capt. Bob E. Houston, assistant inspector general, who commented that the unit's discipline and appearance "exceeds that of any I have seen in the volunteer service."[41]

Initially, there was enthusiasm over the new conscription act and the prospect of finally getting shirkers to the front. G. W. Feagins of the Fifty-ninth Tennessee was jubilant at the news that the draft would be enforced.[42] The *Chattanooga Daily Rebel* spoke out in favor of the September bill, declaring that "a great crisis is upon our country, and to hesitate is to lose all. Our army has to be recruited speedily, otherwise we are lost irrevocably."[43] Two East Tennessee Confederate congressmen, Joseph B. Heiskell and William G. Swan, supported the law, advocating that conscripts be sent to replenish the depleted ranks of units already in the field rather than used to raise new ones. In an open letter to the *Knoxville Register*, both men asserted that the law "has been adopted as a general rule, upon grounds entirely satisfactory to us."[44]

This initial optimism, however, soon evaporated. Events proved that the draft did more damage than good. Although Alfred Bowman of the Sixtieth Tennessee was quite pleased to hear that "there is no chance to doge any longer," many Rebels were disappointed by the draft.[45] "The whole Conscription matter was I think a great mistake," admitted William Stringfield of Thomas's Legion years later. "A miscarriage of reason and justice and right." He argued that "the very idea of building up a Republic—a Republican form of Govt—by forcing 'Citizen Soldiery' into an army" was nothing short of criminal in his estimation.[46] Capt. George Hynds of the Thirty-ninth Tennessee concurred. "The enforcement of the Conscription law in East Tennessee," he lamented, "has either been a failure, or a farce." Hynds figured that the draft had brought few men into the army, and those who were forced in were for the most part Unionist in their sympathy. These men he considered the worst type of recruits, "for you might as well try to make a Christian out of the Devil as a good soldier (Southern) out of a Lincolnite."[47] One member of the Thirty-seventh Tennessee judged conscripts in his regiment "not the very best" of soldiers, most of whom "slipped away in the trying times that followed."[48] Just before Christmas 1862, two entire companies of conscripts seized weapons and escaped from their camp of instruction to a remote part of the North Carolina mountains. Such conduct prompted the *Athens Post* to conclude that it took two hundred loyal Confederate soldiers to keep an eye on one hundred conscripts to "restrain them from breaking for the brush," thereby canceling out any benefit gained from the draft.[49]

A related obstacle for Confederate authorities in obtaining recruits was substitution. As mentioned earlier, the Conscription Act of April 1862 provided an exemption for those able-bodied men who could secure a substitute to take their place. A number of supposedly loyal Confederates took advantage of this loophole to escape military service. For instance, despite his Southern sympathy, John H. Fain of Blountville hired a substitute to fight for him. When the Confederate Congress repealed the substitute law in 1864, Fain fled from East Tennessee to avoid conscription. What his brother-in-law, Maj. James Rhea of the Sixtieth Tennessee, thought of Fain's actions is unknown.[50] Several young residents of Roane County obtained substitutes and went to Georgia but soon came home when they found out that "all [were] being put in the army down there."[51] The wife of Maj. Simeon Reynolds of the Sixty-second Tennessee was worried about a young male relative who could not find a substitute. She confessed to her husband that if the Confederate army came back to

Loudon, the young man would "either have to go in the army or leave home." While she was uncertain how to advise him, she was unequivocal on one point: "We are not at all willing for him to go in the army."[52]

Even some already in the army obtained substitutes or counseled others to find one. Lt. John J. Blair of the Sixty-second Tennessee resigned in January 1863 because of "rheumatism" but still found it necessary to hire a substitute to escape returning to the ranks. His illness did not prevent him from securing a substitute for a friend and then riding to Cumberland Gap from Loudon to bring the hapless recruit to the army.[53] Lt. Sam Saffell of the Sixty-third Tennessee urged his brother-in-law to find a replacement. "I understand that the conscription law is a going to be enforced in E. Tenn. if that be the case you look up a substitute," he admonished.[54] Viewing the problem, the *Bristol Gazette* attacked what it considered the innate unfairness of the policy. "The thing of substitution has been a rare calamity to this Confederacy," the paper complained. "Why pass a law that those veterans shall fight on to a final sacrifice of themselves and families, and that those having substitutes shall stay at home. . . . Are those persons having substitutes the only men who own farms and negroes?"[55]

As debilitating as conscription and substitution were to the Confederate war effort in the Great Valley, an even more serious problem arose out of Richmond's decision to transfer thousands of East Tennessee soldiers to the Deep South. The mistrust of East Tennesseans which Kirby Smith bred in the Davis administration prompted the removal in December 1862 of all local regiments to areas deemed politically safe by the President and his advisors. With Federal forces threatening the Rebel stronghold of Vicksburg, Confederate authorities directed that the seven East Tennessee infantry regiments stationed in the valley—the Third (Provisional Army), Thirty-ninth, Forty-third, and Fifty-ninth Regiments of Brig. Gen. A. W. Reynolds's brigade and the Sixtieth, Sixty-first, and Sixty-second Regiments of John C. Vaughn's brigade—be sent to the Deep South. These troops represented the majority of East Tennesseans in the field; at that time, only five other regiments of infantry were organized, four of which were with the Army of Tennessee near Murfreesboro and were safely distributed among various brigades of Middle and West Tennessee units.

From the government's perspective, Mississippi was an admirable choice. Not only were more men needed to defend the vital river town of Vicksburg, but more important, the Magnolia State was ardently secessionist and therefore would have the desired effect on troops whose loyalty was suspect. By serving in a theater far removed from the undermining

Samuel Saffell, c. 1862. Commissioned as first lieutenant in the Sixty-third Tennessee Infantry in May 1862, Saffell was typical of many East Tennesseans who waited until after the Conscription Act to enlist in the Confederate army. He was mortally wounded near Petersburg in June 1864. Courtesy of Special Collections Department, University of Tennessee Libraries, Knoxville.

influences of Unionists, East Tennessee Confederate soldiers would stiffen their resolve to win Southern independence, or so it was assumed. Had not Kirby Smith himself counseled such a course as the best way to make these men effective soldiers? Who would know better than someone who had personally led them?

And so they went. In December the first of Vaughn's and Reynolds's men boarded trains for the long journey to the Deep South. Yet what may have appeared logical to Richmond turned out to be anything but inspiring for East Tennesseans. Despite predictions by the *Chattanooga Daily Rebel* that "our East Tennessee boys will have a chance to win laurels there," for most Mississippi was a nightmare.[56] The first enemy they faced was not the Federals but the climate. Having spent their entire lives in the mountains and valleys of southern Appalachia, Reynolds's and Vaughn's men were ill-prepared for campaigning in the swamps and bayous of Mississippi. "How it does rain in the swampy country—mud 10 inches deep," complained Lt. John J. Blair of the Sixty-second.[57] Malaria, virtually unknown in East Tennessee, began to take its toll. "The health of the army is very bad," reported Alfred Bowman of the Sixtieth. He admitted that he was quite sick and that the regiment was so exposed to the elements that it was a wonder that any were able for duty.[58] "Our men are taking sick very fast," reported T. A. R. Nelson's son, Stuart, who was serving with the Sixtieth. "We had 75 men when we left Jonesboro & now we have only 51 fit for duty."[59] "I fear your health will not be so good long," predicted a member of the Twenty-sixth Tennessee to Col. Newton J. Lillard of the Third Tennessee, "as I think the climate [of Mississippi] will not suit Tennesseeans."[60] One resident of Monroe County, his body racked with fever and chills, reported to relatives that "sickness is more dreaded than bullets."[61] "There are a good many in the brigade who are sick," observed an East Tennessean visiting Vicksburg. "Two more died in Pitt's Regt [the Sixty-first] yesterday one [was] sick for two days apparently Yellow Fever (tho I hope it was not)."[62] An army chaplain reported to the *Athens Post* that "the fell destroyer still continues his ravages among us, bearing away in his icy arms the soldiers of the Forty-third Tennessee."[63] So many perished from disease that Capt. Reuben Clark of the Fifty-ninth Tennessee recalled that the "greatest mortality in our army during this [Vicksburg] siege—and, indeed, during the Mississippi campaign—was from sickness," rather than enemy fire.[64]

Bad water only added to the misery of the troops. Men accustomed mainly to clear spring water were now forced to consume nothing but rain caught in cisterns. "The water is a little brackish & warm," complained Commissary Agent John Bogle. He observed that the cistern water was supposedly the best available, though "alive with wiggle tails & various tribes of smaller animalculae, which gambal about under your nose quite lively whilst you take a drink."[65] Insects were not only in the water but also in the air. "The muskeeters are getting very numerous," protested Richard Bowman of the Sixtieth. "The water is getting bad I think in alittle time we will have no running water here."[66] Although Lt. Col. David M. Key of the Forty-third Tennessee found few food crops in Mississippi, he noted that "there is one crop that abounds here, mosquitos. None of your small fry either." The Mississippi mosquitos, he declared, "muster Regiments where the other [Tennessee] can only muster squads. The Mississippi fellow is far larger has a larger and sharper bill and though he sings the same tune, he sings it with far greater ferocity."[67] Another Rebel recalled that "there was another foe we had to contend with, more annoying than the enemy's shells—the musquitoes. . . . They would either get on the blanket with you and roll up with you, or they would bite you through the folds."[68] Of course, these pests not only made life uncomfortable but also carried the fever and malaria that incapacitated so many men. Witnessing it all, Lt. John J. Blair summed it up best when he confided to his diary, "I hate Mississippi."[69]

While few East Tennesseans publicly complained of their service in the Deep South, at least one voiced an opinion that probably was shared by others. In a blistering attack on the government's policy published in the *Knoxville Register,* an unidentified soldier summarized his sense of resentment at the poor manner in which Richmond was handling the war in East Tennessee. "Our own Generals and commanders of regiments know the mountains and passes, they know the people, and they should have been in command in East Tennessee all the time and today we would have a better state of affairs around our homes," he charged. "But the authorities in Richmond thought otherwise and some great failures have been committed." He groused that "commanders have been placed over East Tennessee soldiers that looked upon them as nobody and viewed them all with a suspicious eye." The anonymous soldier contended that East Tennesseans would fight better on their own soil, and if sent home, he was "willing to make a contract with the government that [Federal general Ambrose E.] Burnside with his 30,000 men cannot invade it against them." It seemed ridiculous to him that he and his comrades were fighting in Mississippi, because the Great Valley was the most important part of the Confederacy, "more so than Vicksburg, Charleston, Savannah, Port Hudson or Richmond."[70]

Notwithstanding their disappointment with this new assignment, most East Tennesseans prepared to defend Vicksburg to the death. The easy repulse of Gen. William T. Sherman's attempt to seize the city at Chickasaw Bluffs in late December 1862 only fed a perception of Vicksburg as impregnable. Vaughn's troops were under fire only a short time; the

Federals hardly reached within rifle range before being driven back. Perched atop the high bluff and shielded behind breastworks, the East Tennesseans sustained few losses in their baptism of fire.

Total casualties for Vaughn's brigade (Reynolds's men did not reach the field until the fight was over) amounted to eight killed and ten wounded.[71] The Confederate commander, Gen. John C. Pemberton, commended Vaughn's troops for their part in the battle, reporting that "the heavy abattis prevented the approach of the enemy except with sharpshooters who advanced continuously, but were met firmly by his [Vaughn's] East Tennesseans."[72]

After so easy a victory, it was hard to imagine defeat. Indeed, in the minds of many, Vicksburg became the key to Southern success. "Should we be victorious at Vicksburg," declared Lt. William R. Jobe of the Twenty-sixth Tennessee, "the Reconstruction Candidates (& I understand there is not a few of them in East Tennessee) had better try to ride into office upon some other hobby."[73] Ultimate Southern victory was tied to victory at Vicksburg. If the city could be held, the end of the war was nearly at hand. Sgt. Alfred Bowman of the Sixtieth Tennessee considered Vicksburg impregnable. "I think it is impossible for them [the Federals] to land troops at this place on account of high water," he boasted. "If they undertake that our Batterys will sink them as fast as they can land." Bowman thought that the end of the war was close, since the "Yankees are a getting tired of Being whipped so much and not whiping any." He later confided that "the prospect of peace is very good at this time I think we will get to come home by harvest."[74] Colonel Newton J. Lillard of the Third Tennessee agreed with Bowman's assessment, observing that "it will take a tremendous force to accomplish anything here we are well fortified and if we are fully provisioned we can hold out for a long time."[75] When Gen. Ulysses S. Grant finally launched his campaign against the city, John Allen of the Sixty-second advised his wife, "Don't pay any attention to anything you see in the papers or hear, but look on the bright side and [all] will end well we feel sure."[76]

Despite such bravado, the debilitating effect of the Mississippi climate and the resentment of being so far from home must have impaired the East Tennesseans' effectiveness and contributed to their lackluster performance during the Vicksburg campaign. The debacle at the Big Black Bridge exposed just how low morale had dropped in Vaughn's brigade. On May 13, 1863, Vaughn and his men were ordered to hold the left flank of a line of entrenchments constructed to guard the bridge over the Big Black River while the Rebel army retreated into the Vicksburg defenses.[77] When Federal forces launched an at-

tack on the position four days later, Vaughn's command offered little resistance.
The Sixtieth Tennessee raised a white flag when Federal skirmishers were still
two hundred yards away. The entire regiment and its colors, including Lt.
Colonel Gregg, 15 junior officers, and 239 enlisted men, were surrendered to a
lieutenant without the loss of one Federal soldier, according to Union accounts.[78] The Federal officer who spearheaded the assault claimed that "more
men were captured by my brigade than I had men in the charge." The Sixty-
first Tennessee also lost its colors, a member of the Twenty-third Iowa "wrest-
ing them from the rebel color-bearer."[79] Because of the collapse in their sec-
tor, the East Tennesseans precipitated a wild retreat along the entire front. The
Confederate commander, Gen. John C. Pemberton, condemned Vaughn for
the whole fiasco. Pemberton reported after the fight that he considered Vaughn's
brigade fresh and "not demoralized" when he assigned it to the bridge. "Yet
this position was abandoned by our troops almost without a struggle and with
the loss of nearly all our artillery," he lamented.[80] Despite attempts years later
to shift the blame for their failure on construction flaws in the works, it is clear
the East Tennesseans simply lacked the will to fight that day.[81]

Apparently, Pemberton lost all faith in the East Tennesseans after the
battle at the Big Black. When Rebel forces retreated into the Vicksburg
fortifications, Vaughn's and Reynolds's brigades were positioned along quiet
sectors of the line, well away from Federal attempts to storm the works
and capture the city.[82] There they saw little action and suffered few casualties. Reynolds lost only fifty-three men during the entire siege.[83] More
men fell victim to poor diet and the elements than were lost in combat.
One veteran of the Forty-third Tennessee later remembered that his regiment did little fighting, spending most of the time at sharpshooting, and
were issued only one biscuit every twenty-four hours.[84] William Bradford
of the Thirty-ninth recalled that his unit "suffered greatly by privations,"
while the Sixty-first Tennessee's colonel, James G. Rose, claimed that more
died from bad and no food and exposure than battle.[85] When the besieged
defenders were reduced to eating mule meat to survive, Sgt. William H.
Long of the Fifty-ninth was detailed to go down to the slaughter yard and
draw mule rations for his company. When he was unable to stomach his
equestrian dinner, Long gave it to a comrade, as did others of the company. Long claimed that the fellow ate six pounds of mule in one sitting
and remarkably "suffered no inconvenience."[86] Under such conditions, it
is little wonder that during the night men quietly slipped out of the
trenches and made their way to the Federal lines to surrender.[87]

Occasionally, there was something more to fight than hunger and the elements. Colonel Rose described how his regiment was kept continually on the alert. The men slept on their arms within one hundred yards of the trenches, "each company opposite its position in the line, and each soldier knowing his exact position in the works." Upon signal, day or night, the line could be instantly manned.[88] Reynolds's entire brigade was under constant artillery and small arms fire. But only the Forty-third Tennessee appears to have participated in any major fighting. Acting as a mobile reserve, the regiment was sent to reinforce Stephen Lee's division in repulsing a Union breakthrough on May 22. On another occasion, the Forty-third joined the Fifty-seventh Georgia in a sally on the Federal lines, in which they "charged the works with admirable gallantry," according to division commander Carter L. Stevenson, and carried the Federal position. On the whole, however, the East Tennesseans bore little part in the siege fighting, prompting Reynolds to comment that his line was "little harassed by the enemy in front."[89]

When Vicksburg fell on July 4, Vaughn's and Reynolds's brigades were paroled along with the rest of the garrison. Following exchange, Vaughn's men were directed to assemble at Jonesboro in East Tennessee, while Reynolds's were ordered to Braxton Bragg's Army of Tennessee at Chattanooga.[90] Less than half ever returned to the army. "After we were exchanged," recalled Col. William Bradford of the Thirty-ninth Tennessee, "not more that one half of the regiment, or brigade, ever reported for duty."[91] Maj. J. N. Aiken of the Forty-third corroborated Bradford's statement. He admitted that his regiment "entered Vicksburg with more than nine hundred effective men and less than half that number answered the roll-call when it was exchanged."[92] Many of the paroled men returned to homes that were now behind enemy lines, the Federal army having occupied large sections of the valley before their arrival.

Although they were declared exchanged in September, organizational reports for the fall of 1863 confirm that of those regiments formerly belonging to Reynolds's brigade, "few had reported."[93] The situation grew so desperate that Vaughn was forced to confess to President Davis in October, "I am sorry to say that our Vicksburg prisoners in East Tennessee are not reporting for duty. Our people who have been and are within the enemy's lines are very disheartened." He sadly concluded that "out of the seven regiments paroled at Vicksburg we will not get out of the enemy's lines more than three regiments." Vaughn charged that the men would not report, because "they are not yet exchanged and their homes are threatened. I fear one-half will not leave East Tennessee."[94]

Sadly, Vaughn's estimate proved all too true. Hundreds just went home and withdrew from the war entirely. For example, Jesse Reymer of the Sixty-second Tennessee was paroled at Vicksburg, returned home, resumed farming, and never rejoined his regiment. William A. Prince, who had left his job as a contractor in Polk County to join the Forty-third, was elected second lieutenant of his company and "was in active service until the fall of Vicksburg." A Hiwasee College student, James Gilbreath, suspended his studies and enlisted in the Sixty-second in October 1862. After the surrender he returned to Monroe County and quietly took up farming. P. W. Cooper of the Fifty-ninth also went home after his parole to marry and work a five-hundred-acre tract given him by his father. He never reported for duty. Other Vicksburg veterans who bid farewell to the Southern army included Surgeon J. C. Abernathy of the Sixty-second, who took an oath of allegiance to the Federal government when he returned home; Lt. John Pyott of the Forty-third, who headed back to Rhea County and resumed his teaching career; and J. C. Ayres of the Thirty-ninth, who stayed at home six months after Vicksburg and then went to Knoxville, where he remained behind Federal lines (but not in the Federal army) until the close of the war.[95]

Others who were captured at Vicksburg were allowed to take the oath and enlist in the Federal army rather than be exchanged and returned to the South. When Union general S. P. Carter discovered that large numbers of East Tennessee Unionists were among Rebel prisoners of war slated for exchange during the Vicksburg campaign, he pleaded with Gen. Ambrose E. Burnside, commander of the Federal army occupying Knoxville, to intervene. Burnside concurred with Carter that "it would be cruel and unjust to force these loyal East Tennessee conscripts back into the rebel ranks" and took measures to stop their exchange. "East Tennesseans will not be compelled to be exchanged if they wish to remain with us," he assured Carter.[96] Andrew Johnson also took steps to have Vicksburg prisoners enrolled in the Union army. Johnson, with the assistance of Gen. William S. Rosecrans, urged the War Department to allow Rebel prisoners of war to join the Federal ranks. After considerable wavering, Washington finally consented.[97]

The regiments which were surrendered at Vicksburg never overcame the experience. The two Tennessee brigades, raised for infantry service, were mounted during the fall of 1863 and consolidated under Vaughn's command and operated as cavalry for the rest of the war.[98] The united command, depleted by its campaigning in the Deep South, never reached its pre-Vicksburg strength. Although all seven regiments were reported as exchanged by late January 1864, only a fraction ever returned to the field. "It is shameful the way some of our boys have done," groused Samuel H. Wells of the Thirty-ninth Tennessee. "Several of the company here taken the oath and some have joined the tory thieving companys. . . . We have only seven of the company here yet."[99] Capt. Reuben Clark of the Fifty-ninth remembered that the Mississippi debacle disaffected many East Tennessee Rebels, "especially the lower classes," who he complained had suffered so many privations and, "having but little pride or character," preferred "the disgrace which attended to desertion rather than continue in the service."[100] Even a personal plea by Gen. Nathan Bedford Forrest, notifying "all persons captured at Vicksburg that they are exchanged and are expected to rendezvous and rally again around the flag," had little effect.[101] Troop returns for February reveal that the brigade was the smallest in the Department of East Tennessee, only half the size of the three other cavalry brigades.[102]

To make matters worse, many of those who returned soon departed. "The men are destitute and dissatisfied," admitted Adjutant S. A. Key of the Forty-third. "They are collecting slowly—and disappear nearly as fast as they come in." Key related that only seventy of the Forty-third had reported for duty in January 1864 and that the Sixty-first regiment "has gone home" while the Sixty-second was "about 'played out.'"[103] Toward the end of December 1863, even officers were deserting, prompting Vaughn to order Colonel Lillard of the Third Tennessee to arrest all who had left their commands since the evacuation of lower East Tennessee one month earlier.[104]

Under such conditions, discipline and efficiency steadily declined. One officer, Col. J. Stoddard Johnston, chief-of-staff to Gen. John C. Breckinridge, under whose command Vaughn's brigade served during most of 1864, referred to the East Tennesseans as "wild cavalry—the inefficiency of which there was constant complaint almost daily."[105] Archer Anderson, assistant adjutant general to Joseph E. Johnston, reported in April 1864 that "this brigade is in deplorable condition; only about 1,200 effective men. Something will have to be done or the command will be lost." He considered the command "almost a band of marauders." In three regiments, a total of forty-eight men were present.[106] Vaughn's men were said to be deserting "by the hundreds" during March; and even worse, one regiment mutinied in September, and "a captain and a large number of the men" simply rode away and never returned.[107] By the end of 1864, morale had deteriorated so badly that Maj. H. T. Stanton commented that "the predominant idea with Vaughn's men seems to be to get out of reach."[108]

As if their experience at Vicksburg had not been bad enough, Vaughn's East Tennesseans suffered an even more devastating blow, in terms of casualties, at the battle of Piedmont, Virginia, fought on June 5, 1864. Caught in the route of the small Southern army attempting to stem Union general David Hunter's advance down the Shenandoah Valley, Vaughn's brigade was nearly destroyed as an effective fighting force. Of the fifty-six hundred Confederate troops engaged, nearly twenty-five hundred were killed, wounded, or captured at day's end, including the Southern commander, Gen. William E. Jones. Hundreds were simply scooped up by Federal cavalry as they fled the field and were sent northward as prisoners of war.[109] Although it is impossible to determine how many of these were from Vaughn's brigade, casualties in one regiment, the First Tennessee Cavalry, amounted to about 50 percent and were probably typical.[110] Among the killed was sixteen-year-old Arthur Ramsey, youngest son of J. G. M. Ramsey ("our beloved Benjamin," the elder Ramsey styled him), who was serving with the First when his leg was shattered by an artillery shell.[111] The loss was particularly heavy in officers. Col. William Eakin of the Fifty-ninth Tennessee and Maj. James Alexander Rhea, commanding the Sixtieth Tennessee, both fell into enemy hands; and Maj. John B. King and Capt. John Jarnigan of the First Tennessee Cavalry, as well as Capt. James P. Burem of the Thirty-ninth Tennessee, were left dead on the field.[112] The remnant of Vaughn's command continued to participate in the final campaigns, including escort duty with Jefferson Davis as he fled Richmond, but its effectiveness was shattered beyond repair.

Casualties, battlefield reversals, and loss of experienced leaders were not the only reasons for the poor performance by Vaughn's command. Clearly, a large part of the problem was the general himself. Despite his personal bravery—Col. George Dibrell claimed that his Middle Tennessee regiment regarded Vaughn "as one of the bravest of the brave"—Vaughn seems to have lacked the capacity for high command.[113] Adjutant S. A. Key of the Forty-third Tennessee complained that "Genl V. takes no seeming interest in his command. He remains at Bristol [and] gives no directions at all to his Brig."[114] A Rebel surgeon named Long, serving under Vaughn, agreed that the Monroe Countian made himself scarce, adding that he was no cavalryman—just "an infantry general."[115] Lt. Col. Archer Anderson, on an inspection tour of Vaughn's brigade, blamed the general's lack of personal discipline for his unit's problems. "General V. has no idea of discipline," he charged. "From what I can ascertain, the great fault is with the commander of the brigade. Another officer should be put in command of the mounted men, and General V. be made to take the dismounted and be assigned to some infantry division, under a strict officer."[116] After Gen. William E. Jones was killed at Piedmont, Davis and Lee passed over Vaughn for a junior officer more trusted to handle Jones's independent command.[117] Vaughn's poor leadership did little to instill confidence in men whose morale was beaten down by defeat.

In Vaughn's defense, however, it should be noted that the desertions which plagued his command following Vicksburg were not new among East Tennessee troops. Although not unique to East Tennesseans, desertion became a problem earlier in the war for valley regiments than for other Confederate units.[118] Indeed, as early as the spring of 1862, unauthorized leave was a major problem in some commands. The most notable example of mass desertion took place in the Thirty-sixth Tennessee Infantry. Organized in February 1862, the Thirty-sixth was recruited exclusively from lower East Tennessee. One half of the unit's ten companies was raised in heavily Unionist Bradley County alone.[119] The *Chattanooga Gazette and Advertiser* was optimistic about the material of which the new regiment was made, boasting that "they will, when the hour shall come, hurl themselves upon the enemy like an avalanche."[120] Unfortunately, the men of the Thirty-sixth hurled themselves upon the enemy, but not in the manner envisioned by the *Gazette.* Shortly after its organization, the unit was stationed at Cumberland Gap, where many fled across the lines to join family and friends in the Federal army.[121]

While the case of the Thirty-sixth was exceptional, other commands were plagued with desertion problems, albeit on a smaller scale. An examination of the newspapers in East Tennessee during the summer of 1862 reveals that they were filled with notices to absentees to report to their respective commands or "have their names published as deserters and a reward offered for their apprehension."[122] "How many deserters do you suppose there are in East Tennessee?" asked one soldier in February 1863. "Enough to make a small army." He angrily accused them of sneaking about "feeding with tories" and suggested that all such were "liable to be sentenced to death."[123]

After the fall of Vicksburg and the evacuation of East Tennessee, however, desertion increased rapidly, and not just among the units that had been in Mississippi. Men from all commands simply lost the will to continue the struggle and dropped out of the war. One resident of Loudon, John J. Blair, observed in September 1863 that "deserters from Bragg come in by the dozens."[124] Some remained behind when Confederate forces retreated from the region and were picked up by advancing Federals "straggling through the country," while others came forward and surrendered, "all representing that they are deserters from the rebel army," according to Col. William Hoffman of the Third U.S. Infantry and commissary-

John C. Vaughn as a Confederate general, c. 1862. Courtesy of Thomas County Historical Society, Thomasville, Georgia.

general of prisoners for the Department of the Cumberland. These men asked to be allowed to take Lincoln's amnesty oath.[125] During a ten-day period prior to September 2, 1863, eighty-seven soldiers of the Twenty-sixth Tennessee deserted while the regiment was encamped at Loudon near the homes of many in the unit.[126] Sgt. Lewis I. Poats of the Sixty-third Tennessee complained bitterly to his wife in Rogersville that "a large number of men deserted recently from the 19th, 29th, and 63rd all gone to East Tennessee." "You remember the crowd of men from Hancock [County] I got to join Dick Powel's Company?" he asked. "Every rascal of them has deserted. Powel's Company has only 25 or 30 men. Tom Powel is the only officer with the company."[127]

Battlefield reversals throughout the last year of the war only accelerated the hemorrhaging from the ranks. Entire units seemed to be disintegrating. Men often slipped off as quickly as they were gained. For example, in the summer of 1864, twenty-six East Tennesseans, assigned to Marshall's Battery from the Conscript Bureau, were supplied with clothing, to the exclusion of the older members of the unit, and were drilled until all were competent artillerymen. Unfortunately, twenty-four of the twenty-six deserted shortly thereafter, much to the disgust of the other members of the unit.[128] W. C. Brown of the Lookout Artillery confided to his diary in February 1864 that thirty-five men deserted while the unit was en route from Mississippi to Georgia. Six more disappeared during a three-week period in July, and twelve, captured during the retreat from Atlanta, took the oath and "stayed with the Yankees." Brown admitted that by January 1865 the battery had lost more men to desertion than to any other cause. While only two were killed in battle and five more died of disease, fifty-six of Brown's comrades had given up and gone home or crossed over to the enemy.[129]

The despair reflected in these desperate actions ran deep among East Tennessee soldiers. Combating suspicion and insensitivity in Richmond while fighting disease, death, and Yankees on the battlefield proved too much for many. "If they [the Federals] only leave you enough to eat and clothes to keep you comfortable and we could have peace and I could come home," sighed William Thomas of the Thirty-ninth Tennessee. "But no human can tell what the result of this unholy war is to be or when it may end. I hope it will not be long."[130] J. R. Hook of the Nineteenth Tennessee probably voiced the sentiments of those still clinging to the Confederate banner despite the adversity confronting them. "Oh, for that hour when I can bid adieu to Georgia," he exclaimed, "when I can stand once more on my native soil, when I can gaze once more on my own blue mountains, see the rolling Cumberland at my feet, enter again the dear old gate at home and meet dear smiling joyous faces as they welcome me home again to peace and happiness."[131]

Little did he realize the terror that awaited his arrival.

How I Wish We Could Have Peace

On the morning of September 4, 1863, a young Federal officer, Capt. H. S. Chamberlain, quartermaster for Gen. Ambrose E. Burnside's victorious army, stepped out of his quarters on West Church Street in Knoxville to survey the city which had fallen to Union forces the previous day. Chamberlain had not gone far when he was accosted by a citizen who introduced himself as Joseph A. Mabry, a prominent businessman of the city. After exchanging greetings with the Federal, Mabry immediately began to confess his role in supporting the Confederate war effort in East Tennessee. "I am a notorious rebel," he declared. "These people will all tell you that" (apparently motioning to the Unionists who boldly appeared on the city streets now that the Rebels were gone). Mabry recounted for Chamberlain a litany of sins. He admitted that at one time he had been one of ten men who proposed to offer a hundred thousand dollars each to the Confederate treasury. Moreover, he had equipped an entire company of soldiers at his own expense and had operated a successful clothing manufactory furnishing thousands of dollars' worth of uniforms for the Southern army. "I have nothing to conceal concerning my attitude or what I have done," Mabry boldly avowed, "but I am here to tell you that whatever I have that will be of use to your army, you can have it and I shall attempt to conceal nothing." Not surprisingly, Chamberlain was stunned by Mabry's frankness and probably by how easily the Rebel's loyalties were recast.[1]

Mabry's shifting allegiance was not unusual during the late summer of 1863. Indeed, as the war effort began to go badly for the South, Confederate civilians in East Tennessee experienced reactions very similar to the region's Rebel soldiery. Whether because their hearts had never really been committed to winning Southern independence or because they considered the price of achieving this goal simply too high or because they felt unsupported by a government in Richmond that neither understood their problems nor offered a vision of success, secessionist morale began to sag by midwar. As news of Vicksburg's surrender filtered back to the Great Valley, men and women on the home front were devastated by the reversal which had befallen their East Tennessee regiments. Few had anticipated such a calamitous result. Moreover, for many Rebel leaders like Mabry it became increasingly apparent that they had been unable to build upon the prosperity of the prewar years by unifying with the South and to turn secession to their economic advantage. And when the region was abandoned to Federal forces less than three months later severing all trade links with the South, disappointment translated into despair and loss of hope for Confederate victory.

The roots of civilian disaffection are found in the fear of Unionist insurgency which gripped East Tennessee Rebels during the first two years of the war. In fact, as early as summer 1861, Confederate sympathizers were alarmed over the possibility of Unionists rising up and seizing control of the region. Especially was this true following the general elections on August 1 and the subsequent bridge burnings that fall. In the elections, East Tennessee voters, consistent with their earlier rejection of separation, voted overwhelmingly in favor of William H. Polk, instead of incumbent governor Isham G. Harris, rejected ratification of the Confederate constitution, and elected representatives to the United States, rather than the Confederate, Congress. In November 1861, in expectation of a Federal military thrust into the valley, Unionist saboteurs attacked nine major railroad bridges between Bridgeport, Alabama, and the Virginia line. While they were only partially successful (only five of the nine bridges were destroyed), the Unionists had shown that they were willing to, and capable of, lashing out at, and perhaps even overturning, Confederate authority in the region.[2]

This violent disloyalty struck fear into the hearts of Rebel inhabitants. The August elections exposed the anti-Confederate feeling seething just beneath the surface and the bridge burnings demonstrated that Unionists could and would act on that feeling. Suddenly, the specter of a general Tory rebellion became a real possibility and demands were made on Richmond for protection. The citizens of Sneedville in Hancock County, for example, petitioned Confederate commander Brig. Gen. Felix Zollicoffer to station troops in their town. "We do not feel that the lives of ourselves and our families are by any means safe," they complained.[3] Col. W. B. Wood, commanding in Knoxville, shared Sneedvillians' apprehensions: "The Southerners here are considerably alarmed, believing that there is a preconcerted movement amongst the Union men, if by any means the enemy should get into Tennessee."[4] Rumors began to spread that Confederates were being shot at and even killed by Tories, and that Union men were also "tampering with slaves."[5] One East Tennessee Rebel beseeched Confederate authorities in Richmond to introduce martial law. "If we are invaded, every Southern man will be taken prisoner or else murdered in the night-time," warned Madison T. Peoples on November 20, 1861. "Our very existence depends on Mr. Lincoln's ability to invade the State. Under these circumstances ought we not to have all the aid in the power of the government to bestow?"[6]

Others were raising the same question. Confederate Senator and East Tennessean Landon Carter Haynes cautioned Jefferson Davis that if Rebel troops in the region were defeated and the Union army were to seize the railroad, "flames of rebellion will flash throughout East Tennessee . . . and other calamities not necessary to mention will follow."[7] Even after Confederate general Albert Sidney Johnston rushed reinforcements to the valley following the debacle at Mill Springs, Rebel fears persisted. Col. Daniel Leadbetter informed Richmond that "the people here are anxious lest two regiments of East Tennesseans known to be with the enemy should enter the northern counties[,] . . . raise those counties in more open rebellion, destroy the bridges, and inaugurate civil war."[8] Leadbetter's report suggests that Rebels were more fearful of East Tennessee Unionists than they were of the Yankees. Indeed, as late as January 1863, Southern men were still unnerved by Tory activity. "Think of it reader," the *Knoxville Register* observed following the celebration over the Confederate victory on the first day's battle at Murfreesboro, "at that same moment, even in Knoxville, there were plotting scoundrels rejoicing because a body of marauding plunderers were burning bridges and desolating farms."[9]

Dread of Unionist rebellion led Rebels to hold their fellow East Tennesseans with the greatest contempt. Tories were transformed into traitorous demons, deserving severe punishment for defying Confederate authority. In language that later would be applied to themselves, Rebels dehumanized Unionists, characterizing them as the roughest and lowest forms of life and advocating that they be driven from the valley. Many of these characterizations of Unionists sound strangely similar to the perceptions about mountaineers held by middle-class Americans and "local colorists" during the late nineteenth century. During the last decades of the 1800s, writers, reformers, and industrialists "discovered" Appalachia, describing for the nation a mountain culture and people that were "arrested" in their development. Traditionally, historians have held that the stereotype of the Southern highlander as ignorant, backward, and inherently violent did not become popular until the 1880s and 1890s, although a recent study has found the roots of this image in the Tennessee mountains even before the Civil War.[10]

Interestingly enough, East Tennessee Rebels were employing the same pejorative phrases decades before they became popular nationally. "They [the Unionists] are still persisting in their unprincipled and phanatical

courses perpatrating deeds that would make even a devil Blush," ranted a
Meigs County Confederate. He swore that if the authorities discovered
who was disrupting rail connection with Knoxville "they will fair but
midling."[11] One Rebel soldier was even more vindictive, hoping that Unionists "may receive their just deserts, Traitors as they are to their lovely land,
where perhaps first they breathed of life, they deserve to be loathed of
earth, scorned by heaven and hissed by the serpents of hell."[12] A young
Confederate woman remarked that Unionists were "mean enough to travel
at anytime, [but] night suits them better than daylight." When a Unionist was run out of Decatur by a drunken Rebel, she contemptuously commented that the Tory deserved the treatment, "for they ought not to be
allowed to associate with respectible people. I have no feeling for such."[13]
One Greene County Rebel informed Governor Harris that the Union
"party has in it all the ignorant, worthless men in this end of the state."[14]
Similarly, a Confederate soldier belittled East Tennessee Union regiments.
"These pious and puritanical soldiers are composed of the ignorant mountaineers who are too lazy to run and consequently unfit to serve Old Abe
in the Regular Army," he sneered.[15]

The region's Rebel press not only reflected its readers' sentiments, but also
suggested policies for dealing with the "ignorant mountaineers." Reporting
on the Unionists captured in Campbell County heading for Kentucky, the
editor of the *Cleveland Banner* derisively observed that "a meaner looking set
of men will seldom be found in any country. The Bull Run Yankees would
make a respectable looking party if compared with these traitors."[16] The *Chattanooga Rebel* described Union men who fled East Tennessee as "vile miscreants"
and "a corrupt set of men." "They sowed the storm—let them receive the
fury of the whirlwind. They deserve it."[17] The editor of the *Cleveland Banner*
agreed. "They cannot get back to their homes and never will," the paper declared. "If the war was ended, and arrangements were made for their return
they could not live here. They would be looked upon and treated as tories—
loathed and despised."[18] "We can respect the Yankee much more who com-
mits these acts [of vandalism] himself than we can the man born in the South
who rejoices at them," asserted the *Knoxville Register.* "The Yankee has his preju-
dices, and they have made him a barbarian; but the Southerner who sympa-
thizes with him is fired only by the spirit of revenge, and is a *demon.*"[19] The
contempt and extreme vindictiveness expressed in these editorials did not go
unnoticed by Unionists. When the war was over, such language would return
to haunt its authors.

Apprehensive that Unionists might attempt to overthrow Confederate
authority in East Tennessee, Rebels cracked down on known Tories and

others suspected of disloyalty. Confederate leaders persuaded both the state and national governments to institute measures calculated to suppress dissension. The Sequestration Law, loyalty oaths, mass arrests, and martial law were all successively introduced as a means of maintaining minority control over the Unionist majority. Nothing, however, could coerce Unionists' allegiance to the Confederacy. Indeed, it is even questionable that some of the more strident secessionists desired to win the loyalty of Unionists, preferring instead to cement their advantage over their old political rivals by completely destroying them and eliminating them as a potential threat to their domination of the region.[20]

In many ways, the struggle for control of East Tennessee during the Civil War was simply an extension of the old Whig-Democratic rivalry of the prewar years. As noted in chapter 3, a majority of Unionist leaders were members of the Whig party, whereas a corresponding percentage of Rebel leadership was drawn from the ranks of the Democracy. The war offered former Democrats an opportunity to gain a significant, if not lasting, advantage over men who continually scored political victory after victory. In this context, it is not surprising that Rebel repression centered around Knoxville, a Whig stronghold before the war. From there, local Democrats, such as J. G. M. Ramsey, his son J. C. Ramsey, William Churchwell, and John Crozier, were bent on administering a stunning blow to the old Whigs, like William G. Brownlow, Horace Maynard, and O. P. Temple, and thereby destroying Whig ascendancy in East Tennessee.

The vehemence of Rebel attacks launched from the Knoxville area on Unionists was particularly noted by Confederates from other parts of the region and state. For example, Parson Brownlow, the object of so much Rebel antipathy, suggested that Confederate soldiers from Middle Tennessee stationed in the valley were unhappy with how secessionist leaders continually stirred the civil strife and unrest that they were attempting to quell. Brownlow quoted one Confederate soldier as complaining that "the most rabid of secessionists were vehement in their denunciations of the Union men, and rejoiced at the approach of a Confederate force, in as much as it offered them additional opportunity to vent their little spleen at their old political enemies."[21] When the ultrasecessionist *Knoxville Register* criticized Zollicoffer and Caswell for failing to deal more firmly with Unionist insurgents, Brownlow rallied to their defense. Commending the officers for protecting citizens' rights and property, Brownlow declared, "We have not heard their conduct censured, but spoken of in terms of praise except by the *ultra Secession clique* here, who seek to control every thing and every body, for their own base and selfish ends."[22] Surprisingly, the *Athens Post* joined the Parson in denouncing the more fanatical Rebels of the old Second Congressional District who persisted in keeping alive prewar animosities. The paper regretted that "there are places in East Tennessee where both Secessionists and Union men keep themselves constantly employed in cultivating the past, rather than in harmonizing and uniting to prepare for and take care of the future."[23] A West Tennessean, Robertson Topp, informed an acquaintance in Memphis in October 1861 that the mass arrests in East Tennessee were made by "a few malicious, troublesome men in and about Knoxville. . . . It is said that these men have private griefs and malice to gratify, and they aim to bring down the avenging arm of the Government to satiate their passions."[24]

With every effort being made to suppress Unionist unrest in the valley during the fall of 1861 and spring of 1862, and with Southern arms victorious on the battlefield during the second half of 1862, East Tennessee Rebels had every reason to feel increasingly confident of ultimate triumph. Although recognizing that the road to victory would not be easy, the *Chattanooga Advertiser* sounded an optimistic note after the Mill Springs defeat, declaring that "the crisis must come and we are not of those who despair of ultimate success."[25] "The first year of the second war of Independence has closed," noted the *Athens Post* in May, "and although the prospect at present may be less bright and encouraging than some expected, when we grow desponding let us revert to the pages where are recorded the dark and gloomy period through which our fathers passed, and the glorious result that crowned their intense and protracted struggle."[26] By summer, however, the South's prospects for victory had improved decidedly. With Braxton Bragg's army moving toward Kentucky and Robert E. Lee's troops successful in thwarting the Union attack on Richmond, Rebels thought that they could see a change even in their Union adversaries. "We understand that, since the recent Confederate victories, there is not a man in town who owns that he is or ever was a 'Union man,'" the *Greeneville Banner* smugly asserted. "Even the Indigo bag man says he is as good a Southern man as there is in this town. What a change a little time hath wrought."[27] By year's end, the victory at Fredericksburg and Bragg's reclamation of most of Middle Tennessee had brightened hopes for 1863. "Let every Southerner to-day rest assured that the South will triumph," boasted the *Knoxville Register* in December 1862. "Calamities may befall us, and defeat may hurl back our armies, but we have only to bear partially all present and future ills till the North abandons the combat in despair."[28]

As 1863 began, however, Rebel civilians, like their counterparts in the service, looked less to events in Virginia and Middle Tennessee but increasingly placed greater emphasis on the role of Vicksburg in the struggle to achieve Southern independence. Several factors accounted for this. By the spring of that year, a major Federal army, under Gen. Ulysses S. Grant, was vigorously campaigning to capture the Mississippi fortress. In common with other Southerners, East Tennesseans feared the military and political consequences, should the city fall and the Confederacy be cut in two. Even more significant for East Tennesseans, most of the troops from their region were transferred to the Magnolia State during the winter of 1862–63 and were, therefore, engaged in defending Vicksburg from Grant's repeated thrusts. Defeat there would discredit their regiments and perhaps irreparably damage efforts to build political hegemony at home. Following the December 1862 Rebel victory at Chickasaw Bayou, just north of Vicksburg, where many East Tennessee troops received their baptism of fire, the *Chattanooga Rebel* was ecstatic. "Of this, however, all may be assured Vicksburg is ready, and if the vandals again attack her, she will meet the shock unawed, unsubdued, victorious," the paper defiantly proclaimed.[29] When the city came under attack again in May 1863, the *Knoxville Register* prayed for victory: "It is hoped that he [Grant] may fail, and that Vicksburg may still stand a monument to the unequaled heroism of our soldiers and skill of our Generals."[30] "Affairs in the west culminate upon the success of our intrepid Vicksburg army," averred the *Rebel* that spring, "and the fate of Lincolndom trembles in the balance. The race is about 'neck-and-neck,' the nags on the 'home stretch,' and the nation holds its breath on the issue."[31] By June the *Register* expected to hear any day of a bloody battle, "the bloodiest on the continent," that would repel Grant's army. "We have great confidence that Grant will not only be compelled to raise the siege of Vicksburg, but that his army will be routed and probably destroyed," the paper assured its readers.[32]

At the same time that attention was turning to Vicksburg, many eyes in East Tennessee were also refocusing on the defense of the valley. As Grant tightened his stranglehold around Vicksburg, to the north Bragg's army was maneuvered out of Middle Tennessee, bringing Federal troops ever closer to the valley. Indeed, by June, a Union army under the command of Gen. Ambrose Burnside was poised to enter East Tennessee via Cumberland Gap. Of course, Rebels had always considered their region essential to the Southern war effort. Long before East Tennesseans marched off to Mississippi, the *Register* presented the case for holding the region. Under the title "Are We To Be Defended?" the editor contended that the South could not hope to win without East Tennessee. If Federals seized the railroad line, a major communication link would be severed, and Virginia would be cut off from the west. Not only would this hamper troop movements from one theater to another, but it would also mean the loss of the valley's rich food supply.[33] Again, at the height of the Vicksburg campaign, the *Register* argued for the indispensability of East Tennessee and assured its readers that, even though the Federals were closing in, their homes would never be given up.[34]

By the summer of 1863, then, East Tennesseans were growing increasingly apprehensive over the situation both at home and also in Mississippi. As the fighting at Vicksburg settled into a siege, great fear was raised over the fate of the city and the troops defending it. "We are all absorbed in the great siege of Vicksburg," confessed one Rebel in mid-June. "Great God! If Vicksburg falls we are nearly ruined—I would rather see Richmond go a hundred times. . . . All here is anxiety and suspense. We can think of nothing else."[35] Col. David M. Key's sister-in-law expressed similar despair to Mrs. Key. "We have felt much concern for our folks this long while, and still the siege continues, and we cannot know their fate," she complained. "Let us try to keep up brave spirits, and if the worst comes, may God help us."[36] Another Rebel confided that he had "been fearful for some time that they would finally succeed in taking Vicksburg, but I hope it may not be so."[37]

When news came that the city had fallen, the shock was overwhelming. "I am all the time thinking of our poor boys," sighed the sister of one soldier. "The news was so cheering a few days [ago] & is now so sad. How I wish we could have peace."[38] A Bradley County girl confided to her diary that her family was losing hope. "Mother says the South will be subjugated in twelve months," she ruefully recorded, "and she is subjugated now." For days the family discussed the casualties of the Vicksburg campaign and the future of the South.[39] In Loudon, John J. Blair was distraught. "Reported that Vicksburg has fallen if so great was the night thereof." Earlier, Blair had declared that, with the fight at Vicksburg, "the darkest hour of the revolution is upon us." He was certain that "God will not see us defeated our cause being just." Now that the city was surrendered, he could not overcome the pain. "Done nothing but lament over the fall of Vicksburg," he confessed to his journal.[40] The wife of an infantry officer captured with the garrison expressed in her diary the pain felt by many that summer. "What days of darkness almost despair I endured after the fall of Vicksburg," she admitted. Word of her husband's safety helped little to relieve the sense of loss over the city's surrender.[41]

The press joined in expressing its grief and offered words of encouragement. "The fall of Vicksburg, Bragg's retreat, the mendacious accounts of the battle of Gettysburg . . . have all had a depressing tendency upon the public mind and produced an amount of despondency and crooking quite unprecedented," the *Athens Post* sadly proclaimed. The Mississippi fortress "was defended with a heroism and fortitude which has no parallel in modern history," the paper declared, "and its fall is a great calamity."[42] When the valley regiments had marched off the previous winter to the Deep South, the *Knoxville Register* had held bright hopes for success. "If we construe the signs of the times our East Tennessee boys will have a chance to win laurels there," its editors had optimistically predicted.[43] Now, with the defeated remnants of Reynolds's and Vaughn's brigades coming home, as John J. Blair observed, "look[ing] quite feeble," the *Register* attempted to put the best face on the situation. "We cannot honor them now as they deserve," the paper lamented, "but let not the people forget the debt of gratitude that is their due." Elsewhere, the paper spoke more optimistically, attempting to cheer its readers. "The people must arouse themselves to renewal of effort. . . . Let us not sit moodily by our hearthstones and await coming calamities which energy and action can avert."[44] The *Knoxville Southern Chronicle* also refused to be downcast by the disaster in Mississippi. "The noble Hill City, as we have said, 'fell a blessed martyr' to liberty and famous to all history. But the glorious cause of our country fell not with Vicksburg," it defiantly proclaimed.[45] Yet the people had come to expect success, and their disappointment was not so easily assuaged. The *Chattanooga Rebel*, experiencing none of the *Chronicle's* confidence, summed up the sentiment of many. "We believe the coming campaign," the editor warned after Vicksburg, "to be the last of the war."[46]

Indeed, the coming campaign fueled the growing sense of defeatism among East Tennessee Rebels. In June, as fear over Vicksburg's survival was at its height, Federal forces under Gen. William P. Sanders made a raid on Knoxville, the first appearance of Union troops in the valley, throwing the Confederate citizenry into a state of panic. "If they [the Yankees] get possession of East Tennessee such stealing of property, freeing of slaves and insulting of ladies never has been heard of before," predicted a Monroe County Rebel following Sanders's sweep through the region.[47] One Southern woman recorded in her diary that the Federal visit in mid-June constituted "dark days" for East Tennessee, exclaiming, "O God! I beseech thee spare us from such a foe!"[48] Another Rebel woman confessed to her sister that "the news that the Yankees are in E. Ten. at last . . . has created painful excitement throughout this section."[49] As a sign of sagging morale, many of the citizens who assisted in repelling Sanders's attack on Knoxville requested that their names not be published in the official report, perhaps in modesty over their bravery, but more likely out of fear of reprisals if the Federals returned to the region.[50] One of their fellow Knoxvillians insisted that there was far too little starch in many of his neighbors' loyalty now that they had smelled Yankee powder. "But what of our semi-Southern gentry, who, ever since this war broke out, has been pig and pup, hawk and buzz word, astradle the fence and dancing and capering to the music of both sides?" he sardonically asked. "What of them? Poor Devils! They have been striving hard to keep in with their Union friends, so that if Old Abe should pay us a visit, they can say, 'we have not been Southern to hurt!'"[51]

Then, following Sanders's raid and the stunning blow in Mississippi, Confederate troops evacuated the valley, as Federal forces in September pushed their way into Knoxville and Chattanooga. As unnerving and as unbelievable as Sanders's attack and Vicksburg had been, the abandonment of East Tennessee by the Confederate government was almost inconceivable. For months Rebels had heard their leaders assure them that the valley was crucial to Southern victory and, therefore, would never be surrendered. As late as August 1863, with the enemy knocking at the gates, the *Chattanooga Rebel* reaffirmed the region's indispensability to Southern victory. "The mountains of East Tennessee . . . form a breast plate to the Confederacy," the paper insisted. "Pass them and the probe of the enemy at once reaches the guts of the South. Therefore is East Tennessee to be defended at every hazard."[52]

After such assurances the evacuation was staggering. Confederate spirit, already shaken, plunged even lower once Burnside's entire army took possession of the valley. Two months earlier, Rebels had received the sad news that their male friends and relations had been defeated in Mississippi. Now, tragically, their homes were surrendered without a fight. "The disgust and astonishment of the rebels at our presence here is intense," reported one Federal, "and the general feeling is that the blow thus dealt so unexpectedly and vigorously to the Confederacy, is irremediable."[53] One of those astonished Rebels was Ellen Renshaw House. "I think it is outrageous," she cried incredulously. "The Yankees are here. Just think, here—here in Knoxville. Walked in without the least resistance on our part. Bukner evacuated last week, took everything. . . . I never could have believed it."[54] On the same day that Federal troops marched triumphantly into Knoxville, a Confederate soldier in North Carolina attempted to comfort a female friend in Jefferson County. "I cannot agree with you in your belief that the decisive blow will soon be struck and that to our ruin," he averred, obviously in reply to her expressions of defeat.[55] One East Tennessee soldier remembered years later that during the fall of 1863, "the future horizon of the young Confederacy began to look dark and hazy. We had now been battling for two and a half years, and had been driven back by our foes, until our homes were now in the hands and at the mercy of the enemy."[56] Josephine Hooke, who with her family fled Chattanooga when the Federals approached, sadly reported that "we have heard that the enemy occupy the town. O' me, we now feel that our homes are *lost, lost.*" The heartbreaking news was confirmed when a Confederate officer threw a note from a passing train "saying that 'Tenn. is lost.'" Her family was overcome with grief. "I felt as if the judgement day had come and all the world were coming together. Mother cried and Maj. Bransford cried, and Sue and I cried, but crying does not whip the Yankees or bring back our homes."[57]

Indeed, it did not. And those who watched as the Federal columns marched into the valley that September were faced with three options. First, they could grab a few belongings and, like the Hooke family, flee from the advancing Union army, in hopes of returning should Confederate forces retake the valley. Second, they could stay behind, remain true to their Confederate allegiance, and face the consequences. Or, third—and most pragmatically—they could take President Lincoln's amnesty oath of December 1863 and adjust themselves as best as possible to Yankee rule. The fact that so many chose the latter course reflects the shallowness of their original commitment to secession and the economic motivations behind the pro-Confederate rhetoric of some of the most outspoken Rebel leaders.

In fact, military defeat and occupation convinced some Rebels that little chance remained for the South to win its independence. Their support of the Confederacy, once so determined, dwindled the closer Federal troops got to East Tennessee. Although the *Bristol Gazette,* looking back in January 1864 on the events since the Federals invaded the region, claimed that a great many East Tennesseans had been "forced to swallow the Yankee oath at the point of the bayonet," the evidence suggests that many willingly took the oath and actively sought reconciliation with their former foes.[58] For example, Robert McNelly, editor of the rabidly pro-Confederate *Cleveland Banner,* remained behind when the Rebels retreated and took the oath. "The Confederacy kept him alive while he was in it," derisively observed one Unionist, "but when the Confederacy had to leave Bradley [County], so far as he was concerned, it must fight its own battles."[59] In Atlanta, William Gibbs McAdoo learned from refugees that "many *Southern* men remain there [in Knoxville], and seem quite prepared to be on amiable terms with the Yankees." A month later, other refugees reported to McAdoo that "many ardent fire eaters have taken the Yankee oath of allegiance."[60] Five days after the Federals arrived in Loudon, John J. Blair, once so distraught over Vicksburg, swore allegiance to the United States.[61] In Hawkins County, local government officials switched sides as soon as the Yankees hove into view. Three county court judges, the sheriff, and the county court clerk all pledged loyalty so quickly that the Federals were able to hold court on November 2.[62]

Businessmen, once so conspicuous in their support for the Confederacy, also embraced the new order. Apparently, their optimism was not sustainable as the war went badly for the Confederacy. For many, it became increasingly clear that they were unable to turn secession to their economic advantage and that their trade with the South was not going to survive now that the Federals occupied East Tennessee. They seemed willing to cut their losses and to find reconciliation with their enemies. For instance, Joseph A. Mabry, described by the *Knoxville Register* in 1862 as "one of the earliest and staunchest advocates of the Southern cause in this city," wasted little time in seeking Yankee forgiveness.[63] In January 1864 he took the oath, along with 280 other Rebels, and immediately presented the Union provost marshal, Col. F. M. Keith, with two claims in the amount of $643 to be paid by the Federal government for property lost during the war. Not surprisingly, Keith refused to honor the request because, he claimed, Mabry was a notorious Rebel and therefore had no right to restitution. Notwithstanding his Confederate sympathy, Mabry miraculously escaped being "boiled in the ink of Brownlow's press," as his biographer puts it, because he had opposed hanging the Parson when the latter was held in the Knoxville jail in 1862, and obviously was getting along with him now.[64] Similarly, Charles McClung McGhee was a loyal Confederate entrepreneur who took the oath five months after Knoxville fell. This "staunch and unequivocal Southern man," as the *Register* characterized him, ran unsuccessfully for mayor in 1863 and sold pork to the Rebel army from his extensive meat packing establishment—that is, until the Union army arrived, and then he offered to sell his hogs to them.[65] Swiss immigrant Alfred Buffat held a contract to supply corn meal to the Rebels and was even exempted from conscription because of his important trade. When the Federals occupied Knoxville, however, he had no qualms about turning around and selling to his former enemies.[66]

All across the region, previously uncompromising Rebels were getting along famously with their conquerors. When Sanders's command reached Loudon in June, John J. Blair invited Federal soldiers to supper and "re-

ceived the first Green backs that I ever had." He confided to his diary that
"I have long ago since determined to let all fight who want to and attend
to my own business."[67] The pro-Union *Nashville Daily Press* charged that
East Tennessee Southern girls were "seen every day accompanied by our
gay Lotharios to the wonder of Union people and the disgust of real
rebels." The editors complained that "the luke warm patriots who trim
their sails to any squall are exercising too much influence just now. They
feted and dined the Confederate officers, took oaths, raised regiments,
hurrahed for Jeff. Davis and are now delighting our officers with the su-
perabundance of their courtesies."[68] A correspondent for the *Cincinnati
Gazette* reported in September 1863 that Yankee money was winning new
friends for the Union. "Rebels are growing quite amiable under the fasci-
nation of the gay Yankees," he related with manifest amusement, "and
already our officers are quartering themselves among the Secesh, and frat-
ernizing with the fair rebels; who find Yankees and greenbacks are not so
bad as they supposed." He suggested that Confederate sympathy was nearly
dead in East Tennessee. "The last stake of treason is on Bragg, and with
his downfall the discouragement will be complete," he insisted.[69]

But not all Confederates found reconciliation so easy. Either out of fear
of retribution by Yankees and local Unionists or out of a determination
to continue resistance, large numbers of Rebels and their families fled
before the advancing Federal armies. Their destinations varied depending
on the availability of transportation, family and social ties, and the sense
of relative safety offered by a particular locale. J. G. M. Ramsey's family
spent the latter part of the war with relatives in western North Carolina,
as did David M. Key and his family.[70] Lt. Col. William W. Stringfield of
Thomas's Legion celebrated his twenty-seventh birthday in Emory, Virginia, with his mother and sister, who had fled their farm in Jefferson
County.[71] Others, such as the Stakely family of Madisonville, ventured into
Alabama to sit out the war with friends there.[72]

By far the most popular point of refuge, however, was Georgia. It is
impossible to estimate how many East Tennesseans fled to the Peach State,
but clearly hundreds, perhaps even thousands, took shelter there. Several
factors made the state attractive. For one, it was more accessible than other
areas and could be reached simply by catching a train down the East Tennessee and Georgia railroad. It also provided security, inasmuch as exiles
would be shielded by the Confederate Army of Tennessee, which was
operating along the rail line in north Georgia. Furthermore, as suggested
earlier, East Tennesseans had established social and economic ties with

Georgia before the war, and a refugee was certain to find at least a friendly face in cities like Atlanta, Macon, or Augusta, where business associates, friends, and relatives abounded.

Even before the Yankee invasion, Georgia was receiving the flotsam of the war in East Tennessee. In January 1863, Mary Cox, a student at the LaGrange Female College, urged her father in Monroe County to join her. "I am really afraid the Yankees will get into East Tennessee," she warned, "& I write this morning to beg you to come and bring all your family to our house, and Grandfather too." She suggested that he bring all the furniture and farm implements he could transport, because the city was crowded with refugees and anything he offered for sale would go quickly.[73] Once Sanders's Federals advanced into the valley in June 1863, refugees began to pour into Georgia. The wave of homeless, terror stricken noncombatants created near panic among Georgians.[74] J. G. M. Ramsey found Atlanta full of East Tennessee exiles in the fall of 1863, the hotels and private residences overflowing with them. The *Knoxville Register* had set up shop at the home of a Major Good, whose office was the "constant rendezvous of (especially) East Tennessee refugees and army officers."[75] During the same period, William Gibbs McAdoo, who had relocated in Georgia two years earlier, encountered many friends and acquaintances, such as John Sneed, John H. Crozier, and William G. Swan, on the streets of Atlanta.[76] The Hooke family left Chattanooga when the Federals approached that city in late August, and took a crowded southbound train to Georgia. Josephine, who kept a very detailed journal of the sojourn, recorded that Kingston, Cartersville, and Atlanta were all overflowing with East Tennesseans and refugees from other areas. In Atlanta, thousands of soldiers, civilians, slaves, and children climbed all over the cars and popped their heads in every window to get a glimpse of the new arrivals.[77] Even this late in the war, such a mass in-migration could still create quite a sensation.

The life of a refugee was one of privation and constant movement. McAdoo frequently met people en route to other destinations, such as the Stuart family, who with their five children and servants were heading for safety in Montgomery.[78] Josephine Hooke and her family were continually shuttling back and forth between one town or another along the rail line. In a period of only a few months, they traveled to Cassville, Calhoun, Atlanta, and Decatur searching for a temporary residence. Until her father finally purchased a small, cramped dwelling, they lived in a tent or in a box car parked on a side track. Under such conditions, accommodations were quite spartan, especially by the standards they had enjoyed at home. "We have no stove in our cars," she sadly recorded, "and to feel the bleak weather coming on makes us think of the dear old home we have left and all the comforts with which we were surrounded. None but those who have been exiles, wanderers in a strange land, can sympathize." She resented Atlantans, whom she claimed "know nothing of war, they have their elegant mansions, carriages & horses, and dash about the streets as gay and happy" as if the suffering around them did not exist.[79] A Knoxville woman, Elizabeth Baker Crozier, was forced to rent a room in Atlanta and borrow almost every conceivable household item. "Our cooking vessels consisted of one broken skillet which we did our frying and baking in for sometime," she remembered. "Sometimes it [the food] was burnt and others not done." She and her relatives were able to make a few dishes of clay "but nothing tasted good from them."[80]

Despite the hardship, refugees found solace in the company of others who shared their plight. When Greene County native Lt. Col. John B. Johnson of the Twenty-ninth Tennessee died of typhoid fever at Griffin, Georgia, in July 1864, a large funeral was held by East Tennesseans to honor their fallen hero. A similar affair was held the following week for Chattanoogan Francis M. Walker, commander of the Nineteenth Tennessee, who was killed in battle near Atlanta.[81] Josephine Hooke spent her days during the winter of 1863–64 sewing clothes and tobacco bags, praying, and looking for news from the front. She dubbed the family bivouac near Decatur "Camp Exile," which fortunately was located near a staging area for paroled East Tennesseans captured at Vicksburg. Col. James Gillespie and Maj. David M. Key of the Forty-third Regiment were frequent guests with the Hookes, and regimental bands serenaded them in the evenings. "While the troops were here it did us good to see them walk by, for we knew they were men from Tennessee," Josephine recorded after the soldiers were ordered away to the army.[82] In Alabama, William M. Stakely was adjusting to his new surroundings by working the land. "We are putting out cotton, cutting rice, have a good many peas to pick, & sweet potatoes are very fine," he assured his wife.[83] An East Tennessee woman observed to a relative back home that Alabamans had ways different from the folks in the mountains. "I don't want you to conclude from what I have written, that I will find it unpleasant to stay here," she quickly added, "for I think that when I become acquainted with the people & know how to take them & their ways, I will get along finely."[84]

Not all refugees left East Tennessee of their own volition. In January 1864, Federal authorities began banishing from the region or transporting north of the Ohio River Rebel noncombatants who refused to take the oath or who were considered a threat to Union control.[85] "It seems that they are going to turn all the rebels out," Mary Reynolds advised her husband. "I understand that there are several families in Loudon waiting for the boat. They are from Knoxville [and] the military are sending them South because they will not take the oath."[86] "Every family of Southern proclivities has been ordered out of the lines without any time for preparation for the journey," reported the *Bristol Gazette.* According to the editor, seventy families had been or were to be expelled. Among those who had been driven out were the families of Hugh L. McClung, William Cocke, and Samuel Boyd, all prominent Rebels.[87]

The slightest provocation could trigger retaliation. For example, an eld-

Sarah E. Stakely, the daughter of Monroe County's Democratic Party Chairman William Stakely. Sarah found refuge with her family in Georgia and Alabama during the last two years of the war. Courtesy of McClung Historical Collection, Knoxville.

erly woman, Mrs. A. A. Swan, "a most excellent inoffensive and benevolent citizen of Cleveland," was expelled, her crime being that she was the mother of a Rebel soldier and that "the young ladies of her family are understood to sympathize with the South."[88] J. G. M. Ramsey's sixteen-year-old daughter, Sue, was escorted out of Knoxville, after local Unionists reported to Federal authorities that she sewed Confederate flags, flew them on the grounds of her father's estate, and kept a small one secreted in her trunk. Before she was turned over to Confederate troops under a flag of truce, the girl had her baggage and person searched by the Federals, who employed two Unionist women to frisk her and then rifle through her belongings.[89] One Knoxville woman, ordered out of her home by the Federals with less than an hour's notice, concocted a potion to prevent the Yankees from plundering her belongings. Mixing "pickles, sweet-meats, wines, marmalades, preserves, flour, vinegar, mustard, sugar, slops, &c.," she spread the "dish" over her parlor carpets—and then added several buckets of ash and suds for good measure. When the Yankees rushed in minutes after her departure to claim their booty, they were crestfallen to find everything ruined beyond repair.[90]

Some, such as Ellen House, intentionally provoked Federal authorities into deporting them. Bitterly disappointed that her parents refused to voluntarily leave the presence of the hated Yankees, Ellen vented her anger and frustration at being trapped in Knoxville in anyway she could—waving at passing train loads of Confederate prisoners, caring for Southerners held in the Knoxville jail, insulting Union officers and their wives, and openly displaying her contempt for her conquerors (even if, in her opinion, it was unladylike behavior). Her hostile conduct finally got her what she wanted most. In April 1864, she was ordered from the city and boarded a train bound for Virginia, a result she pronounced "glorious indeed." Eventually, she landed in Eatonton, Georgia, where she found other East Tennesseans, including members of the numerous McClung clan of Knoxville.[91]

Many of those considered more dangerous, including Congressman Joseph B. Heiskell of Rogersville, who was captured in upper East Tennessee during the fall of 1864, were sent to prisons in the North. Gen. John C. Vaughn negotiated a deal with Federal Gen. Samuel P. Carter to exchange Heiskell and his fellow captives for Union citizens held by the Rebels, but Secretary of War James Seddon refused to approve the arrangement.[92] Other notorious Rebels, such as *Knoxville Register* editor J. Austin Sperry, were held in confinement in jails in Knoxville and Chattanooga, shackled with ball and chain, and forced to work on the Union fortifications, although neither charged nor convicted of a crime.[93] Such conditions prompted Vaughn to observe in September 1864 that "E. Tenn—no people in this Confederacy have suffered as our Relations & friends have. They are all robbed & imprisoned—not allowed the liberty of Negros."[94]

By the fall of 1864, the last remnants of Confederate nationalism were rapidly deteriorating among the Rebel population of the valley. To be sure, there were diehards such as Ellen House, who confided to her diary on New Year's Day 1865, "We will gain our independence yet," but even she had to admit that her fellow refugees "acknowledge themselves to be whipped."[95] The flood of requests for help in securing release from prison sent to T. A. R. Nelson reflected the growing loss of hope in Southern success. "I will further state to you that my views in regard to the Rebellion have become entirely changed," confessed one Rebel at Johnson's Island, "and I do not desire to be exchanged or sent south under any circumstances."[96] A political prisoner held in the same camp asked Nelson to intercede on his behalf, admitting that "I would be willing to be sent through the federal lines and be a peacible citizen I am willing to [be] governed by Gen. Carter's orders and go home and live peacible with all men."[97] Another Rebel sought Nelson's help in getting her soldier brother out of Fort Delaware, whom she claimed was drafted, "not a Rebel nor a Rebel sympathizer and that was the cause of his being taken for the Rebs has tried to destroy all the honest citizens."[98]

"This war is horrible; when and what will be the end!," sighed Sarah Coffin, sister of Maj. William R. Smith of the Sixtieth Tennessee. "The grave and the prison hold many of our loved ones; and crimson ghastly death hangs over them; families are rudely seperated; and want is now where abundance, luxury and elegance once were. We have merited heavy chastisement," she concluded, "and surely we have received it."[99] But such punishment was only a harbinger of the terror that lay ahead. The harsh policies pursued by the Confederates would be turned against them even before the guns fell silent. "We will be excused if we fail to sympathize with those who behold an act of cruelty in sending persistent rebels South," chided Parson Brownlow. It was his conviction that Confederates were receiving their just desserts after they themselves had "exalted over . . . removal [of the Unionists], and said rebels were doing them right."[100] Clearly, Unionists intended to have their day. If fear and old political rivalries had prompted Rebel leaders to adopt extreme measures, then vengeance would steady the hands of Brownlow and his ilk in settling the score.

We Are Certainly Now
Treading on a Volcano

On a spring day in 1865, former Confederate private Alfred R. Swan rode into the Jefferson County seat of Dandridge in search of tobacco. As he stepped into a general store, two Union veterans silently followed him inside. The war was over and they had won, and now Rebels like Swan must pay the price for fighting against the Federal government. The Unionists warned the store clerk to stay out of the way as they moved toward Swan, declaring that they were going to kill the handsome young traitor. Coolly, Swan stood still and quickly slipped his hand inside his ragged overcoat. His assailants heard a loud, unmistakable "click." Halting in their tracks, the self-appointed Rebel-hunters cursed Swan and then turned away. As they mounted their horses and rode out of town, they did not know that the "weapon" which had backed them down was nothing more than the snapping lid of a tobacco tin which Swan had just purchased.[1]

Scenes such as this were enacted all over East Tennessee during the months following Appomattox, usually with less sanguine results. Once the Confederacy was defeated on the battlefield, former Confederates in East Tennessee suffered an intense and bitter form of retribution unleashed against them by their victorious Unionist neighbors. With Radicals in control of state and local government, a campaign of both private and public terrorism and vengeance was launched against former Rebels. Civilians and returning soldiers alike found themselves the targets of mob violence, criminal and civil suits, and even indictments for treason. Unique among Southerners, many East Tennessee secessionists and their families were forced into hiding or exile, brutally beaten, attacked in the courts, or even killed for having sided with the Confederacy. At times, the streets of towns like Knoxville, Athens, and Morristown and the surrounding countryside resembled a scene from a western novel, as vigilantism, gun fights, horse whippings, lynching, and murder became common occurrences, most of it ignored, if not sanctioned, by local authorities. This situation was a total reversal of conditions in much of the rest of the South, where terrorism and violence were directed toward the victors—native Unionists, carpetbaggers, and blacks—by former Confederates in such extralegal organizations as the Ku Klux Klan.[2]

Postwar conditions in two nearby regions—Middle Tennessee and the Georgia upcountry—stand in sharp contrast to affairs in the Great Valley. In both of these areas, one directly to the west and the other directly to the south, former Confederates used violence and intimidation as a means of asserting control over freedmen and Unionists and as a weapon with which to regain political domination. Vigilantism was common after the close of the war to control black laborers and to settle scores with former Unionists in both Middle Tennessee and northern Georgia; and after 1867 violence took on a more organized form as Democrats sought to offset a series of Republican victories through a campaign of terrorism. Lynching, whippings, murder, and other types of harassment aimed at local white Unionists and blacks, as well as at transplanted Northerners, continued unabated until the end of the decade. In Middle Tennessee, where, according to Stephen Ash, violence was used as "an instrument of racial subjugation," confrontations between Klansmen and politically active blacks sometimes even erupted into full-scale gun battles, as defiant blacks resisted white attempts to reassert their prewar authority.[3]

By way of contrast, the violence that characterized East Tennessee certainly had political overtones, but it was limited to white-on-white, stemming more from a lust for revenge and only secondarily out of political confrontation. Rather than turning to violence as a means of reasserting prewar political power, Unionists were motivated instead by a desire to avenge the harsh policies implemented by East Tennessee's Confederate authorities during the first two and a half years of the war. These iron-fisted measures—arrest of suspected disloyalists and saboteurs, imposition of oppressive confiscation and draft laws, deportation of Unionists leaders and their families, and quartering of Confederate troops in towns across the region—all worked to enflame a deep-seated hatred within the breast of many Unionists and triggered a wave of retaliation as Southern troops withdrew from the Great Valley in early fall 1863. This is not to say that politics were not a factor. Indeed, beneath the violence directed against former Rebels was a desire to see that these people never again controlled the destiny of East Tennessee and, thereby, ensure Radical political domination of the region.

The call for vengeance went up as soon as Union forces occupied the region in the early fall of 1863. Despite the plea of Federal commander Ambrose E. Burnside to loyalists that "while justice should be dealt to persistent rebels, revenge was no part of a magnanimous Government," most Unionists, still stinging from the persecutions of their former masters, had anything but forgiveness on their minds.[4] Proclaiming that "the reign of terror is over," the pro-Union *Knoxville Bulletin* argued for retribution. "Wearied with the long contemplation of scenes of violence, strife and bloodshed, we often feel an intense yearning for amnesty and peace," the editor confessed. "But we cannot and do not pray that any such healing measures may ever reach the remorseless and bloody oppressors of East Tennessee. Any amnesty to be proclaimed by the government should have a long, long list of exceptions, of which East Tennessee would furnish a disproportionately large share."[5]

Loudest among those crying for revenge was Parson Brownlow. Having suffered condemnation, imprisonment, and banishment at the hands of Rebels, Brownlow was in no mood for Christian charity. No one excelled him in stirring passions against secessionists. "A new leaf must be turned over here with all rebels and rebel sympathizers," he asserted not long after returning to Knoxville. "Let them be made to feel the effects of their treason and conduct, and to know that they must go with one party or the other."[6] Returning to Knoxville hard on the heels of the conquering Union army, Brownlow dragged out his old printing press and began to lash out at his foes with even more bitterness than before. Re-christening his old newspaper the *Knoxville Whig* with the new name *Brownlow's Whig and Rebel Ventilator*, the Parson waged a verbal war against Confederates who, he firmly believed, deserved nothing less than the sternest punishment for their sins. "Let our authorities come down on all such," he railed, "and let them be made to feel the consequences of their treason. They labored to bring on this rebellion, caused suffering, deaths, imprisonments and starvation among Union men and families, and now let them be paid back in their own coin."[7]

The Parson resorted to a number of tactics to bring the spirit of revenge to a fevered pitch. He daily reported atrocities committed by unrepentant Rebels and carried lists of staunch secessionists whom he singled out for special treatment. During the final year of the war, the Parson encouraged retaliation by relating tales of robbery, plunder, and murder carried out by Confederate cavalrymen and bushwhackers, and by reducing female secessionists to mere "she-devils" and "she-rebels."[8] While many of the stories undoubtedly were apocryphal, their publication was an ef-

The scourge of East Tennessee Confederates, William G. "Parson" Brownlow. Courtesy of McClung Historical Collection, Knoxville.

fective means of stirring the spirit of revenge against specific Confederates whom Brownlow found particularly obnoxious.

Indeed, Brownlow had no qualms what so ever about identifying old adversaries by name, although he clearly knew that in doing so he was, like a Mafia boss, issuing a call for a "hit" against these foes. For instance, in February 1864, Brownlow published the names of seventy-two Blount

County men who voted for separation in June 1861, so that "our soldiers and officers may appreciate the patriotism of these men when found."[9] He advocated showing no quarter to William Brazelton, Jr., of Jefferson County after he was captured by Federal troops, ranting that "a man having rich parents and relatives [does not] make his murdering and stealing at all lawful."[10] Referring to another notorious Confederate, Brownlow assured his readers that "our Union boys will know how to dispose of him, should they come up with him."[11] Attempting to incite mob action if need be to get rid of his foes, the *Whig* warned Rebel leaders in Blount County to "stay away until these men [Unionists] who were driven out of the country, and had their families robbed, *die of old age!*"[12] Ominously, Brownlow complained that Confederates were being shown leniency and offered protection by Federal officials "when they ought to be imprisoned, or at least sent South to remain during the war. . . . We say tighten the ropes around these vile enemies of the Government."[13]

Such rabble-rousing fell on receptive ears. Although many Union civilians were ready to live in peace, returning Union veterans, especially those who had fled to Kentucky to escape Confederate conscription officers, needed little encouragement to exact retribution. "All *damed* Rebels are *herby* notified to *lieve* at *wonce*," read a notice from former Federal soldiers in New Market. "We are working by the order that you *theving* God forsaken hell deserving Rebels issued four years ago. Union men and Rebels cannot live *togather* which we find not altogather bogus."[14] Similarly, two Union soldiers about to return to East Tennessee requested their father to convey a message to all Rebels in Carter and Washington Counties: "Now we expect to come home shortly and we have concluded that *Seperation* is Best and *thay* must *leav theair* Before we come or we will Kill and *Lintch* them and that without *distinkstion*."[15] Another Unionist, writing under the name "An East Tennessean," also advised driving former Rebels out of the region. "The proud bearing and haughty air that distinguished 'the flower of youth' four years ago changed into humanity and lamb-like gentleness," he observed. "The return of these rebels, who spent four years in the work of destruction, is full of danger for the peace of society. . . . They voted for separation four years ago. If the doctrine was good then it is good yet."[16]

Writing to Union leader T. A. R. Nelson, one former Confederate soldier claimed that former Rebels had good reason to fear Federal soldiers. "I cannot go to the country and go to farming," he noted, "for when those [Union] Tennessee troops return home they will be without restraint & a [Rebel] man wholly unsafe."[17] The widow of Provisional Army general William R. Caswell, who had been murdered by Unionists, informed her son in New Jersey that "a great many southern men have been severely used by the [Union] soldiers Alex Massengill was terribly cowhided—Bob West had his skull broken—Epps was beaten almost to death—and a good many more. . . . I would not have had come back here on any account—at least for some years."[18] Others related similar tales. Joseph L. Burts complained to Andrew Johnson about "discharged union soldiers, who are commiting all maner of cruelty against peaceful & very best citizens of the country," and laid the blame for their actions at Brownlow's feet. "The union Flag *so called* published in Jonesboro [and] the Knoxville Whig," he charged, "are all combined to inflame and incourage these deluded and wicked men, in their lawless conduct."[19] William Gibbs McAdoo agreed. After dining with two East Tennessee Union officers in Georgia following the war, McAdoo was shocked to hear how their attitudes had hardened toward secessionists. "Mother's letter today says she asked them what they would do with me were I to return to East Ten.," he confided to his diary. "They replied, 'Send me to hell where all such people (*rebels*) go.' . . . And after breaking bread with me! Brownlow is the demon that inspires them."[20]

Not all Unionists, however, harbored such ill will toward their former enemies. Some, known as Conservatives, accepted the policy of reconciliation advocated by President Lincoln and later by his successor, Andrew Johnson. In Greeneville, for instance, the *New Era* urged Unionists to restrain their desire for vengeance. "Now what we desire and mean to indicate, is this, that those of our Union citizens who have been aggrieved (and there are many such) by the acts and outrages of the rebels will do well to exercise a philosophic and magnanimous forbearance toward their late vile persecutors," the editor suggested.[21] From the same town, Sam Milligan attacked Brownlow and his allies for stirring hatred against former Rebels. Charging that the Parson was only seeking to perpetuate his own power, Milligan observed to Andrew Johnson that "were it not for the evil influence of such men the country would be at peace."[22] Writing for his brother Thomas, William Crutchfield assured S. A. Key that his brother, David M. Key, would be welcomed back in East Tennessee. "Maj. Key's deportment was such so far as I have been informed to treat all men kindly courteously & gentlemanly regardless of their political opinions—any man in the Rebel Army deporting himself thus has nothing to fear from an honorable high-minded intelligent community," Crutchfield insisted.[23]

Other Unionists called upon their fellow "Tories" to be generous in victory and did what they could to encourage peace. "I have, at the hands of the rebels, suffered arrest, many personal indignities, and pecuniary loss," declared one correspondent of Brownlow's *Whig.* Yet now that the war was over, it was time for peace. "Let us display towards the thousands of our fellow citizens who were engaged in the recent rebellion . . . the same magnanimous spirit which our Government has exhibited," he implored.[24] In Madisonville, two Union men held a party in August 1865 and "invited all 'that had been rebels' to attend; their object was to restore good feelings among the young folks."[25] A group of Washington County Unionists called on President Johnson to use his influence to stop the violence for economic, rather than mere social, reasons. "We are in a state of Anarchy," they cried. "Our citizens are driven off into those states in which after a while we must rely for sale of our entire surplus from which our traders will in turn be driven and we wholly cut off from the use of our productive power—while new immigrants coming to our borders with their enterprise and capital turn away to quieter and more inviting localities."[26]

The lust for vengeance, however, seems to have outweighed any impulse for magnanimity. The quest for revenge began early and took on a variety of forms. Even before Confederate forces evacuated the region, Unionists were lashing out at their oppressors.[27] In fact, Federal occupation seems to have signaled the beginning of open season for Rebel hunting. "Notwithstanding the stringent orders of General Burnside, and the vigilance of General Carter as provost marshal of Tennessee, outrages are constantly committed by the vindictive Tennesseans," reported a correspondent for the *Cincinnati Express.* "The Tennesseans seem to regard the occupation of East Tennessee as an opportunity to retaliate for their own grievances, and complain bitterly that they are not allowed to run riot through rebel property."[28] Tales such as the one related by diarist Ellen House of a Maryville citizen robbed and hanged and his wife threatened with shooting by a gang of Unionists apparently bent on revenge were all too frequent during the last year of the war.[29]

But it was not until the final days of the conflict and the months immediately following its close, as Union troops were mustered out of the service, that instances of violence became widespread and commonplace. All across the region, Union veterans went on a rampage. During the winter of 1865, a gang of Union bushwhackers, composed of "65 of the lowest dam trash of earth" according to one of their victims, made a raid into Hawkins County, plundering numerous homes and killing two Confederate sympathizers. One hapless Rebel, whose life was spared, lost all of his clothes, including the garments in which he slept.[30] In Newport, a former "Secesh" was informed by "a set of lawless, intoxicated men" twice in a three-day period in August 1865 to leave his home or be killed.[31] Similarly, George Caldwell, a Confederate chaplain and Presbyterian minister in Athens, returned to his home after the fighting ended only to be threatened to leave town by morning or be horse whipped. Not easily intimidated, Caldwell went to his gun rack, pulled down a rusty old musket, cleaned it up, and dared anyone to come near him.[32]

Southern soldiers and conscription officers were special targets. Despite the fact that he had taken the amnesty oath, Jake Lawson, a conscription agent in Bradley County, was taken out in the night by "some worthy loyal men whom he had injured," was administered fifty lashes, and ordered out of the state. The very next night, Sam Billings, Lawson's protégé, was "bitten by the same bugbear," according to Parson Brownlow.[33] Returning Federal soldiers broke into the Hynds House in Dandridge and dragged out two former Confederate officers, Robert H. Hynds and P. L. Gammon. The latter was beaten almost to death, while the former was struck once or twice because "he was a Rebel and in bad company, and they said they had a score to settle with his bedfellow."[34] Although horse whippings were a common sight in most towns, sometimes even more primitive weapons were used. William Vestal, a veteran of the Nineteenth Tennessee who apparently possessed more courage than discretion, stood drunk in the middle of Gay Street in Knoxville and swore that "he had fought three years against the d——d Yankees, and was ready to fight that much longer in the same cause." His oration was abruptly brought to a close when a Unionist knocked Vestal down with a rock.[35] Even prominent Unionists participated in the violence, as R. I. Jarnigan found out when he was lured into Clinton by Union colonel L. C. Houk, who having tricked Jarnigan into attending court to handle some legitimate business, raised a mob to attack the former Rebel. Jarnagin managed to escape only after the sheriff intervened on his behalf.[36]

The most brutal and violent form of retaliation was murder, and this too increased in frequency as the war ground to a close. For instance, John Kincaid, described by Brownlow as "a bitter, thorough, and unrelenting rebel," was shot and killed outside the Knox County courthouse by discharged Federal soldiers even after he had taken the oath. With grim determination, the Unionists road up to the courthouse, called Kincaid outside, gunned him down, and then coolly road out of town. Referring to the incident, Brownlow remarked that "injured, insulted and oppressed Union men will redress their own wrongs—and for the life of us, we are not able to see that they are in error."[37] In another act characterized as "Just Retribution" by Parson Brownlow, sixty-five-year-old

Isham Alley attacked and murdered Robert C. West only hours after the latter returned to Knoxville. According to Brownlow, West had several years earlier beaten Alley for proclaiming his hostility to the Confederacy. "So far as we are concerned, we approve of Mr. Alley's course, and venture to predict that he will never be put in the penitentiary," Brownlow remarked, apparently hoping that others would retaliate in similar fashion.[38] A number of former Rebels were killed in Jonesboro, where "a man was shot in the street on monday, and is now lying at the point of death—died this morning," according to one Unionist. "On the friday before on the North side of the County, an old man 70 odd years of age was murdered," he added in shocked disbelief.[39] Numerous threats were made against the lives of Vaughn's returning veterans, and at least one, Deen Anderson of the Third Tennessee, was shot and killed at his farm by unknown Unionists, despite assurances by the local provost marshall that paroled Confederate soldiers would be protected.[40] The reputation of some Unionists was so bad that a Federal officer observed to *Knoxville Register* editor J. Austin Sperry that, had he and his comrades been captured and escorted to Knoxville by East Tennesseans rather than Kentucky troops, they "never would have brought us here alive."[41]

The most spectacular act of violence occurred in September 1865, when Abner Baker was lynched in downtown Knoxville. Baker, a veteran of Ashby's Second Tennessee Cavalry, returned home after the war to find that his father had been killed by East Tennessee Union troops in 1863 at the family estate in west Knox County. Following a brief investigation, the young Baker concluded that William Hall, clerk of the Knox County Court, was responsible for the murder. Determined to avenge his father's death, Baker rode into town, found Hall and gunned him down, for which Baker was immediately arrested and imprisoned in the county jail. Such audacity on the part of a former Rebel was obviously more than many could bear. At 8:00 P.M. a fire bell was sounded and a mob of one thousand vigilantes, with forty advance men, stormed the jail, overpowered the sheriff and jailer, and broke into Baker's cell. Within moments, Baker was hanged to a tree in the jail yard, "quickly and without interruption." The affair must have shocked even many Radicals, for reports of murder declined precipitously thereafter.[42]

A more popular, and peaceful, method of retaliating against former Rebels was to attack them through the court system. Beginning in 1864 and continuing through the end of the decade, Unionists attempted to strike back at their oppressors by bringing suit for a variety of causes. Generally speaking, these actions can be classified in three categories: civil, criminal, and treason. The most common and successful of these were civil suits, actions brought to redress the violation of some private right. Not long after Unionists had reorganized the county courts in East Tennessee, Parson Brownlow began urging Union citizens to find redress for wrongs committed against them through the legal system. "Let every loyal man of the country bring suits for damages, and they will be remunerated," he assured his readers. "Now we say, let justice be done. These traitors have had their day; now let us have ours."[43]

And so they did. Even before the war had ended, Unionists began their legal assault. All across the region, court dockets quickly became crowded with suits against former Rebels. Most of these were instituted for false arrest and imprisonment, a broad sweeping charge which included a variety of wrongs, from enforcing the conscription act to simply suggesting that a seditiously minded Unionist be held under martial law. "Every Union man who was conscripted and forced into the rebel army has a right of action, for false imprisonment, against every person engaged in forcing him into the army," ranted the *Whig*.[44] Taking his cue from Brownlow, one Unionist beseeched T. A. R. Nelson to file a suit for him against several prominent Confederate officials and officers, including Senator Landon Carter Haynes, Col. Henry M. Ashby, and Charles Coffin, for having urged General Zollicoffer to arrest him in 1861.[45] In Bradley County, a number of Union men successfully sued on the grounds of false arrest and imprisonment, one plaintiff obtaining judgments against Congressman William H. Tibbs, Col. James W. Gillespie, and Elizah F. Johnston for twenty thousand dollars. Another twenty thousand was levied against Tibbs and Capt. William L. Brown by a second plaintiff; and a third recovered an additional ten thousand dollars against the same defendants.[46]

Typically, since they had fled the region and were in exile, many defendants were tried in their absence and their real estate attached to satisfy the judgment of the courts. For example, William Bracket brought suit against five different Confederates in Bradley and McMinn counties, claiming false arrest and imprisonment and seeking fifty thousand dollars in damages. When Bracket prevailed in the case, the court ordered the defendants' land and houses seized, since they had "absconded" with all personal property.[47] In fact, by March 1865, the pages of the *Whig* were filled with notices of attachment of real property belonging to exiled Rebel citizens, a good barometer of just how many were sued in absentia or had fled once an unfavorable judgment had been rendered.[48]

Other suits were instituted for loss of personal property during the war. A

Cocke County man successfully brought an action against a former Rebel for trespass after the defendant had relieved him of a gun under an act passed by the state legislature in November 1861 commissioning agents to seize weapons for military use. The state supreme court affirmed the decision of the lower court, reasoning that the defendant's actions were not protected by the 1861 law, since all acts and ordinances passed by the legislature after May 6, 1861, had been declared null and void by the constitutional amendments of February 22, 1865.[49] In the Roane County Circuit Court, one Unionist sued a former Confederate officer for confiscating a wagon laden with corn during the fall of 1863. Although the defendant claimed that he was an officer acting by the rules of war in seizing the property and converting it for Confederate use, the court ruled in favor of the plaintiff, holding that he was a citizen engaged in "ordinary pursuits" and that the defendant, therefore, had no legal right to interfere in his affairs. On appeal, this decision was also affirmed by the state supreme court.[50]

Although secessionists found state and local courts hostile, it is unclear how many really suffered as a result of civil actions brought against them. While the newspapers were filled with notices of attachments, there is some question as to how much property was in fact awarded to and, most significantly, actually taken possession of by aggrieved plaintiffs. This is particularly true because of the numerous cases which flooded the Tennessee state supreme court after the Radicals were expelled from the bench in 1870. Once Reconstruction ended and more moderate men were appointed to the court, Confederates found a sympathetic ear in Nashville. In every instance published in the state reports, previous decisions by Radical courts favoring Unionist plaintiffs were overturned by new supreme court decisions favoring former Confederates appealing unfavorable lower court rulings.

For example, in *Moore v. Birchfield* (1870), the supreme court overturned a judgment of the Jefferson County Circuit Court against the defendant, who was an enrolling officer and had arrested the plaintiff, on the grounds that the case had not been tried before "an impartial and dispassionate jury."[51] Similarly, the court reversed a judgment against William Brazelton of Jefferson County for directing Rebel soldiers to cut timber from the property of a Union man. The court held that there was no trespass and, furthermore, Brazelton incurred no liability because of the wrongful actions of the soldiers.[52] It also overturned the decision of the Anderson County Circuit Court in favor of a Unionist who claimed that he had accepted Confederate money as payment for a real estate transfer under duress and now sought to regain title to his property.[53] And, when a Grainger County court found against a defendant on the basis of testimony that he was a "rebel," the supreme court ordered the judgment reversed because the defendant's sympathy was irrelevant. "The political faith of a party has no pertinence to the issue, more than have his peculiar views on religion," declared Justice J. Turney in delivering the opinion of the court.[54]

Beyond civil litigation, an attempt was also made to bring action against Rebels on the basis of criminal statutes. Unionists managed to secure numerous criminal indictments against their enemies, usually for acts of murder, assault, and robbery committed during Confederate occupation of the region. During 1864 and 1865, the infamous Knoxville jail, "Castle Fox," which had served as the Confederate military prison, was filled with Rebels awaiting trial on various charges. One inmate, Confederate captain Reuben Clark of Grainger County, was arrested for murder and held in a small iron cage within the jail, where, according to Clark, "Federal officers and civilians would come and glare at me through the iron bars, as though I were a monster."[55] In Blount County, Lt. Fredrick A. Lenoir of the Sixteenth Tennessee Cavalry Battalion was accused after the war of shooting and wounding a Louisville farmer named Foster while on a reconnaissance mission in January 1864, a charge which Lenoir vigorously denied.[56] Murder charges were also brought against Sgt. Isaac Fain of the Sixty-third Tennessee, son of Col. Richard G. Fain of Hawkins County, in August 1866 for the slaying of a Union man near Rogersville during the war. His brother, Hiram, and cousin, Sam, also veterans of the Sixty-third, had no sooner bailed him out of jail when Isaac was placed under arrest once again, this time for robbery.[57]

But if civil suits were only partially successful in striking back at Rebels, then those cases brought in the criminal courts proved even less so. Although Unionists had no trouble securing indictments and even arresting accused suspects, they found it nearly impossible to obtain a conviction for a criminal offense, especially murder. This is particularly puzzling, given the attitude toward vigilante justice held by many Unionists. It is little wonder that some simply ignored the judicial process and took the law into their own hands. One noted example of the impotence of Unionists juries was the case of prominent Knoxville Rebel Joseph Mabry, who was acquitted of killing Unionist Charles S. Douglas, even though most loyalists thought he was certainly guilty. After the trial, Mabry announced that "he would as soon be tried by a jury of East Tennessee Union men as a jury of Rebels in Memphis," suggesting how difficult it was to find twelve men who were willing to convict a former Confederate of murder.[58] And even when criminal convictions were obtained, Unionists could foil their own efforts in their zeal to exact retribution, as in the case of Martin Crawford. A veteran of the Thirty-ninth Tennessee, Crawford was found guilty by a Hawkins County court of manslaughter in the April 1865 slaying of a paroled Union soldier. On appeal to the state supreme court, the conviction was overturned because of an error by the lower court judge, who, in his eagerness to put Crawford away, allowed the jury to hear only that part of Crawford's testimony that convicted him, and dismissed the balance.[59]

Probably the most celebrated murder case after the war was that of J. Richard McCann, Reuben Roddie, J. Crozier Ramsey, and William C. Kain for the trial and execution of A. C. Hawn. The accused had served on the court-martial that had found Hawn guilty of sabotage in the bridge burnings of November 1861. Four years later, they were brought to trial in the Knox County Circuit Court on a charge of murder. It appeared to be an open and shut case; few doubted that the accused Rebels would be convicted. "What a jury of this county may do with him, we are not able to say," speculated the *Whig* about Captain Kain after his arrest in Connecticut, "but if he gets justice he will either hang or go to the penitentiary for years!" Yet doubtless to Brownlow's deep chagrin, all four defendants were acquitted of the crime, despite the fact that the jury was considered to be "decidedly Union" in its sentiment.[60]

A third, and even less successful, means of striking back at former Confederates through the legal system was to accuse them of treason. Shortly after Federal forces marched into East Tennessee, Brownlow began calling for treason trials against former Rebels. "These men deserve to be punished, and even disfranchised, for they are guilty of treason against the State, the United States, and of perjury," he railed. He argued that action could be taken against Rebels on the basis of the Tennessee Code, which he quoted as outlawing any who aid the enemies of "the State or the United States."[61] Toward the end of the war, a number of treason cases had already come or were pending before the United States Sixth Circuit Court in Knoxville, presided over by Judge Connally F. Trigg.[62] During 1865, as many as 2,014 Rebels were indicted in East Tennessee for treason and for "giving aid and comfort to the enemy."[63] Among those was John Wood of Cocke County, who was charged with supplying "100 horse, 1,000 pds bacon, 1,000 bushels of corn, 100 hogs, 100 head cattle" to "false traitors." Wood's indictment accused him of "being moved and seduced by the instigation of the devil" to commit such heinous deeds.[64]

The list of those indicted for betraying their country included various figures, both great and small. Among them was J. Austin Sperry, editor of the *Knoxville Register,* who was arraigned for writing treason; John E. Gamble, a former conscription officer in Blount County; William H. Sneed, a prominent attorney and former congressman from Knoxville; and William Gibbs McAdoo, former Confederate officer and fire-eating secessionist. In every case, the charges were dropped when the defendants produced proof that they had taken the amnesty oath or were pardoned by President Johnson.[65] And in those rare instances when there was a conviction, it was quickly overturned, such as the case of Dewitt C. Williams of Jefferson County, who was found guilty in the state courts of "Treason against the State of Tennessee in aiding and abetting the late rebellion." On appeal to the state supreme court, Williams received a *nolle prosequi* on the grounds that his treason was against the United States rather than against Tennessee, and therefore, was not actionable in a state court.[66]

Much of the civil and criminal litigation in which many former Rebels found themselves embroiled came as a result of their exemption from the blanket amnesty proclamation issued by President Johnson on May 29, 1865. The proclamation, which sought a speedy return of the Southern states to the Union, pardoned all persons who had participated in the rebellion, restoring to them their property rights upon subscription to a loyalty oath swearing allegiance to the United States. There were, however, certain important exceptions to the president's amnesty that fell into fourteen broad categories, ranging from holding civil or military office in the Confederate government or army to "aiding or comforting" the rebellion, detainment for "offenses of any kind," and owning twenty thousand dollars or more in taxable property. Persons falling within one or more of these fourteen exemptions, and who were thereby excluded from the general amnesty, were required to appeal in writing to the president or the attorney general for a special pardon. Obtaining presidential clemency was imperative, because it meant the restoration of the petitioner's civil and property rights, and, moreover, offered an avenue of escape from prosecution in the civil and criminal courts.[67]

In all, as many as 652 Tennesseans requested a special pardon from the president. Of this number, fully two-thirds (400) came from heavily Unionist East Tennessee, suggesting that clemency was less important (and necessary) in the middle and western divisions of the state, where Confederates were no longer under attack. Nearly every activity and occupation were represented among the applicants. In the three East Tennessee counties possessing the largest concentration of applicants—Washington (65), Sullivan (63), and Knox (55)—123 pardon seekers were indicted for treason. Of these, 56 had served in the Confederate army, and twenty as petty county officials, such as sheriffs, clerks, tax assessors, and justices of the peace. By far the largest single category represented among all applicants was the 12th exemption, those persons detained or indicted for some offense, usually treason.[68]

Although the majority of Tennessee applicants for special pardon hailed from the eastern section of the state, most of these amnesty seekers were enlisted military personnel, petty officeholders, and minor county officials rather than high-ranking Rebel leaders. In fact, few of the men who led East Tennessee to war in 1861 found cause to request forgiveness from the president. Of the seventy-nine out of one hundred Confederate officers surveyed in chapter 3 who survived the war, only fifteen (19 percent) put forth the effort to apply to Johnson for a pardon. Only three of these applications originated from states other than Tennessee, suggesting that, for the twelve who did apply from within the state, securing a pardon was essential to resuming a normal life. This conclusion is further reinforced by the fact that ten of the fifteen applicants fell into the twelfth exemption, and were facing treason charges at the time they wrote to the president. All but one of the applications was clearly approved (disposition on the application of Luther C. May could not be determined), twelve of the pardon seekers gaining amnesty within a year after the end of the war.[69]

Taken together, the amnesty applications present an interesting profile of the mentality of East Tennessee Rebels during the months immediately following the surrender. Most tried, with varying success, to convince the president that they had either opposed secession or had been lukewarm in their support of the Confederacy. For example, Blount County resident James K. Cox, indicted for treason in Knoxville, claimed that he "was never in the rebel army, never held any office under the so called Confederate states, and never did any act to prevent him from applying for pardon." "At most," Cox asserted, "your petitioner was but a well wisher of the late Rebellion," although Cox had in 1861 requested his name be published in the *Nashville Union and American* as a secessionist.[70] James Miller of Washington County avowed that, while he did support the South, "he never cordially accepted the program of the Southern leaders."[71] Similarly, James W. Gillespie, who assisted Harris in organizing the state's forces and later commanded the Forty-third Tennessee, stated that he "resisted with all his power the dogma of secession in every possible form, believing then as he still believes yet, that it was a *political heresy* and wholly unauthorized by the Constitution, and fearfully dangerous in its tendencies."[72] Another former Confederate declared that he "never voted for secession. . . . I never went into the Rebel army . . . though I was offered high position and big pay," and only "talked about the Southern Confederacy and made them [his neighbors] think I was all right," in order to protect his property. "I never was a rebel at heart."[73]

Other Confederates made no attempt to hide their sympathies. For instance, William M. Cocke of Knoxville boldly stated that, after Lincoln's proclamation, "being a native of the South with all his sympathies enlisted in her behalf, he identified himself with her in her great and unequal contest," although he now acquiesced in the decision of arms.[74] In like fashion, George L. Gillespie of Chattanooga informed the president, "I must be candid enough to acknowledge that . . . when my State went out I entered the service of the Confederate Army, and that my whole sympathy was with the south in the Contest."[75] George R. Powel of Hawkins County put it succinctly: "If it be a fault to have been a Rebel I have been grieviously at fault."[76]

But if some Rebels were willing to admit their loyalties to the South, few, if any, were willing to argue that their cause was right and that they were now unrepentant. Isaac W. George of Blount County confessed that "he committed a great error and political crime, for which he desires to make the best atonement he can by becoming a . . . loyal citizen." His Unionist neighbor, John F. Henry, in endorsing George's application, observed to Johnson that the former Rebel "is completely subjugated."[77] Col. David M. Key, writing from exile in New Jersey, insisted that he, too, was ready to be reconstructed. "You have been triumphant," he averred. "I have fallen. I am completely conquered. . . . I expect to be a faithful and loyal citizen of the Federal Government, fully obedient to its laws and constitution."[78] William W. Stringfield of Thomas's Legion penitently admitted that "he voluntarily entered the late Confederate army[,] . . . but the Sword being the arbiter, and that having been settled against him, he now returns to his allegiance to his mother country—like the prodigal Son Sorry for the evils of the past and wishing to make amends."[79]

While some applicants confessed to serving the Confederacy voluntarily and wholeheartedly, others pleaded that they only supported the South under duress or to avoid some penalty. Such was the case of Cornelius E. Lucky of Jonesboro, who was indicted for treason and requested a pardon on the grounds that he "entered the Rebel service when but a youth, refusing to do so until the Enforcement of the Conscript Law."[80] Similarly, James C. Moses of Knoxville attempted to obtain a pardon for his son, Frank, on the basis that "he is a mere lad, and was at College, when through the influence of his Professor, Capt. [Alexander A.] Blair, since deceased, he was induced to join Blair's Company."[81] P. S . Hale of Hawkins County claimed that "to avoid conscription as well as to serve the public, he accepted the office of Post Master at Rogersville some time in the spring of 1864, but he did this mainly to keep out of the Rebel army."[82] Likewise, Hiram Heartsill of Louisville in Blount County avowed that he consented to serve as an enrolling officer and postmaster to avoid fines and penalties and "as a matter of accommodation, through the solicitation of both Union men & Secessionists."[83] Another resident of Blount County, Hiram Bogle, also claimed that he held the office of postmaster "at an obscure and remote part of said county solely for the accommodation of his neighbors."[84] Fellow civil servant Thomas A. Faw argued that he accepted the post of depot agent at Johnson's Depot in Washington County only to "avoid conscription into the Southern army. . . . I would have gladly come again under the Stars and Stripes," he declared, "but I could not without abandoning my home and family to what might have been a cruel fate."[85]

Even more important in the opinion of former Confederates in legitimizing their right to a pardon was their good treatment of Unionists during the war. Most applicants took great pains to demonstrate that they had in no way persecuted or harmed loyal citizens while the Rebel army had control of the region, hoping perhaps to curry the president's favor by their show of fairness and mercy. Knoxvillian James W. Bowman stressed in his application that "he never engaged in 'guerilla warfare' or in the persecution of Union men or their families; but on the other hand furnished provision to several families whose husbands & sons had gone to Kentucky and joined the Union army also took several Union men out of Rebel prison at this place."[86] David M. Key noted that he "always respected the feelings, persons and property of the Union citizens" and "often labored, and sometimes with effect, for the release of those who were arrested."[87] One prominent Blount County man even argued that he sided with the South so he could protect Union men. "The vote for seperation identifyed me to some extent with the southern cause," H. Talbot Cox declared in a classic case of understatement, "and I suffered it to be so from the fact it placed me in a position the better to protect and defend Union men and their families."[88] In another instance of creative reasoning, Hugh L. McClung contended that he should be pardoned because his wartime activity was restricted to producing salt, most of which helped Union families of East Tennessee, saving them $2 million. McClung reckoned that, since the salt was distributed by agents "at least four fifths of whom were union men," and since "three fourths of the people of East Tenn. are union citizens of course three fourths of the salt made was consumed by union citizens," which he certainly thought exculpated him from any treasonous act.[89]

Government officials were especially careful to point out their good treatment of Tories. Former marshal for the Eastern District of Tennessee, William H. Crouch, informed the president, "I was careful to not trespass upon the rights of my neighbors—I never caused a man to be arrested during the war but in most cases where arrests were made I had them released and sent home."[90] Jefferson County Judge F. W. Turley related a similar tale of mercy and forbearance. He firmly declared that he never "gave offense to Union men" and, in fact, "on many occasions he interceded for Union men . . . improperly arrested sometimes succeeding and at other times failing to procure their release."[91] Jesse G. Wallace of Blount County claimed that he accepted the position of district attorney at the behest of Unionists who were unhappy with his predecessor, John Crozier Ramsey. "I never during the whole of my official career brought the ferst single indictment against a Union man for any political offence," he pleaded, "and I never had any thing to do with the execution of the Confederate Confiscation Law or received a cent in way of fees or commissions from that fund."[92]

Enrolling officers related how they never conscripted a single Union man into the Confederate ranks, all of which must have strained the president's credulity. Former state legislator and Confederate orderly sergeant, William Bayless of Washington County, told how he was appointed enrolling officer "when he quit the army," but "while so acting he never arrested or put into the army in the rebel service, a single man."[93] David Good also claimed that he served as enrolling officer "for the same protection of his Union neighbors," and that "after his acceptance not a single man from his district was put in the Confederate army."[94] Jonesboro resident Alexander McLin, who held the posts of justice of the peace and officer, claimed that "in the latter capacity he frequently favored Union men and never was concerned in informing against or persecuting them." McLin, like so many other Rebels, took the oath when Federal troops arrived in the fall of 1863 and would have done so sooner "if there had been anyone to administer it."[95]

A great number of these pardon applications were submitted from various points of safety outside East Tennessee. Faced with continued threats of violence, many secessionists deemed it prudent to remain in exile rather than return to East Tennessee to face the charges leveled against them.

Indeed, as noted earlier, a great many, if not most, of the civil cases brought against former Confederates were prosecuted in the defendant's absence. "You must know that many of your clients feel some apprehension in going to Knoxville for fear of violence from the mob," John M. King revealed to John Netherland and T. A. R. Nelson, moderate Unionists attorneys who were serving as counsel for many accused Rebels.[96] Among their exiled clients was Joseph Tucker, who was accused of arresting and imprisoning Levi Trewhitt, a Union man, during the war. Tucker had fled to Georgia in 1863 because of violence in his home county of Bradley; in fact, one of his brothers was murdered while he was away. In August 1865, he returned home but left immediately because of anonymous letters notifying him to leave in six hours or face the consequences.[97]

Even pending criminal action could not bring many back home to stand trial. After threats were made against his life, Capt. A. L. Mims of the Fifth Tennessee Cavalry requested a continuance of his trial for treason until the next meeting of the court. His brother assured Nelson that "he wants to come but is afraid of his life and hopes by next court times will be more settled."[98] From Atlanta, William W. Wallace of Blount County also expressed fear of setting foot in East Tennessee, even though he was under bond to appear at the next term of the Federal court upon charges of treason. "I am assured that no one will suppose that I desire to evade the penalty of the Court, but I don't think duty requires me to appear there to be shot down like a dog without provocation as Cox was," he asserted.[99] Few were as brave as Col. Henry M. Ashby, former commander of the Second Tennessee Cavalry, who left his refuge in Atlanta to post bail in Knoxville. After returning to East Tennessee and testing the climate against him, Ashby precipitously fled back to Georgia to await trial for treason and for the murder of Unionist refugees whom he captured fleeing to Kentucky in 1862, charges brought against him by Knox County prosecuting attorney E. C. Camp. Although Ashby was later acquitted of any wrong doing, he made the mistake of seeking revenge against Camp, whom he accosted on the streets of Knoxville in April 1868. Both men struggled over a pistol pulled by Ashby; and before the fray was over, Ashby lay dead in a ditch, shot in the chest and head. Fortunately for Camp, the Knox County coroner was a Brownlow man, so it came as no surprise when Ashby's death was ruled an act of self-defense.[100]

While much of the violence and legal persecution aimed at former Rebels stemmed from actions taken by Confederates during the war, prewar animosities undoubtedly motivated some Unionists to smite their former foes. Now that

Henry M. Ashby. A Chattanooga merchant when the war began, Ashby would become one of Brownlow's most embittered enemies. Ironically, the two old foes are
buried directly opposite each other in Knoxville's Old Gray Cemetery. Courtesy of
Dr. Anthony Hodges.

they had the upper hand, the Radical-Unionist-Whigs were just as determined to solidify their political domination of the region by completely suppressing their old political opponents as had been the Confederate-Secessionist-Democrats when they were in control. David Deaderick claimed that his brother, James, "always a moderate Southern man," was driven out of Jonesboro, not because of his actions during the war, but because he was "obnoxious to certain low men on account of his extensive practice as a lawyer, his success (a rebel) was too much for their *patriotism* to brook."[101] Col. William Brazelton of the Thirty-ninth Tennessee accused District Attorney General J. M. Meek of instituting charges of robbery, larceny, and murder against him simply because Brazelton "had the pleasure of defeating him" in a political contest before the war.[102] Similarly, William Henry Maxwell suggested that old political enmities were behind the violence and suits in Washington County. "There are several Whig enrolling officers (Confed) in this county—Not a single one of whom have been indicted for Treason in a state or Federal court," Maxwell informed Andrew Johnson. "Not a single Whig in the county to my knowledge has been beat ordered off or driven out of the county." On the other hand, "every Democrat in the county occupying respectable positions" had been attacked and indicted for treason "without regard to their conduct in the rebellion. . . . There may be an exceptional Whig but it is an exception who has been indicted to keep up appearances. The plan," he concluded, "is to rid East Tennessee of Democrats."[103]

With conditions so unsettled in East Tennessee, many Confederates opted to remain in exile indefinitely. "The treatment of Southern families throughout this section of the country has been fearful," reported a correspondent for the *Memphis Appeal* a few months after Federal occupation. "The Union neighbors have combined to oppress those who entertained Southern sentiments, and many a private grudge has thus been wiped out in blood, under cover of a so called 'devotion to the Union.'"[104] Faced with such punishment, many cast about in hopes of finding a safe haven until affairs quieted down. "Those who had to fly on account of their opinions, dare not come home," a Greene County woman complained to President Johnson. "Is it not a sad state of things? I would not live in East Tennessee if they were to give me the whole of it, unless there is a change."[105] From Sevier County, Ellen P. Brabson suggested that her exiled brother, William T. Brabson of the Thirty-ninth Tennessee, could return from Middle Tennessee and "get into business as a clerk in Knoxville, and if you *would*, or *could*, come home I don't think there would be danger, but I will not advise you, for one can scarcely trust their dearest friend these days."[106] "I want you to think about the matter & determine where you would like to live," Samuel B. Boyd requested his wife from prison. "I doubt if we could live in K[noxville] for several years." He suggested Louisville or Lexington, Kentucky, because of the good schools and churches in those cities.[107] According to former Confederate General Benjamin F. Cheatham, a number of Rebel soldiers found Kentucky, even with its Unionist majority, to be a genuine point of safety. In an interview with the *Lebanon Register*, Cheatham stated that "all my officers who were from East Tennessee have come here [Louisville] to get into business, the people of that section of the State having driven them from their old homes."[108]

The majority just wanted to get as far away as possible. Common destinations included the states of Alabama and North Carolina and the cities of Memphis and Atlanta, which held promise of business opportunities. Such luminaries as Col. Carrick White Heiskell and his brother, Congressman Joseph B. Heiskell, Senator Landon Carter Haynes, and Dr. Frank A. Ramsey, half-brother of J. G. M., took refuge in Memphis. Only the Ramseys ever returned to East Tennessee.[109] Texas also received its share of expatriate East Tennesseans. Thomas J. Campbell, grandson of Tennessee founding father

Samuel Bell Palmer and John H. Palmer, Knoxvillians who served in W. C. Kain's Tennessee light artillery company. Their removal to Georgia after the war was typical of thousands of East Tennessee Confederates. Courtesy of Van Ness Collection.

Judge David Campbell, had "made himself so obnoxious" to his Unionist neighbors in Bradley County that he "did not deem it prudent to return," and headed to Texas instead.[110] The sons of Judge Robert H. Hynds, all of whom served in the Confederate ranks, scattered their residences between Atlanta and the Lone Star State, never to return to their childhood home in Jefferson County.[111] Others, like William Gibbs McAdoo and Gen. John C. Vaughn, remained in Georgia until all charges were dropped against them, even though Vaughn thought Georgians had "not much sympathy for an East Tenn Rebble."[112] The General advised his friend Ramsey in North Carolina to stay clear of East Tennessee, because with the 1867 election in Tennessee further strengthening Brownlow's power in the state, he warned that "we are certainly now treadding on a volcano."[113]

Some who were not quite so venturesome just crossed the state line into southwestern Virginia. "This Country is crowded with Reffugees from Ten," complained Anderson R. Edwards in Washington County, Virginia, "and they are coming Dayly. They Git orders to Leave in So many days or take the consequences."[114] Still others who wanted to stay in East Tennessee went to Sullivan County, which, while not completely safe, offered some measure of security for those who wished to remain in the region. "Nearly all of our friends from this, and Grainger Counties, have come in," reported a woman in Jefferson County. "I believe *all* but Tom Smith. He was enrolling officer & does not dare come in, but is in Sullivan County."[115] In fact, Sullivan was apparently deemed such a safe haven that a former Confederate chaplain rode all the way from Athens to Bristol on a hand car after finding affairs too hot in McMinn County.[116]

A few Rebels even went north to escape Unionist retribution. The wife of slain state General William R. Caswell sent her son off to school at Princeton in order to spare him the violence at home.[117] Robert B. Reynolds, whom Brownlow described as "active and bitter in trying and imprisoning Union men," left his handsome estate on Kingston Pike in Knox County and crossed the Ohio River into Illinois. From that point of safety, he sought to obtain a pardon from President Johnson.[118] Former Confederate engineer and Swiss immigrant Charles Ducloux went into the mercantile business after the war in New York City, finally returning to Knoxville in 1872.[119] The Stakely and Cox families of Monroe County, refugees in Georgia, even considered leaving the country and going to Mexico. Carrie Stakely swore that "a great many persons here are thinking of going to see that country," but they soon lost the "Mexican fever" once they realized that they could find employment in Georgia.[120]

Not all Confederates fled, however. Some remained behind to face whatever "justice" their victorious neighbors were prepared to dispense. "Well, go, the war is over now and we must drink that bitter cup which we have so long striven in vain to dash from our lips," admitted Col. James G. Rose, commander of the Sixty-first Tennessee, to his girl friend in Virginia. Bravely, Rose returned to Morristown and struggled to rebuild his life amidst the postwar turmoil.[121] A former captain under Rose, J. C. Gallaher, accepted the outcome of the war and the Unionist desire for retribution, while attacking the leading secessionists of Knoxville for going over to the Yankees to save their fortunes. "T'was they who declared that if the South succeeded Union men could not live in Tennessee," he charged. "And it was they who first bowed obsequiously to the Federal masters, and now, sycophant like, ask to be taken into full Federal communion." Gallaher informed Brownlow that he would accept Union oppression and disfranchisement, boldly declaring that "if we had succeeded, [I] would have favored the passage of laws that would have precluded from citizenship men who left their homes and took up arms against us. And I cannot reprobate in others, what I would have considered just in myself."[122]

Not all who remained submitted to Unionist punishment so uncomplainingly. In Hamilton County, former Rebels demanded that Tories be legally ordered to discontinue whipping and driving them out of the region.[123] Some even struck back with equal violence, like the "scouts" who attacked and beat a justice of the peace in Sullivan County who was attempting to prosecute former Confederates.[124] In Jonesboro, an unsuccessful effort was made to burn the office of the Radical newspaper, the *Union Flag*, by throwing lighted paper soaked with turpentine through the windows.[125] And others, like the group of former Confederate soldiers who published an open letter to Brownlow after he was elected governor, called for protection and warned of the consequences if their plea for justice was ignored. Writing under the name "MANY SO-CALLED REBELS," they demanded that those committing crimes against former Confederates be arrested and prosecuted. If they were not, the Confederates vowed to take the law into their own hands. "We are hunted down and driven from our homes, not by the authorities, but by the vulgar, cowardly, and unprincipled class who never placed themselves in any danger. . . . & you have never tried to suppress it, but we *will* suppress it, if we have to suppress their worthless lives." Insisting that "we have forbore with a certain class until forbearance has ceased to be a virtue," they declared that "we have sworn to put an end to them" if the persecution did not stop.[126]

Fortunately for them, by 1870 the volcano described by Vaughn had finally cooled. Although there were reports of scattered violence and a few cases still pending before the courts in Knoxville at the close of the de-cade, they were the exception rather than the rule. With Brownlow in Washington serving as Senator, and with the "redemption" of the state that year from Radical control, the physical and legal assault finally tapered off. The new Democratic legislature reenfranchised former Confederates, breaking the lock which Unionists had held for five years on the state's political system, while the recast state supreme court was overturning un-favorable rulings against Rebel defendants.

All of this effectively brought the persecution to a close. Still, most of East Tennessee's secessionist leaders had not returned, and indeed, never would. Of the one hundred officers surveyed in chapter 3, only twenty-four had returned to the region by the end of the 1860s. Twenty-one had died during the war from a variety of causes, including disease and com-bat-inflicted wounds. Five were residing in the friendly territory of West Tennessee, while fifty, fully half the sample, had removed to other states or had died since the close of the war.[127] That meant that a majority of the men who had led East Tennessee to war were no longer living within the region's boundaries. Brownlow had complained bitterly in 1865 about "rebels in our midst" and had advocated driving the "traitors" out of the valley.[128] To a large extent, he and his followers had succeeded.

Epilogue: They Never Hoped to Do Great Things

The Confederate experience in East Tennessee was distinctive, if not unique, differing not only in degree but also in kind from that of other Southerners. Just as their economy and culture had diverged from the mainstream of antebellum Southern society, so too did the wartime role played by mountain Rebels deviate from that of the majority of Confederates.[1] Led to war by a young merchant-professional class that saw secession as an avenue for enhancing their personal and regional economic and political fortunes, East Tennessee Confederates reluctantly took up the sword to fight along side Georgians, South Carolinians, and Virginians, people with whom they had little in common except for mutually beneficial economic ties.

Besieged by enemies from without and within, East Tennessee Rebels found themselves poorly supported by a Richmond administration that failed to understand their problems or appreciate the magnitude of the sacrifice they were being called upon to make. When Unionist hostility eventually erupted into open rebellion, Rebels, out of fear for their own political hegemony, adopted a harsh policy toward local Tories. At the same time, Confederate authorities, viewing the disloyalty of the Tennessee mountain district from afar, failed to distinguish between the loyal and the disloyal and came to suspect all East Tennesseans of lacking a strong commitment to Southern independence. As a result, thousands of Confederate soldiers from the Great Valley were ordered to the Deep South, where they suffered defeat, sickness, and ridicule from their comrades in the field.

Mistrusted and abandoned by Confederate authorities in Richmond, and unable to turn secession to their economic advantage, Rebel morale sagged and eventually collapsed as Federal occupation quickly followed the military debacle at Vicksburg. As a consequence, many soldiers and civilians lost confidence in Southern victory, quietly withdrawing their support or seeking reconciliation with their conquerors. Others fled before the advancing columns of the enemy out of fear of Unionist retribution or in hopes of continuing the struggle for Southern independence as exiles.

Ironically, war's end brought them no peace. A vindictive and vengeful foe bent on exacting revenge and completely destroying Rebels as a threat to Unionist political domination unleashed a campaign of terrorism and intimidation. The resulting oppression took on many forms, including violence, civil suits, treason charges, and criminal prosecution. Although thousands of treason and criminal proceedings were either dropped or overturned, Rebels were beaten, horsewhipped, and even murdered, and lost much property as a result of civil litigation. All of this compelled many to flee the region once again, scattering their residence across the South and elsewhere.

Of course, Parson Brownlow and his Radical vigilantes could not keep them out forever. Slowly at first, and then with increasing speed, the expatriates wound their way back to the valley from their many points of exile. While it is almost impossible to calculate how many Confederate refugees finally came home, it is clear that many, especially the enlisted men and junior officers who had held no leadership roles, eventually found it safe to return. As numbers of former Rebels ventured back to East Tennessee after the violence had subsided, they attempted to resume their lives and to assimilate into society. Surprisingly, given the bitterness and hatred generated by the war, most former Unionists apparently were willing to forgive their enemies and allow them to come home and live in peace. Indeed, Unionists not only tolerated Rebels but even sought their help in rebuilding the valley's economic and political fortunes. Around the region, previously devoted Confederates were accepted back into the life of the valley, moving once again into business, social, and religious affairs.

Most revealing of how welcomed former Rebels were in East Tennessee was the fact that many began winning political office soon after their return. In Morristown, for instance, former Confederates found little trouble in easing their way back into political activities. There, Capt. John C. Hodges returned with his refugee family from North Carolina in 1866 and resumed his law practice. By 1874, he had become so popular in the community that he was elected to the Tennessee General Assembly for one term.[2] After Hamblen County was formed in 1870, two former enemies, Union major John Murphy and Confederate major George Folsom, worked together to build a courthouse in the new county seat. Folsom was eventually appointed president of the Morristown branch of the First National Bank.[3] In neighboring Hawkins County, Christopher C. Spears, formerly a soldier in the Nineteenth Tennessee, was elected sheriff on the Democratic ticket in 1870, 1872, and 1874, after which he joined the Republican Party and ran successfully for circuit court clerk and coroner in 1878 and 1887, respectively.[4]

In other heavily Unionist areas, former Rebels were gaining political office, even while running as Democrats. In McMinn County, for example, William M. Bradford, who had fought for three years as colonel of the Thirty-ninth Tennessee, ran as a Democrat and defeated D. C. Trewhitt, a Union man and Republican, for the office of chancellor of the Third Chancery District.[5] Staunchly Republican Blount County residents elected Capt. William H. Henry as superintendent of public instruction in 1875 and justice of the peace in 1882, despite Henry's Confederate record and Democratic affiliation.[6] After returning to Sweetwater in 1873, Confederate veteran Jacob Warren served two terms as sheriff of Monroe County and, in 1882, was elected county trustee.[7] Most remarkable of all, Gen. John C. Vaughn was elected in 1871 as a Democrat from Monroe, Meigs, Polk, and McMinn Counties to the general assembly, where he served one term as speaker of the senate.[8]

But not all fit in so easily. The most prominent Rebels, especially those who had served as high-ranking officers and government officials, never returned. Even Vaughn eventually went back to Georgia and to his wife's home town of Thomasville, where he spent the remainder of his life as the lord of a great south Georgia plantation. The loss of so many merchants and professionals like Vaughn and their entrepreneurial skills and capital is difficult to assess. The flight to Atlanta and Augusta of many of East Tennessee's wealthiest and most ambitious citizens, the region's "displaced persons," who before the war financed the railroad, directed the region's trade, and built the cities and towns, clearly had some impact on the region's postwar development, but in what manner is less clear. East Tennessee families like the Inmans and the Allens which fled to Georgia after the war made significant contributions to the growth of what has become the economic goliath of Atlanta. These business leaders of antebellum East Tennessee were supplanted by a new class of men, primarily composed of East Tennesseans who before the war had been outside the traditional mainstream of power; and former Northern soldiers, who had seen the region's natural resources while marching through the valley and then returned after the war to exploit them.[9]

The war swept away the traditional economic leadership and created a vacuum which new men from below and afar quickly filled. The coalition of men such as Unionist L. C. Houk and Yankee John T. Wilder took the region down a path different from that which J. G. M. Ramsey and Vaughn were headed. Houk, the former Blount County carpenter who became a Union colonel and Republican political boss during the last decades of the nineteenth century and Wilder, the former Ohioan and Union general who pioneered East Tennessee's iron and coal mining industries, did not share the vision of a prosperous, commercialized, agricultural economy envisioned by their Democratic opponents Ramsey and Vaughn. Under their leadership, East Tennessee became increasingly industrialized, Republican, and impoverished. It may have been a different place during the postwar years, perhaps even veered from the road to industrialization and economic dependency recently described by Paul Salstrom, if the war had not so badly damaged agriculture in what he terms "old Appalachia" (the Tennessee Valley region) and removed the old merchant-professional class which had previously directed its development toward commercial agriculture. On the other hand, the destruction of the region's farming interests may have been so great that, even in political and military victory, Ramsey and his followers could not have turned the tide against dependency. Whatever the economic outcome, the region certainly would have been Democratic in its political affiliation if Ramsey and Vaughn were in charge of its destiny. Instead, under Houk and Wilder (not to mention Brownlow and his sons), East Tennessee became known as the staunchest Republican stronghold in the South, the land of the "Lilly White" faction of the party, a reputation which it retains to this day.[10]

Judging from how quickly those former Rebels who did return won political office and power, it is evident that few gloried in their war records. Most seemed willing to forget the terrible suffering of the war and to concede ideological hegemony to the Unionists. In only a few locations was there any attempt to memorialize the sacrifice or to participate actively in Confederate veterans' affairs. By the end of the century, there existed only fifteen United Confederate Veterans (UCV) camps in the region, concentrated primarily in the area between Knoxville and Chattanooga. In the counties above Knoxville, so few Rebels were interested in remembering the war years of the 1860s that only a single organization, christened the Confederate Veterans Association of Upper East Tennessee, was formed. Encompassing the vast territory of the First and Second Congressional Districts, the association attracted a scattered membership of only several hundred. Chattanooga, which had received an influx of soldiers from other states, had only one camp located there. Vast stretches of central East Tennessee never organized a veterans' group at all. There were, however, some pockets of intense UCV activity. For example, camps and "bivouacs" were scattered about the Rhea-Meigs-Monroe area, but those counties had voted for secession and therefore could be expected to participate with more enthusiasm in the Lost Cause celebration. Similarly, so many veterans had located or returned to Knoxville after the war that the city could boast of two UCV camps, named after local heroes, Fred Ault and Felix Zollicoffer. On the whole, though, organized or institutionalized Confederate veterans' activity was sporadic and was customarily limited to specific prosecession communities, where former Rebel soldiers congregated in relatively large numbers.[11]

The sister organization to the UCV, the United Daughters of the Confederacy (UDC), enjoyed a bit more success in mobilizing East Tennesseans to participate in the Lost Cause. Organized simultaneously with the UCV, the UDC quickly emerged as a leading institution in celebrating the Confederate experience. By 1900, five chapters, including a Knoxville Ladies Memorial Association founded in 1868, had been formed or were in the process of organizing, primarily in places like Chattanooga and Knoxville. By 1920, when the celebration of the Confederacy was at its height, sixteen chapters had been chartered up and down the valley; after that date, an additional fifteen were organized. But many of these disappeared within only a few years, their membership so reduced that the state division dropped them from the rolls. Apparently, some chapters, such as that named in honor of Capt. Roby Brown in Mountain City, realized that they were fighting a losing battle in the midst of a Unionist majority. The chapter's historian confessed that "they never hoped to do great things for the cause located as they were, the outpost of the state . . . where most of the people were on the other side." During the period between 1896, when the first chapters were organized in Knoxville and Chattanooga, and the 1930s, a few chapters did attempt to mark soldiers' graves, place portraits of Confederate heroes in schools and libraries, and prepare rosters of soldiers from their communities, but many, especially those organized in the major urban areas during the First World War, were mere social and civic clubs and quietly died out after a short time.[12]

While the Union majority may have dampened most efforts, in one instance it galvanized Rebel women into action. After Johnson City was selected in 1903 as the site for a new federally operated veterans hospital, Union soldiers converged upon the small Washington County town. The presence of so many of their former enemies prompted local ladies into forming a UDC chapter the following year. "The real urge and need for a

UDC chapter," commented the division historian, "was felt even more strongly because of the 'blue coats' that had descended upon the city and much feeling was aroused at the sight of same." The ladies went to work immediately erecting monuments and placing paintings and books in local schools to counteract the effect of so many Yankees, home-grown and otherwise, on their community.[13]

Monument erection, which became such an obsession and a cornerstone of the Lost Cause, received scant attention in East Tennessee. Unlike most parts of the South, where seemingly every courthouse lawn was graced with a stone figure of a Southern soldier during the period between the 1890s and the first decade of the twentieth century, the people of the valley seemed little interested in thus memorializing the war. Even heavily Confederate Rhea, Meigs, and Monroe Counties were immune to the monument fever. Only eight Confederate monuments were ever erected in East Tennessee, and many of these, oddly enough, after the Lost Cause celebration had passed its zenith.[14] Such indifference extended even to headstones and grave markers. Few veterans chose to immortalize their service by carving any mention of their rank, unit, or Confederate affiliation upon their tombstones, as was common practice in other regions of the South. And today's visitor to East Tennessee's cemeteries rarely encounters the iron Maltese-cross grave markers, or "Southern Crosses of Honor," which so dominate the old graveyards, both great and small, from Virginia to Texas.

What is striking about all of this is that East Tennessee Confederates, having suffered so greatly during the war, seemed little interested in memorializing their sacrifice. As a minority situated among a hostile and bitter majority, East Tennessee Rebels had risked more and, in many ways, endured more than most Southerners. Even so, they were hesitant, even reluctant, to embrace the flag waving and sentimentalism of the cult of the Lost Cause. While, as Charles Reagan Wilson has shown, other Southerners sought to give meaning to their sacrifice by creating a civil religion that fused the imagery and symbolism of the Confederacy with that of Christianity, East Tennesseans who had sided with the South seemed content merely to watch from the sidelines.[15] It was as if the ambivalence so many had shown about the fight for Southern independence carried over into the postwar attempts to glorify that unsuccessful struggle. The loss of hope and the disillusionment that had afflicted so many by midwar continued to exert a controlling influence over their perception of the past, their attitude toward the role they played in the defining moment in American history.

Of course, it would be unfair to expect people, surrounded as they were by a victorious Union majority, to proclaim loudly their loyalty to a cause and a revolutionary movement that had never received their full support. Although Gaines Foster argues that the postwar memorialization of Southern patriotism was nothing more than an attempt on the part of the former Confederates to bring their section back into the mainstream of American society, East Tennesseans viewed the matter differently.[16] The Lost Cause was for them not an avenue to reunion but a divisive factor between themselves and the Unionists with whom they now had to live peacefully for the economic and social benefit of both sides. Little could be gained by keeping alive old memories which might antagonize or alienate former enemies, who were now business partners, neighbors, and even friends.

Sadly, though, few could have realized that by distancing themselves from their Confederate experience, they had doomed themselves to near oblivion. Future historians and scholars would focus not on the secessionists and their cause, but on the Unionists and their rebellion against rebellion. The story of East Tennessee's Confederate people would become shrouded and eventually lost in the myths and stereotypes of mountain Unionism. Undoubtedly, it was a result that would have given Parson Brownlow no little satisfaction.

Notes

1. A Land that Can Flow with Milk and Honey

1. A description of the events surrounding the driving of the final spike in the East Tennessee and Virginia can be found in James W. Holland, "The Building of the East Tennessee and Virginia Railroad," *East Tennessee Historical Society's Publications* 4 (1932): 99–100 (hereafter referred to as *ETHSP*).

2. While I differentiate between the Tennessee Valley proper and the Sequatchie Valley, for the sake of convenience I refer to the whole region as the Tennessee, or Great, Valley.

3. For a discussion of the effects of geography on the trade and agriculture of East Tennessee, see J. B. Killebrew, *The Resources of Tennessee* (Nashville, 1874), 431–32; Lewis C. Gray, *History of Agriculture in the Southern United States to 1860*, 2 vols. (Washington, D.C., 1933), 2:882–85; David Hsuing, "Isolation and Integration in Upper East Tennessee, 1780–1860: Historical Origins of Appalachian Characterizations" (Ph.D. diss., Univ. of Michigan, 1991); Donald Buckwalter, "Effects of Early Nineteenth Century Transportation Disadvantages on the Agriculture of East Tennessee," *Southeastern Geographer* 27 (1987): 18–37; and Stanley J. Folmsbee, *Sectionalism and Internal Improvements in Tennessee, 1796–1845* (Knoxville, 1939), 10–14.

4. Hilliard, *Hog Meat and Hoecake: Food Supply in the Old South* (Carbondale, Ill., 1972), 193–94.

5. Edmund C. Burnett, "Hog Raising and Hog Driving in the Region of the French Broad River," *Journal of Agricultural History* 20 (1946): 87–88.

6. Wilma Dykeman, *The French Broad* (New York, 1955), 140–41.

7. Burnett, "Hog Raising and Hog Driving," 89.

8. *Confederate Veteran* 2 (1894): 310.

9. Killebrew, *Resources of Tennessee*, 356.

10. Gray, *History of Agriculture* 2:840; Hilliard, *Hog Meat and Hoecake*, 186.

11. William L. Barney, *The Secessionist Impulse: Alabama and Mississippi in 1860* (Princeton, N.J., 1974), 33; Hilliard, *Hog Meat and Hoecake*, 107–8.

12. Robert E. Gallman, "Self-Sufficiency in the Cotton Economy of the Antebellum South," *Agricultural History* 44 (1970): 5–23; William K. Hutchinson and Samuel H. Williamson, "The Self-Sufficiency of the Antebellum South: Estimates of the Food Supply," *Journal of Economic History* 31 (1971): 591–612; Diane Lindstrom, "Southern Dependence upon Interregional Grain Supplies: A Review of the Trade Flows, 1840–1860," *Agricultural History* 64 (1970): 101–14.

13. For an example of a typical East Tennessee market report, see the *Knoxville Southern Citizen*, Mar. 18, 1858.

14. The traditional argument for a subsistence economy in East Tennessee can be found in Killebrew, *Resources of Tennessee*, 353; William F. Rogers, "Life in East Tennessee Near the End of the Eighteenth Century," *ETHSP* 1 (1929): 27–42; Thomas P. Abernethy, *From Frontier to Plantation in Tennessee: A Study in Frontier Democracy* (Chapel Hill, N.C., 1932), 144–63; and Blanche Henry Clark, *The Tennessee Yeomen, 1840–1860* (Nashville, 1942). Among the recent scholarship that has challenged the idea of Appalachian isolation are Christopher Warren Baker, "East Tennessee Within the World Economy (1790–1850): Pre-Capitalist Isolation or Peripheral Capitalism?" (Master's thesis, Univ. of Tennessee, 1991); Durwood Dunn, *Cades Cove: Life and Death of a Southern Appalachian Community* (Knoxville, 1988); John C. Inscoe, *Mountain Masters, Slavery, and the Sectional Crisis in Western North Carolina* (Knoxville, 1989); and John S. Otto, *Southern Frontiers, 1607–1860: The Agricultural Evolution of the Colonial and Antebellum South* (New York, 1989).

15. Frederick L. Olmsted, *A Journey in the Back Country* (London, 1860), 230; Killebrew, *Resources of Tennessee*, 447; John Morgan, *The Log House in East Tennessee* (Knoxville, 1990), 59–78; Killebrew, *Resources of Tennessee*, 354.

16. Robert Tracy McKenzie, *One South or Many? Plantation Belt and Upcountry in Civil War–Era Tennessee* (New York, 1994); Frank L. and Harriet C. Owsley, "The Economic Structure of Rural Tennessee, 1850–1860," *Journal of Southern History* 8 (1942): 173.

17. Paul Salstrom, *Appalachia's Path to Dependency: Rethinking a Region's Economic History, 1730–1940* (Lexington, 1994), 20–40.

18. Bureau of the Census, *Eighth Census of the United States: 1860* (Washington, D.C., 1864).

19. Chase C. Mooney, *Slavery in Tennessee* (Bloomington, Ind., 1957), 124–25.

20. Gray, *History of Agriculture* 2:873.
21. Paul Salstrom, "The Agricultural Origins of Economic Dependency, 1840–1880," in *Appalachian Frontiers: Settlement, Society, and Development in the Preindustrial Era,* ed. Robert D. Mitchell (Lexington, 1990), 265.
22. Bureau of the Census, *Seventh Census of the United States: 1850* (Washington, D.C., 1853); Bureau of the Census, *Eighth Census of the United States: 1860*; Inscoe, *Mountain Masters,* 87–114.
23. Robert Y. Hayne, *An Address in Behalf of the Knoxville Convention to the Citizens of the Several States Interested in the Proposed Louisville, Cincinnati, and Charleston Rail Road* (Charleston, 1836), 26.
24. Stanley J. Folmsbee, "The Beginnings of the Railroad Movement in East Tennessee," *ETHSP* 5 (1933): 85.
25. For Ramsey's position on railroads, secession, and states' rights, see William B. Hesseltine, ed., *Dr. J. G. M. Ramsey: Autobiography and Letters* (Nashville, 1954), 18–32, 93–97. As will be discussed in chapter 2, there were painfully few people in East Tennessee who advocated Southern nationalism and separation from the Union prior to April 1861.
26. James W. Holland, "The East Tennessee and Georgia Railroad, 1836–1860," *ETHSP* 3 (1931): 98–107.
27. *Knoxville Register,* June 28, 1855.
28. See Holland, "East Tennessee and Virginia Railroad," 83–101.
29. *Knoxville Register,* May 20, 1858.
30. Bureau of the Census, *Eighth Census of the United States: 1860.* For the accelerated development of wheat as a commercial crop after the coming of the railroad, see also Donald L. Winters, *Tennessee Farming, Tennessee Farmers: Antebellum Agriculture in the Upper South* (Knoxville, 1994), 62–64. For an examination of a parallel development of wheat and commercial agriculture in a neighboring section of Appalachia as a result of railroad construction, see Kenneth W. Noe, *Southwest Virginia's Railroad: Modernization and the Sectional Crisis* (Urbana, Ill., 1994), 31–52.
31. *Rogersville (Tenn.) Times,* Aug. 14, 1851.
32. *Knoxville Register,* July 30, 1857.
33. See *Jonesboro Union,* Sept. 22, 1860; *Kingston Gazette,* Apr. 7, 1855; and *Loudon Free Press,* Oct. 11, 1854; *Athens (Tenn.) Post,* Feb. 4, 1859; *Jonesboro East Tennessee Herald,* Oct. 17, 1856; *Maryville East Tennessean,* Aug. 14, 1857; *Chattanooga Advertiser,* Jan. 8, 1857; *Greeneville American Presbyterian,* Sept. 29, 1858. For further discussion of East Tennessee's wheat trade with Southern markets, see also Paul M. Fink, "The Railroad Comes to Jonesboro," *Tennessee Historical Quarterly* 36 (1977): 161–80; Lindstrom,

"Southern Dependence upon Interregional Grain Supplies," 101–14; and James M. Russell, *Atlanta, 1847–1890: City Building in the Old South and New* (Baton Rouge, 1988), 20–25.

34. *Knoxville Southern Citizen,* June 3, 1858.
35. Killebrew, *Resources of Tennessee,* 433.
36. *Knoxville Register,* Sept. 20, 1855.
37. *Knoxville Southern Citizen,* Mar. 18, 1858.
38. *Maryville East Tennessean,* Aug. 14, 1857.
39. Fink, "Railroad Comes to Jonesboro," 177; Hilliard, *Hog Meat and Hoecake,* 198; Russell, *Atlanta,* 26–27.
40. Hilliard, *Hog Meat and Hoecake,* 160–68; Killebrew, *Resources of Tennessee,* 96, 355, 433. Other parts of the mountain South, including the Valley of Virginia and the Piedmont regions, were also unsuitable for McCormick's reaper. In fact, it was for that very reason that the inventor transferred his company to Chicago in the 1850s. See Clement Eaton, *History of the Old South,* 3d ed. (New York, 1975), 431.
41. Bureau of the Census, *Eighth Census of the United States: 1860.*
42. *Knoxville Register,* June 28, 1855.
43. See ibid., Aug. 14, 1857, for the proceedings of and reaction to the convention.
44. Zella Armstrong, *The History of Hamilton County and Chattanooga, Tennessee,* 2 vols. (Chattanooga, 1931), 1:147; Roy G. Lillard, ed., *The History of Bradley County* (Cleveland, Tenn., 1976), 50–51; Inez Burns, *History of Blount County, Tennessee, 1795–1955* (Maryville, Tenn., 1957), 87–88.
45. See Nathalia Wright, "Montvale Springs under the Proprietorship of Sterling Lanier," *ETHSP* 19 (1947): 48–63, for a history of the Springs in the late 1850s.
46. *Maryville East Tennessean,* Aug. 14, 1857.
47. Wright, "Montvale Springs," 50.
48. William Gibbs McAdoo diary, Special Collections Library, University of Tennessee, Knoxville (hereafter cited as McAdoo diary).
49. Bureau of the Census, *Eighth Census of the United States: 1860.*
50. Mary U. Rothrock, ed., *The French Broad–Holston Country* (Knoxville, 1946), 84–89; Killebrew, *Resources of Tennessee,* 354.
51. Goodspeed's Publishing Company, *A History of Tennessee from the Earliest Times to the Present, East Tennessee Edition* (Nashville, 1887), 854.
52. Lillard, *History of Bradley County,* 38–39, 57–58.
53. *Morristown (Tenn.) Intelligencer,* May 14, 1858. On Morristown's founding and growth, see Goodspeed's *History of Tennessee,* 869. For Bristol's

development, see Oliver Taylor, *Historic Sullivan County* (Bristol, Tenn., 1909), 312–17.

54. W. B. Lenoir, *History of Sweetwater Valley* (Richmond, 1916), 199–201, 221–26.

55. *Rogersville (Tenn.) Times,* June 12, 1851.

56. Lewis E. Atherton, *The Southern Country Store, 1800–1860* (Baton Rouge, 1949), 90–100; Russell, *Atlanta,* 43–44; *Knoxville Southern Citizen,* Jan. 21, 1858; Gray, *History of Agriculture* 2:839–42. For a study of a parallel development of a merchant class in western North Carolina, see Inscoe, *Mountain Masters,* 25–58.

57. Atherton, *Southern Country Store,* 99–100.

58. Ibid., 98–99; Lenoir Family Papers, Special Collections Library, University of Tennessee, Knoxville.

59. Lillard to Patton, Mar. 22, 1854, Letter Book, Lillard Family Papers, Tennessee State Library and Archives, Nashville (hereafter cited as Lillard Family Papers). See also Account Books for Lillard Family Store, 1850–60, ibid.

60. Rothrock, *French Broad–Holston Country,* 76.

61. *Maryville East Tennessean,* July 16, 1858.

62. *Knoxville Register,* June 28, 1855.

63. Quoted in Daniel E. Sutherland, ed., *A Very Violent Rebel: The Civil War Diary of Ellen Renshaw House* (Knoxville, 1996), xviii.

64. For a history and description of nineteenth-century Roane County, see Goodspeed's *History of Tennessee,* 821–28.

65. Bureau of the Census, "Eighth Census of Tennessee: 1860," Free Inhabitants MSS Schedule for Roane County (quotation marks here and below indicate that the data comes from unpublished manuscript census records). These statistics are based on heads of households rather than totals in these occupational categories. For a discussion of professional/merchant class development in the towns of Appalachian Kentucky and southwestern Virginia, see Mary Beth Pudup, "Social Class and Economic Development in Southeast Kentucky, 1820–1860," in Mitchell, *Appalachian Frontiers,* 235–60.

66. On antebellum Blount County, see Morgan, *Log House,* 75–76.

67. Bureau of the Census, "Eighth Census of Tennessee: 1860," Free Inhabitants MSS Schedule for Roane County. These statistics are based on heads of households.

68. *Knoxville Register,* June 23, 1855.

69. *Chattanooga Advertiser,* June 23, 1857.

2. They Made Me a Rebel

1. Armstrong, *History of Hamilton County and Chattanooga* 1:125.
2. Ramsey to L. W. Spratt, Apr. 29, 1858, quoted in Hesseltine, *Dr. J. G. M. Ramsey,* 95. For Ramsey's attitude toward the Union, see ibid., 83–97.
3. R. P. Fickle to T. A. R Nelson, Mar. 8, 1860, T. A. R. Nelson Papers, McClung Historical Collection, Lawson McGhee Library, Knoxville (hereafter cited as Nelson Papers).
4. "Henry Melville Doak Memoirs" (hereafter cited as "Doak Memoirs"), typescript, p. 7, Confederate Collection, Tennessee State Library and Archives, Nashville (hereafter cited as Confederate Collection).
5. "Reminiscences of Robert M. Rhea," typescript, Chickamauga-Chattanooga National Military Park Library, Ft. Ogelthorpe, Ga.
6. "Hiwassee College Annual Celebration of the Literary Societies, January 30, 1861," program in possession of Malcolm Rogers, Knoxville.
7. *Confederate Veteran* 21 (1913): 81; 34 (1926): 345.
8. McAdoo to W. S. Patton, Nov. 8, 1860, Edward P. Clark Collection, Special Collections Library, University of Tennessee, Knoxville.
9. "Doak Memoirs," 8.
10. A. A. Kyle to T. A. R. Nelson, Jan. 14, 1861, Nelson Papers.
11. Mortimer F. Johnson to Andrew Johnson, Dec. 31, 1860, in LeRoy P. Graf, Ralph W. Haskins, and Paul H. Bergeron, eds., *The Papers of Andrew Johnson,* 14 vols. to date (Knoxville, 1967–), 4:107 (hereafter cited as Papers of Andrew Johnson).
12. Charles Johnson to Andrew Johnson, Jan. 1, 1861, ibid., 110–11.
13. W. P. Hunt to T. A. R. Nelson, Feb. 2, 1861, Nelson Papers.
14. Ramsey to Lyman Draper, Jan. 14, 1861, quoted in Hesseltine, *Dr. J. G. M. Ramsey,* 98–99.
15. *Knoxville Register,* Dec. 6, 1860.
16. McAdoo diary, Dec. 12, 1860.
17. Ramsey to Draper, Feb. 12, 1861, quoted in Hesseltine, *Dr. J. G. M. Ramsey,* 99.
18. *Knoxville Register,* Mar. 7, 1861.
19. Ibid.
20. John C. Love to Andrew Johnson, Feb. 18, 1861, *Papers of Andrew Johnson* 4:309–10.
21. Blackston McDannel to Andrew Johnson, Mar. 18, 1861, ibid., 404.

22. R. M. Edwards to Andrew Johnson, Apr. 4, 1861, ibid., 469–70.

23. William C. Kyle to Andrew Johnson, Apr. 3, 1861, ibid., 456–57; William Dawes to Johnson, Mar. 13, 1861, ibid., 387.

24. *Athens (Tenn.) Post,* Mar. 22, 1861.

25. *Knoxville Register,* Dec. 6, 13, 20, 1860.

26. Ibid., Dec. 6, 1860, Jan. 10, 1861.

27. *Nashville Republican Banner,* Feb. 19, 1861.

28. *Knoxville Whig,* Jan. 22, 1861.

29. Ibid., Feb. 2, 1861.

30. *Knoxville Register,* Jan. 31, 1861.

31. *Chattanooga Advertiser,* Jan. 24, 1861.

32. *Knoxville Register,* Jan. 31, Feb. 7, 1861. For Brownlow's attitude on East Tennessee's relationship with the South, see Knoxville Whig, Jan. 26, 1861.

33. *Jonesboro Express,* Jan. 25, 1861.

34. Quoted in *Knoxville Whig,* Jan. 26, 1861. See also William R. Sevier to Andrew Johnson, Jan. 22, 1861, *Papers of Andrew Johnson* 4:183–84.

35. Daniel W. Crofts, *Reluctant Confederates: Upper South Unionists in the Secession Crisis* (Chapel Hill, N.C., 1989), 104–6.

36. Ibid., 105.

37. J. Peck to T. A. R. Nelson, Feb. 14, 1861, Nelson Papers.

38. Laura Maynard to George S. Hillard, Nov. 16, 1860, Horace Maynard Papers, Special Collections Library, University of Tennessee, Knoxville.

39. *Knoxville Whig,* Jan. 26, 1861.

40. J. Peck to Nelson, Feb. 14, 1861, Nelson Papers.

41. Crofts, *Reluctant Confederates,* 105.

42. *Greeneville Democrat,* Nov. 27, 1860.

43. *Knoxville Whig,* Dec. 15, 1860.

44. *Athens (Tenn.) Post,* Dec. 14, 1860.

45. Robert McCorckle to Nelson, Jan. 10, 1861, Nelson Papers.

46. William M. Lowry to Andrew Johnson, Dec. 29, 1860, *Papers of Andrew Johnson* 4:101.

47. While numerous sources exist, in this study I have used returns for state elections in Mary Emily Robertson Campbell, *The Attitude of Tennesseans Toward the Union, 1847–1861* (New York, 1961), 288–90. For returns on the delegates, see the *Nashville Republican Banner,* Feb. 16, 19, 1861. A strong argument in favor of examining the votes for or against specific convention delegates rather than simply the pro- or anti-

convention vote can be found in Marc W. Kruman, *Parties and Politics in North Carolina, 1836–1865* (Baton Rouge, 1983), 273–78. Since there were Unionists who supported the call for a convention, the vote for or against the convention did not necessarily reflect local attitudes toward secession. Delegates, however, usually took a clear stand on the separation issue.

48. Campbell, *Attitude of Tennesseans,* 288–90.

49. *Knoxville Whig,* Feb. 16, 1861.

50. *Nashville Union and American,* Mar. 9, 1861.

51. Alexander B. Small to Andrew Johnson, Feb. 18, 1861, *Papers of Andrew Johnson* 4:312.

52. C. H. Mills to Andrew Johnson, Feb. 10, 1861, ibid., 268.

53. Blackston McDannel to Andrew Johnson, Feb. 16, 1861, ibid., 294–95.

54. William H. Maxwell to Andrew Johnson, Mar. 29, 1861, ibid., 452; *Knoxville Register,* Apr. 4, 1861.

55. Samuel Evans to Andrew Johnson, Apr. 6, 1861, *Papers of Andrew Johnson* 4:468–69.

56. *Athens (Tenn.) Post,* Apr. 12, 1861.

57. W. R. Sevier to T. A. R. Nelson, Apr. 26, 1861, Nelson Papers.

58. "W. W. Stringfield Memoirs," handwritten manuscript, pp. 28–33, 50, William W. Stringfield Collection, North Carolina Department of Archives and History, Raleigh (hereafter cited as "W. W. Stringfield Memoirs").

59. A. W. Howard to T. A. R. Nelson, Apr. 17, 1861, Nelson Papers.

60. Henry [?] to Elizabeth Key, Apr. 15, 1861, David M. Key Papers, Chattanooga–Hamilton County Bicentennial Library, Chattanooga. (hereafter cited as Key Papers, Bicentennial Library).

61. *Athens (Tenn.) Post,* Apr. 19, 1861.

62. N. M. Hicks to Nelson, Apr. 24, 1861, Nelson Papers.

63. W. H. Crouch to L. C. Haynes, Apr. 24, 1861, Nelson Papers.

64. Ada Smith to Carrie Stakely, Apr. 4, 1861, Hall-Stakely Papers, McClung Historical Collection, Lawson McGhee Library, Knoxville (hereafter cited as Hall-Stakely Papers).

65. W. M. Stakely to Carrie Stakely, Apr. 27, 1861, Hall-Stakely Papers.

66. *Knoxville Register,* May 2, 1861.

67. *Athens (Tenn.) Post,* Apr. 26, 1861.

68. For a history of events in the legislature and around the state at this time, see Jonathan M. Atkins, *Parties, Politics, and Sectional Conflict in*

Tennessee, 1832–1861 (Knoxville, 1997), 244–58. Tennessee's legislature was one of the few bold enough to submit its action to a popular referendum.

69. A list of those legislators voting for and against the secession ordinance can be found in O. P. Temple, *East Tennessee and the Civil War* (Cincinnati, 1899), 222–23.

70. For example, Union men in Blount County demanded the immediate resignation of S. T. Bicknell for his support of Harris and the secession ordinance. See *Knoxville Whig,* May 25, 1861.

71. *Nashville Union and American,* May 11, 1861.

72. *Knoxville Register,* May 18, 1861.

73. *Nashville Union and American,* May 11, 1861.

74. *Athens (Tenn.) Post,* May 10, 1861.

75. See Atkins, *Parties, Politics, and Sectional Conflict,* 247–53; Vernon M. Queener, "East Tennessee Sentiment and the Secession Movement, November 1860–June 1861," *ETHSP* 20 (1948): 59–83; and Charles F. Bryan Jr., "The Civil War in East Tennessee: A Social, Political, and Economic Study" (Ph.D. diss., Univ. of Tennessee, 1978), 34–73.

76. Quoted in the *Nashville Union and American,* May 11, 1861.

77. *Athens (Tenn.) Post,* May 31, 1861.

78. *Cleveland (Tenn.) Banner,* May 24, 1861.

79. *Knoxville Register,* May 18, 23, 1861.

80. For a schedule of the speaking circuit, see ibid., May 18, 1861.

81. John C. Gaut to T. A. R. Nelson, May 26, 1861, Nelson Papers.

82. *Knoxville Register,* June 5, 1861.

83. Ibid., May 25, 1861.

84. Ibid., May 23, 1861.

85. *Nashville Republican Banner,* May 22, 1861.

86. *Knoxville Register,* May 23, 1861.

87. *Knoxville Whig,* May 25, 1861.

88. John C. Gaut to T. A. R. Nelson, May 26, 1861, Nelson Papers.

89. *Knoxville Register,* June 5, 1861.

90. For the results, see Campbell, Attitude of Tennesseans, 291.

91. David M. Key to Elizabeth Key, June 10, 1861, Key Papers, Bicentennial Library.

92. *Knoxville Register,* June 11, 1861.

93. For an examination of Clingman's role in western North Carolina, see John C. Inscoe, "Thomas Clingman, Mountain Whiggery, and the Southern Cause," *Civil War History* 33 (1987): 42–62.

94. Temple, East Tennessee and the Civil War, 542.
95. David M. Key to Elizabeth Key, May 6, 1861, Key Papers, Bicentennial Library.
96. Ramsey to Harris, Apr. 24, 1861, William Rule Papers, McClung Historical Collection, Lawson McGhee Library, Knoxville.
97. Queener, "East Tennessee Sentiment and the Secession Movement," 73.
98. *Nashville Banner*, June 13, 1861.
99. *Knoxville Register*, June 11, 1861.
100. For antebellum voting returns, see Anne H. Hopkins and William Lyons, *Tennessee Votes: 1799–1976* (Knoxville, 1978); and for a discussion of party politics in prewar East Tennessee, see Atkins, *Parties, Politics, and Sectional Conflict*; and Paul H. Bergeron, *Antebellum Politics in Tennessee* (Lexington, 1982), 9–34.
101. Bureau of the Census, *Eighth Census of the United States: 1860* (Washington, D.C., 1864).
102. The methodology used for tables 2, 3, and 4 was complex and, therefore, requires a brief explanation. Data on population and various economic indicators—agricultural production, farm size (in terms of total acreage), value of farms, and numbers of farms—were gleaned from the published 1850 and 1860 U.S. Census. Twenty-eight East Tennessee counties were included in the sample: Anderson, Bledsoe, Blount, Bradley, Campbell, Carter, Claiborne, Cocke, Grainger, Greene, Hamilton, Hancock, Hawkins, Jefferson, Johnson, Knox, McMinn, Marion, Meigs, Monroe, Morgan, Polk, Rhea, Roane, Scott, Sevier, Sullivan, and Washington. Three additional counties—Cumberland, Sequatchie, and Union—were omitted because they were created during the 1850s, rendering it impossible to measure changes between 1850 and 1860. Two present-day counties—Hamblen and Loudon—were also omitted, since they were not created by the general assembly until 1870.

The counties were grouped according to percentage of secession vote in the June 8, 1861, referendum. Five counties favored secession by a vote of 50 percent and greater and can be classified as solidly Confederate: Meigs (64.3), Monroe (58.6), Polk (69.9), Rhea (64.1), and Sullivan (71.7). Eleven others favored separation by a vote of between 25 and 49 percent and can be classified as divided in loyalty: Bledsoe (28.3), Bradley (26.8), Cocke (30.4), Grainger (28.2), Hamilton (40.4), Hancock (30.7), Hawkins (38.3), Knox (27.7), McMinn (44.1), Marion (40.8), and Washington (41.4). The remaining twelve counties registered votes of less than 25 percent favoring secession and can be classified as solidly Unionist: Anderson (7.0), Blount (19.1), Campbell (5.6), Carter (6.0), Claiborne (16.7), Greene (21.7), Jefferson (23.3), Johnson (12.4), Morgan (5.7), Roane (22.4), Scott (3.5), and Sevier (3.8).

Data for counties in each of these three categories were collected, and percentage changes between 1850 and 1860 for each county were figured. The average of those counties in each voting category was then computed and presented in the tables. Regional figures were based on the average of all twenty-eight county percentages, regardless of voting category. This method assigns an equal weight to all counties and, in the process, presents a clearer picture of what was happening across the region as a whole than could be obtained by simply averaging the three category averages.

103. Salstrom, *Appalachia's Path to Dependency*, 1–40.
104. Ibid., 110–13, 127; Bryan, "Civil War in East Tennessee," 48; John C. Inscoe, "Mountain Unionism, Secession, and Regional Self Image: The Contrasting Cases of Western North Carolina and East Tennessee," in *Looking South: Chapters in the Story of an American Region*, ed. Winifred B. Moore Jr. and Joseph F. Tripp (New York, 1990), 123–27.
105. W. R. Smith to Nelson, Aug. 5, 1861, Nelson Papers.

3. The Social Origins of East Tennessee's Confederate Leadership

1. Samuel C. Williams, "John Mitchel, the Irish patriot, Resident of Tennessee," *ETHSP* 10 (1938): 47.
2. Fred Bailey came close but still missed the mark. His *Class and Tennessee's Confederate Generation* (Chapel Hill, N.C., 1987) does not deal with leadership as defined in this essay. Of the 770 respondents to the Tennessee Veterans Questionnaires, only 30 held the rank of captain or above. This is not surprising since the Questionnaires were completed fifty years after Appomattox; most respondents, therefore, were too young during the war to have held positions of leadership. See pp. 147, 160.
3. Among the most recent in a long list of studies dealing with East Tennessee Unionism is Bryan, "Civil War in East Tennessee"; Crofts, *Reluctant Confederates*; Inscoe, "Mountain Unionism"; Peter Wallenstein, "Which Side Are You On? The Social Origins of White Union Troops

from Civil War Tennessee," *Journal of East Tennessee History* 63 (1991): 72–103; Walter Lynn Bates, "Southern Unionists: A Socio-economic Examination of the Third East Tennessee Volunteer Infantry Regiment, U.S.A.," *Tennessee Historical Quarterly* 50 (1991): 226–37; Richard N. Current, *Lincoln's Loyalists: Union Soldiers from the Confederacy* (Boston, 1992); Noel C. Fisher, *War at Every Door: Partisan Politics and Guerrilla Violence in East Tennessee, 1860–1869* (Chapel Hill, N.C., 1997); and Durwood Dunn, *An Abolitionist in the Appalachian South: Ezekiel Birdseye on Slavery, Capitalism, and Separate Statehood in East Tennessee, 1841–1846* (Knoxville, 1997).

4. For more on the myth of mountain Unionism, see Kenneth W. Noe, "Toward the Myth of Unionist Appalachia, 1865–1883," *Journal of Appalachia Studies Association* 6 (1994): 73–80. While Current observes that Union soldiers from the South generally have received little scholarly attention, Unionism itself has not been ignored. This is especially true for East Tennessee, as the works of Bryan, Dunn, Crofts, Fisher, Inscoe, Wallenstein, and Bates makes clear. Current, *Lincoln's Loyalists*, ix.

5. O. P. Temple, *East Tennessee and the Civil War* (Cincinnati, 1899), 200.

6. *Knoxville Whig*, Feb. 9, 1861.

7. Ibid., June 15, 1861.

8. Ibid., May 4, 1861. While Brownlow was correct in ascribing secession sympathy to merchants and railroad men, his observation is less accurate about indebtedness to the north. His was a commonly held assumption by many in the South about planters and others who, it was reasoned, favored separation as a means of breaking the cycle of debt to Northern money houses accumulated as a part of the cotton trade. For further discussion of the link between Southern debt and secession, see C. Stuart McGehee, "Wake of the Flood: A Southern City in the Civil War: Chattanooga, 1838–1878" (Ph.D. diss., Univ. of Virginia, 1985).

9. James B. Campbell, "East Tennessee during Federal Occupation, 1863–1865," *ETHSP* 19 (1947): 65.

10. *Nashville Banner*, June 11, 1861.

11. Thomas W. Humes, *The Loyal Mountaineers of Tennessee* (Knoxville, 1888), 91.

12. Campbell, "East Tennessee during Federal Occupation," 65.

13. Willene B. Clark, ed., *Valleys of the Shadow: The Memoir of Captain Reuben G. Clark* (Knoxville, 1994), xvii.

14. For a study of the Knoxville Convention, see Bryan, "Civil War in East Tennessee," 43–48.

15. Ibid., 48.

16. The names of these officers and the units they commanded were selected from Tennessee Civil War Centennial Commission, *Tennesseans in the Civil War,* 2 vols. (Nashville, 1964), vol. 1 (hereafter cited as *Tennesseans in the Civil War*). Additional information was gleaned from Compiled Service Records of Confederate Soldiers Who Served from the State of Tennessee, RG 109, National Archives (hereafter cited as Compiled Service Records, RG 109). While use of the term "separationists" is borrowed from Crofts, *Reluctant Confederates,* it was frequently employed in Tennessee in 1861 to describe secessionists.

17. Robert C. Kenzer, *Kinship and Neighborhood in a Southern Community: Orange County, North Carolina, 1849–1881* (Knoxville, 1987), 71–74; Martin Crawford, "Volunteering and Enlistment in Ashe County, North Carolina, 1861–1862," *Civil War History* 37 (1991): 37–39. See also Bell I. Wiley, *The Life of Johnny Reb: The Common Soldier of the Confederacy* (Indianapolis, 1943), 18–20. It cannot be denied that there is a certain measure of inexactness in comparing military with political leaders, even if those military men are drawn from the ranks of civilian leadership. However, it would be a mistake simply to characterize doing so as nothing more than comparing the proverbial apples and oranges. Maybe it is more like comparing oranges to tangerines.

18. The units were selected from *Tennesseans in the Civil War,* vol. 1, in which they are listed by numerical designation and by county. The counties represented in the sample of officers are: Bledsoe, Blount, Bradley, Claiborne, Cocke, Cumberland, Grainger, Greene, Hamilton, Hancock, Hawkins, Jefferson, Knox, McMinn, Marion, Meigs, Monroe, Polk, Rhea, Roane, Sequatchie, Sullivan, and Washington.

19. Computed from Bureau of the Census, "Eighth Census of Tennessee: 1860," Free Inhabitants MS Schedule for various counties. Locations of rail lines, major roads and turnpikes, and rivers, as well as location, size, and other information used to determine whether a community qualified as a town in 1861, was obtained from a variety of sources. These include John L. Mitchell, *Tennessee State Gazetteer and Business Directory for 1860–61* (Nashville, 1860); *Atlas to Accompany the Official Records of the Union and Confederate Armies* (Washington, D.C., 1891–95), plates 25:3, 142, 149; and the following maps: Thomas Cowperthwait, "New Map of Tennessee. . . ." (n.p., 1850); J. Johnson, "Johnson's Kentucky and Tennessee" (New York, [1860?]); and E. Mendenhall, "Railway and County Map of Tennessee. . . ." (Cincinnati, 1864).

20. For more on internal improvements and the coming of the railroad to East Tennessee, see W. Todd Groce, "Mountain Rebels: East Tennessee Confederates and the Civil War, 1860–1870" (Ph.D. diss., Univ. of Tennessee, 1992), 8–26. Although the terms "urban" and "city" are employed here, probably only Knoxville qualified as a city by northeastern U.S. standards. Most East Tennessee towns were mere villages in 1860. Nevertheless, they were the region's main centers of transportation, communication, government, and commerce. For a similar argument about towns in other sections of antebellum Appalachia, see Inscoe, *Mountain Masters*, 27–37; and Noe, *Southwest Virginia's Railroad*, 53–66.

21. Bureau of the Census, "Eighth Census of Tennessee: 1860," Population Schedules for various counties.

22. Clement A. Evans, ed., *Confederate Military History, Extended Edition*, 12 vols. (Atlanta, 1899), 8:315, 339.

23. Robert M. McBride et al., comps., *Biographical Directory of the Tennessee General Assembly*, 5 vols. (Nashville, 1975–), 1:324–25, 742–43; 2:329 (hereafter cited as *BDTA*).

24. Charles Freeling Welker Papers, McClung Historical Collection, Knoxville; T. J. Campbell, *Records of Rhea: A Condensed County History* (Dayton, Tenn., 1940), 132.

25. For an examination of the prevailing antiaristocratic, republican ideology prevalent in East Tennessee and in the upper South in general during the antebellum period, see Crofts, *Reluctant Confederates*, 158–59; and J. Mills Thornton III, "The Ethic of Subsistence and the Origins of Southern Secession," *Tennessee Historical Quarterly* 48 (1989): 67–85. See also Clement Eaton, *The Growth of Southern Civilization, 1790–1860* (New York, 1961), 1–3, 221–22. On highland farmers with additional occupations, see Inscoe, *Mountain Masters*, 7–8, 37–39. On storekeepers moving in and out of merchandising, see Atherton, *Southern Country Store*, 98. It also should be noted that the census enumerators were instructed to record only one occupation per entry.

26. Bureau of the Census, "Eighth Census of Tennessee: 1860," Population Schedules for various counties; Compiled Service Records, RG 109.

27. Bureau of the Census, "Eighth Census of Tennessee: 1860," Slave Schedules for various counties.

28. Ibid.

29. Bureau of the Census, "Eighth Census of Tennessee: 1860," Slave Schedule for Hawkins County, Tennessee.

30. Temple, *East Tennessee and the Civil War*, 542.

31. Bureau of the Census, *Eighth Census of Tennessee: 1860*, Population Schedules for various counties.

32. In his unpublished memoirs, H. M. Doak of the Nineteenth Tennessee Infantry mentions serving with the younger Nelson and Arnold. See "Doak Memoirs." Biographies of Heiskell's sons, Carrick W. and Joseph B., both of whom were prominent Rebels, can be found in Evans, *Confederate Military History* 8:532–35. Kyle's sons, Robert and William, served in cavalry companies raised in Hawkins County. Details of Judge Lucky's unsuccessful attempt to keep his son from enlisting in the Confederate army are given in *Confederate Veteran* 30 (1922): 347. Knoxvillian David A. Deaderick had four sons who served in the Southern ranks, three of whom joined up prior to their eighteenth birthdays, despite their father's strong Unionist proclivities. See "Register of Events," David Deaderick Papers, Special Collections Library, University of Tennessee, Knoxville (hereafter cited as Deaderick Papers).

33. Gary W. Gallagher, *The Confederate War* (Cambridge, Mass., 1997), 72, 96–111; and Peter S. Carmichael, *Lee's Young Artillerist: William R. J. Pegram* (Charlottesville, 1995), 2–6.

34. Evans, *Confederate Military History* 8:535–36.

35. William S. Speer, *Sketches of Prominent Tennesseans* (Nashville, 1888), 189.

36. For a study of the connection between age and wealth, see Lee Soltow, *Men and Wealth in the United States, 1850–1870* (New Haven, Conn., 1975), 69–74; and Randolph B. Campbell and Richard G. Lowe, *Wealth and Power in Antebellum Texas* (College Station, Tex. 1977), 57–60, 65, 135.

37. Bureau of the Census, "Eighth Census of Tennessee: 1860," Population and Slave Schedules for various counties.

38. For a more detailed examination of the role of the merchant in East Tennessee's economic and social development, see Groce, "Mountain Rebels," 20–26.

39. A good example of a highland merchant who established numerous contacts and ties while purchasing inventory in the Deep South is William H. Thomas. Although a western North Carolinian, Thomas's experiences were not unlike those of East Tennessee businessmen. See E. Stanley Godbold Jr. and Mattie U. Russell, *Confederate Colonel and Cherokee Chief: The Life of William Holland Thomas* (Knoxville, 1990), 17–35. Inscoe, *Mountain Masters*, 37, 40–44, also explores this contact between highland merchants and Southern coastal cities.

40. Biographies of Cowan, Deaderick, and Dickinson can be found in Rothrock, *French Broad–Holston Country*, 401–2, 409–12.

41. Party affiliation was gleaned from biographical sketches in *BDTA*, various county histories, and Evans, *Confederate Military History*. Unfortunately, the relative obscurity of most of those in the sample prevented all thirty-five officeholders from being positively linked to a political organization. In some cases, party affiliation was attributed to members of the sample who hailed from counties with strongly traditional Democratic or Whig voting patterns. Information on Powel and Vaughn was obtained from the 1860 census and from *BDTA* 1:598, 2:934. For a discussion of party loyalty and organization in prewar Tennessee, see Bergeron, *Antebellum Politics in Tennessee*, 64–102.

42. A closer look at the psychology of mountain Unionism can be found in Bryan, "Civil War in East Tennessee," 48; and Inscoe, "Mountain Unionism," 123–28. An argument similar to mine about the youthfulness and radicalism of secessionists is offered in Barney, *Secessionist Impulse*, 267–316, and again by William L. Barney in "Towards the Civil War: The Dynamics of Change in a Black Belt Community," in *Class, Conflict, and Consensus: Antebellum Southern Community Studies*, ed. Orville Vernon Burton and Robert C. McMath (Westport, Conn., 1982), 146–72. In these studies, Barney found, for Alabama and Mississippi, evidence of a correlation between Democratic (Breckinridge) party affiliation, rising levels of wealth, youth, and secessionist sympathy.

43. *Knoxville Register*, Dec. 12, 1862. During the height of the railroad craze, the *Register* attacked Andrew Johnson as an opponent of railroads, claiming that he repeatedly had voted and spoken against them as a member of the legislature and as governor. "Who ever thinks of the word 'Railroad' in connection with Andrew Johnson?" the editor asked his readers. "The idea is most ridiculous." *Knoxville Register*, July 26, 1855.

44. For an examination of the prevailing sense of moral superiority among East Tennessee Unionists, see Inscoe, "Mountain Unionism," 123–24.

45. Hesseltine, *Dr. J. G. M. Ramsey*, 18.

46. McAdoo diary, Dec. 12, 1860.

47. Sam Houston Hynds to Ann Hynds, June 23, 1861, in Tennessee Historical Records Survey, *Civil War Records of Tennessee*, 3 vols. (Nashville, 1939), 1:88 (hereafter cited as *Civil War Records of Tennessee*).

48. Evans, *Confederate Military History* 8:577–78; Stewart Lillard, *Meigs County, Tennessee* (Sewanee, Tenn., 1975), 68–104; Lillard Family Papers.

49. Military backgrounds were gleaned from biographical material in *BDTA*; various county histories; and the Tennessee State Militia Officer Commission Book, Tennessee State Library and Archives, Nashville.

50. Data on political experience were more readily available than on military. Sources used include *BDTA*; Goodspeed's, *History of Tennessee*; Mitchell, *Tennessee State Gazetteer*; and various county histories. Goodspeed's Publishing Company is particularly useful, since it lists all local officeholders by county, beginning with the formation of the county through the Civil War.

51. Crawford, "Volunteering and Enlistment in Ashe County," 39.

52. Hopkins and Lyons, *Tennessee Votes*, 43.

53. *BDTA* 1:598, 638–39. The vote in Hawkins County was 38 percent in favor of secession; in Hancock it was 31 percent.

4. East Tennesseans Are Willing to Fight

1. Evans, *Confederate Military History* 8:339.

2. "Reminiscences of Robert M. Rhea," 2.

3. *Jonesboro Union*, May 4, 1861.

4. "Reminiscences of Robert M. Rhea," 3.

5. Cora Davis Brooks, *History of Morristown, 1787–1936* (Nashville, 1940), 24.

6. Francis Young Schumaker, "Confederate History of Hawkins County, Tennessee," typescript, p. 3, Special Collections Library, University of Tennessee, Knoxville.

7. "Civil War Diary of George W. Clemmer," *Cleveland (Tenn.) Daily Banner*, n.d., Cleveland Public Library, Cleveland, Tenn.

8. William Boyce to R. G. Fain, July 16, 1861, RG 4, Army of Tennessee Collection, Tennessee State Library and Archives, Nashville (hereafter cited as Army of Tennessee Collection).

9. Michael L. Patterson to Andrew Johnson, July 29, 1861, *Papers of Andrew Johnson* 4:652–53.

10. Hesseltine, *Dr. J. G. M. Ramsey*, 163–64.

11. *Knoxville Register*, May 24, 29, 1861.

12. Ibid., May 25, 1861.

13. *Nashville Republican Banner*, May 22, 1861.

14. Martin Crawford, "Confederate Volunteering and Enlistment in Ashe County, North Carolina, 1861–1862," *Civil War History* 37 (1991): 29–50.

15. *Tennesseans in the Civil War* 1:214–15.

16. Wiley, *Life of Johnny Reb*, 15–19; Gerald F. Linderman, *Embattled Courage: The Experience of Combat in the American Civil War* (New York, 1987), 7–20; Reid Mitchell, *Civil War Soldiers: Their Experiences and Their Expectations* (New York, 1988), 1–11.

17. James A. Caldwell to Carrie Stakely, June 5, 1861, Hall-Stakely Papers.

18. Richard Saffell to John Bogle, Oct. 13, 1861, Saffell Papers, Special Collections Library, University of Tennessee, Knoxville (hereafter cited as Saffell Papers).

19. Hannibal Paine to "Jennie," Sept. 3, 1861, Paine Family Papers, Tennessee State Library and Archives, Nashville (hereafter cited as Paine Family Papers).

20. A. L. Burem to J. L. Cain, July 1861, *Civil War Records of Tennessee* 2:33.

21. George P. Faw to Thomas A. Faw, Oct. 27, 1861, Faw Family Papers, Archives of Appalachia, East Tennessee State University, Johnson City.

22. Hannibal Paine to "Jennie," July 26, 1861, Paine Family Papers.

23. James Scruggs to Carrie Stakely, Mar. 29, 1862, Hall-Stakely Papers.

24. Sam Houston Hynds to Ann Hynds, June 23, 1861, *Civil War Records of Tennessee* 1:84.

25. Catherine Watterson to William H. Watterson, May 20, 1861, in Schumaker, "Confederate History of Hawkins County," 2–3.

26. Larry Daniel, *Soldiering in the Army of Tennessee: A Portrait of Life in a Confederate Army* (Chapel Hill, N.C., 1991), 14.

27. Humes, *Loyal Mountaineers of Tennessee*, 96–97.

28. J. A. Caldwell to Carrie Stakely, Feb. 25, 1862, Hall-Stakely Papers.

29. William Lillard to T. J., J. M., and N. J. Lillard, July 8, 1861, Lillard Family Papers.

30. *Chattanooga Gazette and Advertiser*, Feb. 6, 1862.

31. James Stakely to Carrie Stakely, Mar. 21, 1862, Hall-Stakely Papers.

32. Samuel L. Lyle to J. M. Lyle, Jan. 23, 1862, William R. Caswell Papers, Southern Historical Collection, University of North Carolina, Chapel Hill (hereafter cited as Caswell Papers).

33. J. A. Caldwell to Carrie Stakely, May 5, 1861, Hall-Stakely Papers.

34. Peter Wallenstein, "Which Side Are You On? The Social Origins of White Union Troops from Civil War Tennessee," *Journal of East Tennessee History* 63 (1991): 84–86; *Tennesseans in the Civil War*, vol. 1, various regiments. For the number of East Tennesseans who were conscripted,

see the report of John S. Preston, Superintendent of the Bureau of Conscription, Feb. 1865, *War of the Rebellion: A Compilation of the Official Records of the Union and Confederate Armies* (hereafter cited as *OR*), 70 vols. (Washington, D.C., 1880–1901), ser. 3, vol. 5, p. 701. J. G. M. Ramsey recalled that Georgia recruiting officers operated in East Tennessee before the state seceded, enlisting young men into Georgia regiments. See Hesseltine, *Dr. J. G. M. Ramsey*, 128–29. In addition, two full companies and various individuals enlisted in Thomas's North Carolina Legion and remained with that unit during the entire war (three additional companies were transferred to Tennessee cavalry units). See Vernon H. Crow, *Storm in the Mountains: Thomas' Confederate Legion of Cherokee Indians and Mountaineers* (n.p., 1982), 149–235. For purposes of this study, I have included Sequatchie County in East Tennessee, although according to Tennessee law, it is today officially a part of Middle Tennessee. Culturally and geographically, Sequatchie has identified with East Tennessee since its organization in 1857. Furthermore, its voting returns traditionally have been tabulated with those of the eastern counties.

35. Report of William R. Caswell to W. C. Whitthorne, July 19, 1861, RG 4, Army of Tennessee Collection; *Tennesseans in the Civil War* 1:9; John B. Lindsley, *Military Annals of Tennessee: Confederate* (Nashville, 1886), 521.
36. Bruce S. Allardice, *More Generals in Gray* (Baton Rouge, 1995), 54.
37. *Tennesseans in the Civil War* 1:235–53.
38. R. S. Garnett to E. K. Smith, May 21, 1861, *OR*, ser. 1, 2:860–61.
39. *Knoxville Register*, May 29, 1861.
40. W. H. Carroll to Judah P. Benjamin, Dec. 13, 1861, *OR*, ser. 1, 7:764–66.
41. W. H. Warren to W. H. Carroll, Dec. 13, 1861, *OR*, ser. 1, 7:766–67.
42. Carroll to Benjamin, Dec. 13, 1861, *OR*, ser. 1, 7:764–66.
43. G. B. Crittenden to S. Cooper, Dec. 19, 1861, *OR*, ser. 1, 7:774.
44. *Tennesseans in the Civil War* 1:268.
45. Lindsley, *Military Annals of Tennessee*, 499.
46. W. S. Brown to Carrie Stakely, May 29, 1862, Hall-Stakely Papers.
47. Humes, *Loyal Mountaineers of Tennessee*, 304–5.
48. Lindsley, *Military Annals of Tennessee*, 434.
49. Ibid., 584.
50. Ibid., 139.
51. *Knoxville Register*, July 11, 1862.
52. Lindsley, *Military Annals of Tennessee*, 434.

53. L. B. Headrick to Harris, Mar. 18, 1862, William G. Brownlow Papers, Special Collections Library, University of Tennessee, Knoxville (hereafter cited as Brownlow Papers).

54. *Greeneville Banner,* June 4, 1862.

55. Quoted in *Athens (Tenn.) Post,* Jan. 24, 1862.

56. Ibid., Apr. 3, 1863.

57. *Chattanooga Gazette and Advertiser,* Jan. 4, 1862.

58. Benjamin F. Taylor to parents, July 8, 1861, photocopy of original in possession of Betty Broyles, Dayton, Tenn.

59. McHenry Howard, *Recollections of a Maryland Confederate Soldier and Staff Officer* (Baltimore, 1914), 59–60. Howard remembered that when anyone visited the Tennessee camp and was halted by the sentinels, "he was in the next breath directed where to go to get the best cakes or liquor."

60. Lindsley, *Military Annals of Tennessee,* 437.

61. Ibid., 435. Out of seven units in the brigade, the Twenty-ninth sustained 25 percent of the total casualties.

62. *Confederate Veteran* 3 (1895): 187.

63. An examination of *Tennesseans in the Civil War,* vol. 1, reveals that regimental organization continued strong in Middle and West Tennessee during the fall and winter of 1861, while dropping off precipitously in East Tennessee.

64. Hannibal Paine to Virginia Royal, Nov. 26, 1861, Paine Family Collection.

65. Ramsey to Davis, Nov. 4, 1861, *OR,* ser. 1, 4:511.

66. *Chattanooga Gazette and Advertizer,* Jan. 4, 24, 1862.

67. James Stakely to Carrie Stakely, Mar. 21, 1862, Hall-Stakely Papers.

68. For a more in-depth look at the effect of the bridge burnings and Mill Springs on Confederates in East Tennessee, see Charles F. Bryan Jr., "'Tories' Amidst Rebels: Confederate Occupation of East Tennessee, 1861–1863," *ETHSP* 60 (1988): 9–10.

69. L. B. Headrick to Harris, Mar. 18, 1862, Brownlow Papers.

70. A. G. Graham to Jefferson Davis, Nov. 12, 1861, OR, ser. 1, 4:239.

71. *Chattanooga Gazette and Advertizer,* Jan. 4, 26, 1862.

72. *Athens (Tenn.) Post,* Mar. 7, 1862.

73. *Knoxville Register,* Dec. 24, 1861.

74. *Cleveland (Tenn.) Banner,* Mar. 14, 1862.

75. Report from Headquarters, 1st Div. Tenn. Militia, to W. C. Whitthorne, Mar. 24, 1862, RG 4, Army of Tennessee Collection.

76. L. B. Headrick to Harris, Mar. 18, 1862, Brownlow Papers.

77. Ezra J. Warner, *Generals in Gray: Lives of the Confederate Commanders* (Baton Rouge, 1959), 279–80; Joseph H. Parks, *General Edmund Kirby Smith, CSA* (Baton Rouge, 1954). The only indication that Smith may have had a problem with Vaughn's men is in *OR*, ser. 1, 2:945, where Smith complained about "the inefficient state of the Tennessee regiment" which had been assigned to his brigade.

78. Although Zollicoffer was not a native of East Tennessee, he launched his career in Knoxville working for the *Register*. A former Whig congressman, his appointment was welcomed by many East Tennesseans. See Bryan, "'Tories' Amidst Rebels," 5.

79. E. K. Smith to S. Cooper, Mar. 13, 1862, *OR*, ser. 1, vol. 10, pt. 2, p. 321.

80. Smith to Cooper, Apr. 2, 1862, *OR*, ser. 1, vol. 10, pt. 2, pp. 385–86.

81. Smith to Cooper, Mar. 13, 1862, *OR*, ser. 1, vol. 10, pt. 2, p. 321.

82. Smith to Cooper, Apr. 2, 1862, *OR*, ser. 1, vol. 10, pt. 2, pp. 385–86.

83. Report of Smith to Cooper, Mar. 15, 1862, *OR*, ser. 1, vol. 10, pt. 1, p. 21.

84. Smith to Jefferson Davis, Mar. 10, 1862, *OR*, ser. 1, vol. 10, pt. 2, p. 309.

85. Smith to Cooper, Mar. 23, 1862, *OR*, ser. 1, vol. 10, pt. 2, pp. 355–56.

86. Cooper to Smith, Mar. 31, 1862, *OR*, ser. 1, vol. 10, pt. 2, p. 376.

87. Tennesseans in the Civil War 1:48–49, 251–52.

88. Smith to Cooper, Mar. 15, 1862, *OR*, ser. 1, vol. 10, pt. 1, pp. 20–21.

89. E. K. Smith to D. Leadbetter, Mar. 26, 1862, *OR*, ser. 1, vol. 10, pt. 1, p. 366.

90. Report of E. K. Smith to S. Cooper, Apr. 23, 1862, *OR*, ser. 1, vol. 10, pt. 1, p. 649.

91. The three units were the Thirty-first (later known as the Thirty-ninth) and Fifty-ninth Infantry Regiments and Captain William C. Kain's artillery company. *Tennesseans in the Civil War* 1:133, 259, 298.

5. A *Damned* Stinking Cotton Oligarchy

1. Quoted in William C. Davis, ed., *The Confederate General*, 6 vols. (New York, 1991), 4:115.

2. Emory Thomas, *The Confederate Nation, 1861–1865* (New York, 1979), 152–53.

3. E. K. Smith to S. Cooper, Apr. 2, 1862, *OR*, ser. 1, vol. 10, pt. 2, pp. 385–86.

4. *Cleveland (Tenn.) Banner*, Mar. 14, 1862.

5. *Knoxville Register*, Apr. 3, 1862.

6. *Athens (Tenn.) Post,* Feb. 28, 1862.

7. *Cleveland (Tenn.) Banner,* Apr. 25, 1862.

8. T. W. White to Carrie Stakely, May 2, 1862, Hall-Stakely Papers.

9. *Bristol (Tenn.) Southern Advocate,* Aug. 14, 1862.

10. Report to W. C. Whitthorne, Mar. 24, 1862, RG 4, Army of Tennessee Collection.

11. *Athens (Tenn.) Post,* Apr. 18, 1862.

12. *Tennesseans in the Civil War* 1:298–300. Although the Sixty-third Regiment was organized in June, it was composed mainly of companies raised in the spring of 1862, along with members of the Twenty-sixth Regiment not captured at Fort Donelson in February. See *Tennesseans in the Civil War* 1:305–6.

13. Jefferson Davis to E. K. Smith, May 13, 1862, *OR,* ser. 1, vol. 10, pt. 2, p. 521.

14. *Chattanooga Rebel,* Aug. 9, 1862.

15. *Athens (Tenn.) Post,* June 13, 1862.

16. *Knoxville Register,* Sept. 18, 1862.

17. *Greeneville Banner,* July 25, 1862.

18. G. W. Randolph to Samuel Jones, Sept. 19, 1862, *OR,* ser. 1, vol. 16, pt. 2, p. 851.

19. Notices appeared during September and October in the *Cleveland (Tenn.) Banner, Athens (Tenn.) Post, Knoxville Register,* and *Greeneville Banner.* For a typical conscription notice, see *Chattanooga Daily Rebel,* Sept. 12, 1862.

20. *Greeneville Banner,* Oct. 24, 1862.

21. Samuel Jones to G. W. Randolph, Sept. 24, 1862, *OR,* ser. 1, vol. 16, pt. 2, pp. 868–69.

22. Dunbar Rowland, ed., *Jefferson Davis, Constitutionalist: His Letters, Papers, and Speeches* (Jackson, Miss., 1923), 360.

23. Jones to Randolph, Oct. 17, 1862, *OR,* ser. 1, vol. 16, pt. 2, p. 953.

24. Histories of the units can be found in *Tennesseans in the Civil War* 1:298–305.

25. Report of the Superintendent of Bureau of Conscription, Feb. 1865, *OR,* ser. 3, 5:700.

26. Manassas veterans P. L. Bible, W. W. Grubb, W. R. Smith, and William Parker had all served in Vaughn's Third Regiment before joining the Sixty-second. *Tennesseans in the Civil War* 2:38, 181, 314, 375.

27. The two for whom no previous Confederate service can be found are Maj. Nathan Dodd of the Sixty-first and John H. Crawford of the Sixtieth.

28. *Tennesseans in the Civil War* 1:325.

29. See ibid., vols. 1 and 2 for more on the command structure of these regiments.

30. Ibid. 1:300–301.

31. Petition to Jefferson Davis from citizens of Washington County, Tennessee, Feb. 1862, John H. Crawford Papers, Archives of Appalachia, East Tennessee State University, Johnson City (hereafter cited as Crawford Papers).

32. J. S. Shannon to John H. Crawford, Sept. 20, 1862, Crawford Papers.

33. C. S. Newman to Crawford, Sept. 10, 1862, Crawford Papers.

34. James C. Hodges to Crawford, Sept. 9, 1862, Crawford Papers.

35. W. A. Wash to Crawford, Sept. 10, 1862, Crawford Papers.

36. *Jonesboro Express,* Aug. 15, 1862.

37. Ibid., June 6, 1862.

38. S. R. Gammon to John H. Crawford, Sept. 14, 1862, Crawford Papers.

39. James C. Hodges to Crawford, Sept. 29, 1862, and W. A. Wash to Crawford, Oct. 1, 1862, Crawford Papers.

40. *Tennesseans in the Civil War* 1:300.

41. Ibid., 301.

42. G. W. Feagins to wife, Sept. 14, 1862, Franklin P. Baxter Papers, Archives of Appalachia, East Tennessee State University, Johnson City.

43. *Chattanooga Daily Rebel,* Oct. 7, 1862.

44. Quoted in ibid., Oct. 10, 1862.

45. Alfred Bowman to Joseph Bowman, Feb. 25, 1863, Bowman Family Collection, Archives of Appalachia, East Tennessee State University, Johnson City (hereafter cited as Bowman Family Collection).

46. "W. W. Stringfield Memoirs," 51–52.

47. George W. Hynds to Ann Hynds, Jan. 6, 1863, *Civil War Records of Tennessee* 1:82.

48. Lindsley, *Military Annals of Tennessee,* 503.

49. See *Athens (Tenn.) Post,* Nov. 7, Dec. 5, 26, 1862.

50. Fannie A. Fain diary, Archives of Appalachia, East Tennessee State University, Johnson City.

51. Mary Reynolds to Simeon D. Reynolds, Jan. 10, 1864, Reynolds Letters, Special Collections Library, University of Tennessee, Knoxville (hereafter cited as Reynolds Letters).

52. Mary Reynolds to Simeon D. Reynolds, Jan. 26, 1864, Reynolds Letters.

53. John J. Blair diary, typescript, Confederate Collection (hereafter cited as Blair diary).

54. Sam Saffell to John Bogle, July 31, 1862, Saffell Papers.

55. *Bristol (Tenn.) Gazette*, Feb. 18, 1864.

56. *Chattanooga Daily Rebel*, Dec. 30, 1862.

57. Blair diary, Jan. 18, 1863.

58. Alfred Bowman to Joseph Bowman, Feb. 25, 1863, Bowman Family Collection.

59. Stuart Nelson to T. A. R. Nelson, Dec. 15, 1862, Nelson Papers.

60. Joseph A. Hammell to Newton J. Lillard, Jan. 1, 1863, Lillard Family Papers.

61. Nannie [?] to Carrie Stakely, June 18, 1862, Hall-Stakely Papers.

62. J. C. M. Bogle to Bess Bogle, May 11, 1863, Saffell Papers.

63. *Athens (Tenn.) Post*, Apr. 4, 1863.

64. Clark, *Valleys of the Shadow*, 25.

65. J. C. M. Bogle to Bess Bogle, May 9, 1863, Saffell Papers.

66. Richard Bowman to Joseph Bowman, Mar. 18, 1863, Bowman Family Collection.

67. David M. Key to Elizabeth Key, Apr. 25, 30, 1863, Key Papers, Bicentennial Library.

68. W. J. Worsham, *Old Nineteenth Tennessee Regiment, CSA* (Knoxville, 1902), 59.

69. Blair diary, Jan. 29, 1863.

70. *Knoxville Register*, Apr. 28, 1863.

71. Robert U. Johnston and Clarence C. Buel, eds., *Battles and Leaders of the Civil War*, 3 vols. (New York, 1887), 3:471.

72. Report of J. C. Pemberton, Feb. 1863, *OR*, ser. 1, vol. 17, pt. 1, p. 668.

73. H. R. Jobe to Joseph Offield, June 4, 1863, quoted in Leona Taylor Aiken, "The Letters of the Offield Brothers, Confederate Soldiers of East Tennessee," *ETHSP* 46 (1974): 116–25.

74. Alfred Bowman to Joseph Bowman, Feb. 25, Mar. 13, 1863, Bowman Family Collection.

75. Newton J. Lillard to Crate Lillard, Mar. 13, 1863, Lillard Family Papers.

76. John Allen to wife, May 8, 1863, quoted in Brooks, *History of Morristown*, 33.

77. J. C. Pemberton to J. C. Vaughn, May 13, 1863, *OR*, ser. 1, vol. 24, pt. 3, p. 874.

78. Report of Stephen G. Burbridge, May 24, 1863, *OR*, ser. 1, vol. 24, pt. 2, p. 32; *Tennesseans in the Civil War* 1:301.

79. Report of Michael K. Lawler, May 26, 1863, *OR*, ser. 1, vol. 24, pt. 2, p. 138.
80. Report of J. C. Pemberton, Aug. 2, 1863, *OR*, ser. 1, vol. 24, pt. 1, p. 267.
81. Lindsley, *Military Annals of Tennessee*, 140, 575–76.
82. Vaughn's men were stationed near the impregnable Fort Hill on the north end of the line; Reynolds's brigade was positioned below the Hall Ferry Road.
83. Johnston and Buel, *Battles and Leaders of the Civil War* 3:549.
84. *Chattanooga Times*, Jan. 30, 1927.
85. Lindsley, *Military Annals of Tennessee*, 465, 575–76.
86. "Autobiography of William H. Long," *Civil War Records of Tennessee* 1:54–55.
87. Reports of John C. Vaughn, June 9–11, 1863, *OR*, ser. 1, vol. 24, pt. 2, pp. 693–94.
88. Lindsley, *Military Annals of Tennessee*, 574.
89. Reports of Carter L. Stevenson, July 29, 1863, and A. W. Reynolds, July 1863, *OR*, ser. 1, vol. 24, pt. 2, pp. 345, 355–56.
90. Special Orders No. 197, Aug. 19, 1863, *OR*, ser. 2, 6:218–19.
91. Lindsley, *Military Annals of Tennessee*, 466.
92. Ibid., 525.
93. Robert Ould to S. A. Meredith, Sept. 11, 1863, *OR*, ser. 2, 6:279–80; Report of the Organization of the Army of Tennessee, Nov. 20, 1863, *OR*, ser. 1, vol. 31, pt. 2, p. 662.
94. J. C. Vaughn to Jefferson Davis, Oct. 23, 1863, *OR*, ser. 1, vol. 31, pt. 2, pp. 581–82; Vaughn to Davis, Aug. 27, 1863, ser. 1, vol. 30, pt. 4, p. 560.
95. Goodspeed's, *History of Tennessee*, 993–1293.
96. A. E. Burnside to William Hoffman, June 19, 1863; Burnside to S. P. Carter, June 20, 1863, *OR*, ser. 2, 6:28, 31.
97. Andrew Johnson to Thomas M. Vincent, July 6, 1863, *Papers of Andrew Johnson* 6:285; W. S. Rosecrans to William Hoffman, Aug. 28, 1863, *OR*, ser. 3, 6:735; Hoffman to Rosecrans, Aug. 29, 1863, *OR*, ser. 3, 6:737–38.
98. Braxton Bragg to C. L. Stevenson, Nov. 4, 1863, *OR*, ser. 1, vol. 31, pt. 3, p. 633.
99. Samuel H. Wells to Felix W. Wells, Oct. 29, 1863, in M. Archer, "A Southern Part of East Tennessee," *Tennessee Ancestors* 3 (1987): 206.
100. Clark, *Valleys of the Shadow*, 25.
101. *Knoxville Whig and Rebel Ventilator*, Nov. 18, 1863.

102. Abstract from Return of the Dept. of East Tennessee, Feb. 29, 1864, *OR*, ser. 1, vol. 32, pt. 2, p. 822.

103. S. A. Key to David M. Key, Jan. 11, 15, 1864, David M. Key Papers, Southern Historical Collection, University of North Carolina, Chapel Hill (hereafter cited as Key Papers, SHC).

104. John C. Vaughn to Newton J. Lillard, Dec. 28, 1863, Lillard Family Papers.

105. J. Stoddard Johnston, "Sketches of Operations of General John C. Breckinridge," *Southern Historical Society Papers* 7 (1879): 319.

106. Report of Archer Anderson, Apr. 29, 1864, *OR*, ser. 1, vol. 32, pt. 3, pp. 844–46.

107. R. A. Crawford to William Schofield, *OR*, ser. 1, vol. 32, pt. 3, p. 174; John Echols to S. Cooper, Sept. 7, 1864, *OR*, ser. 1, vol. 45, pt. 1, p. 831.

108. H. T. Stanton to J. Stoddard Johnston, Dec. 19, 1864, *OR*, ser. 1, vol. 43, pt. 2, p. 865. For an evaluation of Vaughn's command on the 1864 Valley campaign, see Robert K. Krick, "'The Cause of All My Disasters': Jubal A. Early and the Undisciplined Valley Cavalry," in *Struggle for the Shenandoah*, ed. Gary W. Gallagher (Kent, Ohio: 1991), 77–106.

109. Report of Vaughn, June 6, 1864, *OR*, ser. 1, vol. 37, pt. 1, p. 151. The fullest account of the fight at Piedmont is Marshall Moore Brice, *Conquest of a Valley* (Charlottesville, Va., 1965).

110. *Confederate Veteran* 22 (1914):397.

111. Hesseltine, *Dr. J. G. M. Ramsey*, 191–93.

112. W. Todd Groce, "Confederate Faces in East Tennessee: A Photographic Essay," *Journal of East Tennessee History* 65 (1993): 28; Clark, *Valleys of the Shadow*, 31; Lindsley, *Military Annals of Tennessee*, 607; *Confederate Veteran* 22 (1914):397.

113. Report of George G. Dibrell, Oct. 27, 1863, *OR*, ser. 1, vol. 31, pt. 1, p. 12.

114. S. A. Key to David M. Key, Jan. 15, 1864, Key Papers, SHC.

115. Possibly Washington Long, assistant surgeon, Nineteenth Tennessee Cavalry. W. P. Sanders to John G. Parke, Nov. 6, 1863, *OR*, ser. 1, vol. 31, pt. 3, p. 67.

116. Report of Archer Anderson, Apr. 29, 1864, *OR*, ser. 1, vol. 32, pt. 3, pp. 844–46.

117. R. E. Lee to Jefferson Davis, Aug. 9, 1864; Davis to Lee, Aug. 10, 1864, *OR*, ser. 1, vol. 43, pt. 1, pp. 990–92.

118. For recent examinations of desertion in the Confederate army, see Daniel, *Soldiering in the Army of Tennessee,* 126–47; and Kevin Conley Ruffner, "Civil War Desertion from a Black Belt Regiment: An Examination of the 44th Virginia Infantry," in *The Edge of the South: Life in Nineteenth Century Virginia,* ed. Edward L. Ayers and John C. Willis (Charlottesville, Va., 1991), 79–108.
119. *Tennesseans in the Civil War* 1:251.
120. *Chattanooga Gazette and Advertiser,* Jan. 15, 1862.
121. E. K. Smith to S. Cooper, Apr. 28, 1862, *OR,* ser. 1, vol. 10, pt. 2, pp. 460, 511–12; *Tennesseans in the Civil War* 1:268.
122. *Greeneville Banner,* July 25, 1862.
123. *Athens (Tenn.) Post,* Feb. 27, 1863.
124. Blair diary, Sept. 14, 1863.
125. William Hoffman to George H. Thomas, May 9, 1864, *OR,* ser. 2, 7:131.
126. R. H. G. Minty to P. P. Oldershaw, Sept. 2, 1863, *OR,* ser. 1, vol. 30, pt. 3, pp. 306–7.
127. Lewis I. Poats to Annie Poats, Nov. 15, 1863, quoted in Schumaker, "Confederate History of Hawkins County," 9–10.
128. Lindsley, *Military Annals of Tennessee,* 829.
129. W. C. Brown diary, Feb. 23, June 23–July 25, Sept. 10, 1864, Jan. 11, 1865, Chattanooga–Hamilton County Bicentennial Library.
130. William S. Thomas to Minerva Thomas, Dec. 8, 1863, *Civil War Records of Tennessee* 1:63.
131. J. R. Hook to Josephine Hook, Oct. 22, 1863, ibid. 2:57–63.

6. How I Wish We Could Have Peace

1. The story of Mabry's encounter with Chamberlain can be found in the *Knoxville Journal,* May 7, 1893.
2. Affairs in the region prior to Federal invasion are examined in Bryan, "'Tories' Amidst Rebels," 3–22.
3. F. M. Turner et al. to Felix Zollicoffer, Sept. 9, 1861, *OR,* ser. 1, 4:404–5.
4. W. B. Wood to Zollicoffer, Oct. 28, 1861, *OR,* ser. 1, 4:482–83.
5. Madison T. Peoples to Judah P. Benjamin, Nov. 20, 1861, *OR,* ser. 1, 7:686.
6. *OR,* ser. 1, 7:686.
7. Landon C. Haynes to Davis, Nov. 8, 1861, *OR,* ser. 1, 4:529–30.

8. D. Leadbetter to S. Cooper, Jan. 26, 1862, *OR*, ser. 1, 7:848.

9. *Knoxville Register*, Jan. 2, 1863.

10. Henry David Shapiro, *Appalachia on Our Mind: The Southern Mountains and Mountaineers in the American Consciousness* (Chapel Hill, N.C., 1978); David C. Hsiung, *Two Worlds in the Tennessee Mountains: Exploring the Origins of Appalachian Stereotypes* (Lexington, 1997).

11. D. C. Blevins to Benjamin F. Taylor, Aug. 3, 1861, photocopy of original in the possession of Betty Broyles, Dayton, Tenn.

12. Hannibal Paine to Virginia Paine, Aug. 8, 1861, Paine Family Collection, TSLA.

13. Kate Leuty to Benjamin F. Taylor, Aug. 22, 1861, in the possession of Betty Broyles, Dayton, Tenn.

14. L. B. Headrick to Isham G. Harris, Mar. 18, 1862, Brownlow Papers.

15. Sam H. Hynds to Ann Hynds, May 27, 1862, *Civil War Records of Tennessee* 1:93.

16. *Cleveland (Tenn.) Banner*, Apr. 25, 1862.

17. *Chattanooga Daily Rebel*, Aug. 9, 1862.

18. Quoted in ibid.

19. *Knoxville Register*, Mar. 3, 1863.

20. For a history of Confederate repression of Unionists, see Bryan, "'Tories' Amidst Rebels," 6–13.

21. The soldier's letter, which first appeared in the *Nashville Banner*, was quoted in the *Knoxville Whig*, Aug. 31, 1861.

22. *Knoxville Whig*, Sept. 7, 1861.

23. *Athens (Tenn.) Post*, Sept. 9, 1861.

24. Robertson Topp to Robert Gasselyn, Oct. 26, 1861, *OR*, ser. 1, 4:476–77.

25. *Chattanooga Advertiser*, Feb. 13, 1862.

26. *Athens (Tenn.) Post*, May 5, 1862.

27. *Greeneville Tri-Weekly Banner*, July 25, 1862.

28. *Knoxville Register*, Dec. 25, 1862.

29. *Chattanooga Daily Rebel*, Feb. 19, 1863.

30. *Knoxville Register*, May 21, 1863.

31. *Chattanooga Daily Rebel*, May 26, 1863.

32. *Knoxville Register*, June 17, 1863.

33. Ibid., July 11, 1862.

34. Ibid., May 10, 1863.

35. A. C. Hickey to Talbot Greene, June 16, 1863, Nelson Papers.

36. E. K. B. to Elizabeth Key, June 21, 1863, Key Papers, Bicentennial Library.

37. F. J. Paine to Mary L. Paine, July 10, 1863, Confederate Collection.

38. Margaret to Carrie Stakely, July 11, 1863, Hall-Stakely Papers.

39. Myra Inman diary, July 27, 1863, Southern Historical Collection, University of North Carolina, Chapel Hill.

40. Blair diary, May 29, 31, July 8, 9, 1863.

41. Susan Heiskell McCampbell diary, Sept. 4, 1863, McCampbell Family Collection, Tennessee State Library and Archives, Nashville (hereafter cited as McCampbell diary).

42. *Athens (Tenn.) Post,* July 17, 1863.

43. *Knoxville Register,* Dec. 25, 1862.

44. Blair diary, July 25, 1863; *Knoxville Register,* July 29, 1863.

45. *Knoxville Daily Southern Chronicle,* July 11, 1863.

46. *Chattanooga Daily Rebel,* July 26, 1863.

47. James Scruggs to Carrie Stakely, June 24, 1863, Hall-Stakely Papers.

48. McCampbell diary, June 26, 1863.

49. E. K. B. to Elizabeth Key, June 21, 1863, Key Papers, Bicentennial Library.

50. Report of Milton A. Haynes, June 21, 1863, *OR,* ser. 1, vol. 23, pt. 1, p. 393.

51. *Knoxville Register,* July 29, 1863.

52. *Chattanooga Daily Rebel,* Aug. 6, 1863.

53. *Nashville Daily Press,* Sept. 19, 1863.

54. Sutherland, *Very Violent Rebel,* 4.

55. Charles F. Davis to Harriet Davis, Sept. 6, 1863, *Civil War Records of Tennessee* 1:19.

56. Worsham, *Old Nineteenth Tennessee Regiment,* 104.

57. Josephine Hooke diary, Sept. 8–9, 1863, typescript, Special Collections Library, University of Tennessee, Knoxville (hereafter cited as Hooke diary).

58. *Bristol (Tenn.) Gazette,* Feb. 18, 1864.

59. J. S. Hurlbut, *History of the Rebellion in Bradley County, East Tennessee* (Indianapolis, 1866), 143–44.

60. McAdoo diary, Sept. 2, Oct. 20, 1863.

61. Blair diary, Sept. 9, 1863.

62. Schumaker, "Confederate History of Hawkins County," 9.

63. *Knoxville Register,* Apr. 3, 1862.

64. Jerome G. Taylor, "The Extraordinary Life and Death of Joseph A. Mabry," *ETHSP* 42 (1972): 42–46.

65. *Knoxville Register,* Jan. 3, 1863, William J. MacArthur Jr., "The Early Career of Charles McClung McGhee," *ETHSP* 45 (1975): 12–13.

66. Rothrock, *French Broad–Holston Country*, 387–88.

67. Blair diary, June 15, Sept. 4, 1863.

68. *Nashville Daily Press*, Oct. 10, 1863.

69. Quoted in ibid., Oct. 2, 1863. At the time, Gen. Braxton Bragg's Army of Tennessee was besieging Chattanooga, attempting to starve the Federals out.

70. Hesseltine, *Dr. J. G. M. Ramsey*, 220–35. See also "Journal of Mrs. J. G. M. Ramsey," J. G. M. Ramsey Papers, Southern Historical Collection, University of North Carolina, Chapel Hill (hereafter cited as Ramsey Papers); and David M. Abshire, *The South Rejects a Prophet: The Life of Senator David M. Key, 1824–1900* (New York, 1967), 53–54. Key also resided in New Jersey near the end of the war.

71. Vernon M. Crow, "The Justness of our Cause: The Civil War Diaries of William W. Stringfield," *ETHSP* 56–57 (1984–85): 86.

72. For the travails and wanderings of the Stakely family, see William M. Stakely diary, Hall-Stakely Papers. Stakely, a resident of Madisonville, was chairman of the Monroe County Democratic Party before the war, a secessionist, and father of a Confederate soldier. He kept a journal of his activities as a refugee in Alabama during 1864.

73. Mary Cox to "Father," Jan. 9, 1863, Hall-Stakely Papers.

74. McAdoo diary, Aug. 30, 1863.

75. Hesseltine, *Dr. J. G. M. Ramsey*, 123.

76. McAdoo diary, Aug. 31, Sept. 3, 7, 10, Oct. 3, 9, 20, 21, 26, 1863.

77. Hooke diary, Aug. 30, Sept. 13, 1863.

78. McAdoo diary, Sept. 10, 1863.

79. Hooke diary, Sept. 17–21, Oct. 23–26, 1863.

80. Elizabeth Baker Crozier journal, typescript, pp. 10–11, Special Collections Library, University of Tennessee, Knoxville.

81. *Chattanooga Daily Rebel*, July 18, 25, 1864.

82. Hooke diary, Sept. 24, 28, Oct. 1, Nov. 12, 1863.

83. William M. Stakely to "wife," Oct. 16, 1864, Hall-Stakely Papers.

84. Margaret to Carrie Stakely, Feb. 23, 1865, Hall-Stakely Papers.

85. For an examination of conditions after Confederate evacuation, see Campbell, "East Tennessee During Federal Occupation," 64–80.

86. Mary Reynolds to Simeon Reynolds, Jan. 28, 1864, Reynolds Papers, Special Collections Library, University of Tennessee.

87. *Bristol (Tenn.) Gazette*, Feb. 18, 1864.

88. Undated news clipping, Ramsey Papers, Special Collections Library, Univ. of Tennessee.

89. Hesseltine, *Dr. J. G. M. Ramsey*, 165–66; newspaper clipping, dated Aug. 9, 1864, Ramsey Papers, Special Collections Library, Univ. of Tennessee.

90. *Bristol (Tenn.) Gazette*, Feb. 18, 1864.

91. Sutherland, *Very Violent Rebel*, 87, 117, 127.

92. Article of Agreement Respecting Exchange of Non-combatants, Dec. 1, 1864; James A. Seddon to John C. Vaughn, Dec. 15, 1864, *OR*, ser. 2, 7:1175, 1229.

93. Paul W. Prindle, *Ancestry of William Biencke* (n.p., 1974), 258–59. An autobiography of Sperry can be found in this work about a Sperry descendant, Biencke. On Rebel political prisoners forced to labor on Federal fortifications, see *Knoxville Whig and Rebel Ventilator*, Dec. 7, 1864.

94. John C. Vaughn to David M. Key, Sept. 28, 1864, Key Papers, SHC.

95 Sutherland, *Very Violent Rebel*, 139.

96. Samuel L. Kerr to Nelson, Sept. 16, 1864, Nelson Papers.

97. John Murrell to Nelson, Oct. 30, 1864, Nelson Papers.

98. Mariah J. Harrison to Nelson, Oct. 3, 1864, Nelson Papers. See also B. Bryant to Nelson, June 27, 1864, W. N. Clarkson to Nelson, June 2, 1863, Francis S. Blair to Nelson, Oct. 24, 1864, and Samuel Ghormley to Nelson, Oct. 30, 1864, all Nelson Papers. See also R. B. Rosenburg, ed., *"For the Sake of My Country": The Diary of Col. W. W. Ward, 9th Tennessee Cavalry, Morgan's Brigade, CSA* (Murfreesboro, Tenn., 1992), 118.

99. Sarah A. Coffin to T. A. R. Nelson, Dec. 7, 1864, Nelson Papers.

100. *Knoxville Whig*, Feb. 6, 1864.

7. We Are Certainly Now Treading on a Volcano

1. Swan's story is based on an interview with Edna Swan Carter, Morristown, Tenn., Oct. 1985. See Sandra S. Wilson and Dennis L. Snapp, eds., *Broken Hearts—Broken Lives: Jefferson County, Tennessee, 1860–1868: Civilian Life in the Civil War* (Jefferson City, Tenn., 1986), 109–10.

2. For a fuller examination of conditions in postwar East Tennessee, see Bryan, "Civil War in East Tennessee," 160–86; and Thomas B. Alexander, "Neither Peace Nor War: Conditions in Tennessee in 1865," *ETHSP* 21 (1949): 44–48.

3. Steven Hahn, *The Roots of Southern Populism: Yeoman Farmers and the Transformation of the Georgia Upcountry, 1850–1890* (New York, 1983), 212–16; Stephen V. Ash, *Middle Tennessee Society Transformed, 1860–1870: War and Peace in the Upper South* (Baton Rouge, 1988), 204–5, 22.

4. *Nashville Daily Press,* Sept. 14, 1863.

5. Quoted in ibid., Sept. 16, 1863.

6. *Knoxville Whig and Rebel Ventilator,* Feb. 6, 1864.

7. Ibid., Nov. 30, 1864.

8. Ibid., Feb. 6, Nov. 23, 1864, Mar. 15, 1865.

9. Ibid., Feb. 6, 1864.

10. Ibid., Mar. 15, 1865.

11. Ibid., Mar. 5, 1864.

12. Ibid., Sept. 6, 1865.

13. Ibid., July 29, 1864.

14. "Special Order No. 1," July 24, 1865, Nelson Papers.

15. John C. and David G. Boren to D. L. Boren, July 28, 1865, Boren Family Papers, McClung Historical Collection, Lawson McGhee Library, Knoxville.

16. *Knoxville Whig and Rebel Ventilator,* Oct. 17, 1865.

17. A. M. Brown to T. A. R. Nelson, July 25, 1865, Nelson Papers.

18. Mrs. William R. Caswell to William Caswell, June 19, 1865, Caswell Papers.

19. Burts to Johnson, Oct. 10, 1865, *Papers of Andrew Johnson* 9:215–16.

20. McAdoo diary, Nov. 11, 1865.

21. *Greeneville New Era,* Sept. 16, 1865.

22. Milligan to Johnson, Mar. 29, 1866, *Papers of Andrew Johnson* 10:331.

23. Crutchfield to S. A. Key, July 28, 1865, Key Papers, Bicentennial Library.

24. *Knoxville Whig and Rebel Ventilator,* June 7, 1865.

25. Margaret Stakely to Carrie Stakely, Aug. 8, 1865, Hall-Stakely Papers.

26. Petition from Washington County Citizens to Andrew Johnson, Apr. 20, 1866, *Papers of Andrew Johnson* 10:435–36.

27. For an example of violence perpetrated against Rebel citizens before Federal occupation, see the *Chattanooga Daily Rebel,* Aug. 9, 1862, where it is reported that retired Provisional Army general William R. Caswell was murdered near his home by a gang of unknown assassins. James K. McAnnally was murdered in Jefferson County on June 2, 1863, under circumstances similar to those surrounding Caswell's slaying. See *Chattanooga Daily Rebel,* June 3, 1863. For other instances of early violence, see *Knoxville Register,* Mar. 3, Apr. 26, 1863.

28. Quoted in *Nashville Daily Press,* Oct. 4, 1863.

29. Sutherland, *Very Violent Rebel,* 111.

30. H. Wax to "Cousin App," Feb. 25, 1865, H. G. Wax Papers, Special Collections Library, University of Tennessee, Knoxville.

31. Robert S. Roadman to T. A. R. Nelson, Aug. 20, 1865, Nelson Papers.

32. Taylor, *Historic Sullivan County*, 309–10.

33. *Knoxville Whig and Rebel Ventilator*, Sept. 21, 1864.

34. The story of the assault on Hynds and Gammon is based on an interview with Ruth Swan Goddard, Dandridge, Tenn., Sept. 1985, in Wilson and Snapp, *Broken Hearts—Broken Lives*, 123.

35. *Knoxville Whig and Rebel Ventilator*, Sept. 20, 1865.

36. *Cincinnati Enquirer*, Aug. 31, 1866.

37. *Knoxville Whig and Rebel Ventilator*, Feb. 22, 1865.

38. Ibid., May 10, 1865.

39. William Henry Maxwell to Andrew Johnson, Dec. 12, 1865, *Papers of Andrew Johnson* 9:336–337.

40. Margaret Stakely to Carrie Stakely, Apr. 21, 22, 1865, Hall-Stakely Papers.

41. "Diary of Jacob Austin Sperry," in Prindle, *Ancestry of William Biencke*, 249.

42. *Knoxville Whig and Rebel Ventilator*, Sept. 6, 1865; Digby Seymour, *Divided Loyalties: Fort Sanders and the Civil War in East Tennessee*, 2d ed. (Knoxville, 1982), 235.

43. *Knoxville Whig and Rebel Ventilator*, Mar. 5, 1864; May 17, 1865.

44. Ibid., Mar. 5, 1864.

45. Patterson to Col. Butler, Oct. 10, 1864, Nelson Papers.

46. *Knoxville Whig and Rebel Ventilator*, May 17, 1865.

47. Indictment against John S. Carmichael, Christopher Graves, Moses Bonner, B. Brocke, and William J. Johnston, May 31, 1865, Nelson Papers.

48. *Knoxville Whig and Rebel Ventilator*, Mar. 1, 1865.

49. *Smith v. Ishenhour* (1866), *Tennessee Reports*, 3 Caldwell, 214–18.

50. *Yost v. Stout* (1867), ibid., 4 Caldwell, 205–14.

51. *Moore v. Burchfield* (1870), ibid., 1 Heiskell, 203–7.

52. *Smith v. Brazelton* (1870), ibid., 1 Heiskell, 45–67.

53. *Wilkerson v. Bishop* (1866), ibid., 7 Caldwell, 26–31.

54. *Starnes v. Hubbs* (1870), ibid., 1 Heiskell, 196–97.

55. Clark, *Valleys of the Shadow*.

56. F. A. Lenoir to A. G. Welker, Aug. 21, 1865, Nelson Papers.

57. *Knoxville Whig*, Aug. 29, 1866.

58. Ibid., Oct. 10, 1866.

59. *Crawford v. State* (1867), *Tennessee Reports*, 4 Caldwell, 190–95.

60. *Knoxville Whig and Rebel Ventilator*, June 28, 1865, June 20, July 4, 1866; *Nashville Republican Banner*, Nov. 14, 1865. See also William G. Brownlow

to Andrew Johnson, May 25, June 14, 25, 1865, *Papers of Andrew Johnson* 8:107, 236, 287–88; and Brownlow to Johnson, Nov. 10, 1865, ibid. 9:367–68.

61. *Knoxville Whig and Rebel Ventilator,* Nov. 18, 1863.

62. Ibid., Nov. 30, 1864.

63. Persons Indicted or Prosecuted for Treason in the United States Court of the Eastern District of Tennessee, Records of the Department of Justice, RG 60, NA; Bryan, "Civil War in East Tennessee," 166–67.

64. *U.S. v. Wood,* Nelson Papers.

65. *Nashville Republican Banner,* Oct. 19, Nov. 14, Dec. 27, 1865; *Knoxville Whig and Rebel Ventilator,* May 31, June 21, Sept. 6, Dec. 20, 1865; Petition of W. H. Sneed to United States Court for the Eastern District of Tennessee, Dec. 10, 1867, Nelson Papers; McAdoo diary, Nov. 25, 1867.

66. Bryan, "Civil War in East Tennessee," 171.

67. For an overview of the Johnson pardon program, see Jonathan T. Dorris, *Pardon and Amnesty under Lincoln and Johnson: The Restoration of the Confederates to Their Rights and Privileges* (Chapel Hill, N.C., 1953). See also Amnesty Proclamation, May 29, 1865, *Papers of Andrew Johnson* 8:128–30.

68. R. B. Rosenburg, "Reconstructed Rebels: Tennessee Pardon-seekers under Johnson's Plan" (seminar paper, Univ. of Tennessee, Knoxville, 1984), 15–17.

69. Amnesty Papers (M1003, rolls 48–51), Tenn., RG 94, NA; *House Executive Documents,* 39 Congress, 2 Session, No. 116, pp. 46–47, 79 (ser. 1293).

70. James K. Cox to Andrew Johnson, Feb. 23, 1866, Amnesty Papers (M1003, roll 48), Tenn., James K. Cox, RG 94, NA. The list of Blount County secessionists published in the *Union* can be found in the *Knoxville Whig and Rebel Ventilator,* Feb. 6, 1864.

71. James Miller to Andrew Johnson, Oct. 30, 1865, Amnesty Papers (M1003, roll 50), Tenn., James Miller, RG 94, NA.

72. James W. Gillespie to Andrew Johnson, Oct. 2, 1865, Amnesty Papers (M1003, roll 49), Tenn., James W. Gillespie, RG 94, NA.

73. N. R. Meroney to Andrew Johnson, May 7, 1866, Amnesty Papers (M1003, roll 50), Tenn., N. R. Meroney, RG 94, NA.

74. William M. Cocke to Andrew Johnson, Sept. 5, 1865, Amnesty Papers (M1003, roll 48), Tenn., William M. Cocke, RG 94, NA.

75. George L. Gillespie to Andrew Johnson, July 12, 1866, *Papers of Andrew Johnson* 10:677–78.

76. George R. Powel to Andrew Johnson, Aug. 22, 1865, ibid. 8:643.

77. Isaac W. George to Andrew Johnson, Aug. 28, 1865, Amnesty Papers (M1003, roll 49), Tenn., Isaac W. George, RG 94, NA.

78. David M. Key to Andrew Johnson, May 25, 1865, Amnesty Papers (M1003, roll 50), Tenn., D. M. Key, RG 94, NA.

79. William W. Stringfield to Andrew Johnson, June 29, 1865, Amnesty Papers (M1003, roll 51), Tenn., W. W. Stringfield, RG 94, NA.

80. Cornelius E. Lucky to Andrew Johnson, June 27, 1865, Amnesty Papers (M1003, roll 50), Tenn., Cornelius E. Lucky, RG 94, NA.

81. James C. Moses to Andrew Johnson, Mar. 19, 1866, *Papers of Andrew Johnson* 10:278.

82. P. S. Hale to Andrew Johnson, July 10, 1865, Amnesty Papers (M1003, roll 49), Tenn., P. S. Hale, RG 94, NA.

83. Hiram Heartsill to Andrew Johnson, Aug. 3, 1865, Amnesty Papers (M1003, roll 49), Tenn., Hiram Heartsill, RG 94, NA.

84. Hiram Bogle to Andrew Johnson, Sept. 8, 1865, Amnesty Papers (M1003, roll 48), Tenn., Hiram Bogle, RG 94, NA.

85. Thomas A. Faw to Andrew Johnson, May 17, 1865, Amnesty Papers (M1003, roll 49), Tenn., Thomas A. Faw, RG 94, NA.

86. James W. Bowman to Andrew Johnson, Sept. 2, 1865, Amnesty Papers (M1003, roll 48), Tenn., James W. Bowman, RG 94, NA.

87. David M. Key to Andrew Johnson, May 25, 1865, *Papers of Andrew Johnson* 8:109.

88. H. Talbot Cox to Andrew Johnson, June 17, 1865, ibid., 250–51.

89. Hugh L. McClung to Andrew Johnson, June 27, 1865, ibid., 302.

90. William H. Crouch to Andrew Johnson, July 1, 1865, Amnesty Papers (M1003, roll 48), Tenn., William H. Crouch, RG 94, NA.

91. F. W. Turley to Andrew Johnson, Oct. 5, 1865, Amnesty Papers (M1003, roll 51), Tenn., F. W. Turley, RG 94, NA.

92. Jesse G. Wallace to Andrew Johnson, July 6, 1865, *Papers of Andrew Johnson* 8:366.

93. William Bayless to Andrew Johnson, Aug. 4, 1865, Amnesty Papers (M1003, roll 48), Tenn., William Bayless, RG 94, NA.

94. David Good to Andrew Johnson, c. Aug. 1865, Amnesty Papers (M1003, roll 49), Tenn., David Good, RG 94, NA.

95. Alexander McLin to Andrew Johnson, Aug. 12, 1865, Amnesty Papers (M1003, roll 50), Tenn., Alexander McLin, RG 94, NA.

96. John M. King to John Netherland and T. A. R. Nelson, Oct. 23, 1865, Nelson Papers. David M. Key reported to his wife that on the first

day of court in Chattanooga, "several poor rebels—mostly old men—were severely beaten." He himself was warned "to keep a sharp look out—as I was threatened." Fortunately, he managed to escape unscathed. D. M. Key to Elizabeth Key, Feb. 14, 1866, Key Papers, Bicentennial Library.

97. Joseph Tucker to T. A. R. Nelson, Sept. 8, 1865, Nelson Papers.

98. M. J. Mims to T. A. R. Nelson, Nov. 11, 1865, Nelson Papers.

99. W. W. Wallace to T. A. R. Nelson, Aug. 23, 1865, Nelson Papers.

100. *Knoxville Whig*, Aug. 8, 1866; July 16, 1868. Ashby had incurred the wrath of Brownlow for his raid on a band of Unionists attempting to cross the Cumberland Mountains into Kentucky in April 1862. Approximately four hundred Tories were captured and sent southward to Monticello, Georgia. See the *Whig*, June 20, 1866.

101. David Deaderick, "Register of Events," typescript, p. 77, in Deaderick Papers.

102. William Brazelton to Robert Johnson, Aug. 8, 1865, Andrew Johnson Papers, Library of Congress, Washington, D.C.

103. William Henry Maxwell to Andrew Johnson, Nov. 2, 1865, *Papers of Andrew Johnson* 9:336–37.

104. *Memphis Appeal*, Jan. 1, 1864.

105. Maria S. Wofford to Andrew Johnson, Sept. 11, 1865, *Papers of Andrew Johnson* 9:69.

106. Ellen P. Brabson to William T. Brabson, June 25, 1865, Brabson Family Papers, Special Collections Library, University of Tennessee, Knoxville.

107. Samuel B. Boyd to "wife and family," Apr. 12, 1865, Samuel Boyd Papers, Special Collections Library, University of Tennessee, Knoxville.

108. *Lebanon Register*, Oct. 26, 1865.

109. Evans, *Confederate Military History* 8:533–35; Joshua W. Caldwell, *Sketches of the Bench and Bar of Tennessee* (Knoxville, 1898), 331; *Knoxville Whig*, Jan. 31, 1866.

110. Goodspeed's, *History of Tennessee*, 801.

111. *Civil War Records of Tennessee* 1:69, 79, 83.

112. Evans, *Confederate Military History* 8:341; McAdoo diary, Nov. 25, 1867; John C. Vaughn to J. G. M. Ramsey, Ramsey Papers, Special Collections Library.

113. John C. Vaughn to J. G. M. Ramsey, Aug. 8, 1867, Ramsey Papers.

114. Andrew R. Edmonds to Andrew Johnson, Sept. 9, 1865, *Papers of Andrew Johnson* 9:12–14.

115. Ada Smith to Carrie Stakely, May 28, 1865, Hall-Stakely Papers.

116. Taylor, *Historic Sullivan County,* 309–10.

117. Mrs. W. R. Caswell to William Caswell, June 19, 1865, Caswell Papers.

118. *Knoxville Whig,* Feb. 21, 1866; Robert B. Reynolds to Andrew Johnson, c. Feb. 10, 1866, Amnesty Papers (M1003, roll 50), Tenn., Robert B. Reynolds, RG 94, NA. As of this writing, the home still stands, an island in the midst of Kingston Pike's strip malls and urban sprawl.

119. Evans, *Confederate Military History* 8:457.

120. Carrie Stakely to Margaret Stakely, Jan. 25, 1866, Hall-Stakely Papers.

121. James G. Rose to Josephine Thomas, June 1865, *Civil War Records of Tennessee* 1:67.

122. *Nashville Daily Press,* July 4, 1865.

123. *Knoxville Whig and Rebel Ventilator,* Aug. 30, 1865.

124. Ibid., Sept. 6, 1865.

125. *Knoxville Whig,* Aug. 8, 1866.

126. *Knoxville Whig and Rebel Ventilator,* Sept. 13, 1865.

127. Sources used to determine the location of the sample include the *Ninth Census of Tennessee: 1870,* Free Inhabitants MSS Schedule; Compiled Service Records, RG 109; and the Memorial Rolls in Lindsley, *Military Annals of Tennessee.*

128. *Knoxville Whig and Rebel Ventilator,* Mar. 8, 1865.

Epilogue

1. It should be noted that situations similar to that in East Tennessee existed in parts of Kentucky and Missouri. For instance, see Michael Fellman, *Inside War: The Guerrilla Conflict in Missouri during the American Civil War* (New York, 1989). Conditions there differed, however, in that the Federal army quickly occupied those states, whereas in East Tennessee it was not until 1863 that Union troops seized control.

2. Goodspeed's, *History of Tennessee,* 1206.

3. Ibid., 1202; Hamblen County Centennial Celebration, *Historic Hamblen, 1870–1970* (Morristown, Tenn., 1970), 27.

4. Goodspeed's, *History of Tennessee,* 1236.

5. Speer, *Sketches of Prominent Tennesseans,* 133.

6. Lenoir, *History of Sweetwater Valley,* 281–82.

7. Goodspeed's, *History of Tennessee,* 1092.

8. *BDTA* 2:934–35.

9. An interesting account of the Allen family and how East Tennessee

contributed to the rebirth of postwar Atlanta can be found in Gary
M. Pomerantz, *Where Peachtree Meets Sweet Auburn: The Saga of Two Families
and the Making of Atlanta* (New York, 1986).

10. For a closer examination of the war's impact on the economic and
political development of East Tennessee, see Robert Tracy McKenzie,
"'Oh! Ours Is a Deplorable Condition': The Economic Impact of
the Civil War in Upper East Tennessee," in *The Civil War in Appalachia:
Collected Essays*, ed. Kenneth W. Noe and Shannon H. Wilson
(Knoxville, 1997), 199–226; Gordon B. McKinney, *Southern Mountain
Republicans, 1865–1900: Politics and the Appalachian Community* (Chapel Hill,
N.C., 1978); and Salstrom, *Appalachia's Path to Dependency.*

11. *Confederate Veteran* 1 (1893): 343; 3 (1895): 277; 5 (1897): 593; 8 (1900): 17;
15 (1907): 28–29.

12. Anne Cody, *History of the Tennessee Division of the United Daughters of the
Confederacy* (Nashville, n.d.), 259–336; Confederate Southern Memorial
Associations, *History of the Confederate Memorial Associations of the South*
(New Orleans, 1904), 247–48.

13. Cody, *History of the Tennessee Division*, 287.

14. Ralph W. Widner Jr., *Confederate Monuments: Enduring Symbols of the South
and the War Between the States* (n.p., 1982), 189–97. Monuments erected
before 1920 were those to the Confederate soldiers in Knoxville (1892),
Cleveland (1911), Tazewell (1917), and the A. P. Stewart statue in Chattanooga (1919). Post-1920 memorials include those to the Confederate
soldiers of Blountville in Sullivan County (1938), Erwin in Unicoi
County (1930), and stones to John Hunt Morgan in Greeneville (1932)
and Abner Baker in Knoxville (1926).

15. Charles Reagan Wilson, *Baptized in Blood: The Religion of the Lost Cause,
1865–1920* (Athens, Tenn., 1980), 1–17.

16. Gaines M. Foster, *Ghosts of the Confederacy: Defeat, the Lost Cause, and the
Emergence of the New South* (New York, 1987), 1–8.

Bibliography

Primary Materials

Manuscripts

Archives of Appalachia, East Tennessee State University, Johnson City
  Bowman Family Collection
  Fannie A. Fain Diary
  Faw Family Papers
  Franklin P. Baxter Papers
  John H. Crawford Papers
Chattanooga–Hamilton County Bicentennial Library, Chattanooga, Tennessee
  David M. Key Papers
  W. C. Brown Diary
Chickamauga-Chattanooga National Military Park Library, Ft. Oglethorpe, Georgia
  "Reminiscences of Robert M. Rhea"
Cleveland Public Library, Cleveland, Tennessee
  George W. Clemmer Diary
Library of Congress, Washington, D.C.
  Andrew Johnson Papers
McClung Historical Collection, Lawson McGhee Library, Knoxville
  Boren Family Papers
  Hall-Stakely Papers
  T. A. R. Nelson Papers
  William Rule Papers
National Archives, Washington, D.C.
  Amnesty Papers (M1003, Rolls 48-51), Tenn. RG 94.
  Compiled Service Records of Confederate Soldiers Who Served from the State of Tennessee. RG 109.

Persons Indicted or Prosecuted for Treason in the United States Court of the Eastern District of Tennessee. Records of the Department of Justice. RG 60.

U.S. Bureau of the Census, "Eighth Census of Tennessee: 1860." Population and Slave Schedules.

U.S. Bureau of the Census, "Ninth Census of Tennessee: 1870." Population Schedules.

North Carolina Department of Archives and History, Raleigh
    William W. Stringfield Collection
Private Collection of Betty Broyles, Dayton, Tennessee
    Benjamin F. Taylor Letters
Southern Historical Collection, University of North Carolina, Chapel Hill
    David M. Key Papers
    J. G. M. Ramsey Papers
    Myra Inman Diary
    William R. Caswell Papers
Special Collections Library, University of Tennessee, Knoxville
    Brabson Family Papers
    David Deaderick Papers
    Edward P. Clark Collection
    Elizabeth Baker Crozier Journal
    H. G. Wax Papers
    Horace Maynard Papers
    Josephine Hooke Diary
    Lenoir Family Papers
    Reynolds Letters
    Saffell Papers
    Samuel Boyd Papers
    William G. Brownlow Papers
    William Gibbs McAdoo Diary
Tennessee State Library and Archives, Nashville
    Army of Tennessee Collection
        RG 4
    Confederate Collection
        "Henry Melville Doak Memoirs"
        John J. Blair Diary
    Lillard Family Papers
    McCampbell Family Collection
    Paine Family Papers
    Tennessee State Militia Officers Commission Book

Published Works

Aiken, Leona Taylor. "The Letters of the Offield Brothers, Confederate Soldiers of East Tennessee." East Tennessee Historical Society's *Publications* 46 (1974): 116–25.

Caldwell, Joshua W. *Sketches of the Bench and Bar of Tennessee.* Knoxville, 1898.

Clark, Willene B., ed. *Valleys of the Shadow: The Memoir of Confederate Captain Reuben G. Clark.* Knoxville, 1994.

Confederate Veteran. 40 vols. Nashville, 1893–1932.

Crow, Vernon M. "'The Justness of Our Cause': The Civil War Diary of William W. Stringfield." East Tennessee Historical Society's *Publications* 56–57 (1984–85): 71–101.

Dunn, Durwood. *An Abolitionist in the Appalachian South: Ezekiel Birdseye on Slavery, Capitalism, and Separate Statehood in East Tennessee, 1841–1846.* Knoxville, 1997.

Evans, Clement A., ed. *Confederate Military History, Extended Edition.* 12 vols. Atlanta, 1899.

Goodspeed's Publishing Company. *A History of Tennessee from the Earliest Times to the Present, East Tennessee Edition.* Nashville, 1887.

Graf, LeRoy P., Ralph W. Haskins, and Paul H. Bergeron, eds. *The Papers of Andrew Johnson.* 15 vols. to date. Knoxville, 1967–.

Greene, Talbot. *The Bivouac: Or, Life in the Central Army of Kentucky.* Bowling Green, Ky., 1861.

Hayne, Robert Y. *An Address in Behalf of the Knoxville Convention to the Citizens of the Several States Interested in the Proposed Louisville, Cincinnati, and Charleston Rail Road.* Charleston, 1836.

Hesseltine, William B., ed. *Dr. J. G. M. Ramsey: Autobiography and Letters.* Nashville, 1954.

Hiwassee College Annual Celebration of the Literary Societies, January 30, 1861. Private Collection.

Howard, McHenry. *Recollections of a Maryland Confederate Soldier and Staff Officer.* Baltimore, 1914.

Humes, Thomas W. *The Loyal Mountaineers of Tennessee.* Knoxville, 1888.

Hurlbut, J. S. *History of the Rebellion in Bradley County, East Tennessee.* Indianapolis, 1866.

Johnston, J. Stoddard. "Sketches of Operations of General John C. Breckinridge." *Southern Historical Society Papers* 7 (1879): 317–23.

Johnston, Robert U., and Clarence C. Buel, eds. *Battles and Leaders of the Civil War.* 3 vols. New York, 1887.

Killebrew, J. B. *The Resources of Tennessee.* Nashville, 1874.

Lenoir, W. B. *History of Sweetwater Valley.* Richmond, 1916.

Lindsley, John B. *Military Annals of Tennessee: Confederate.* Nashville, 1886.

Mitchell, John L. *State Gazetteer and Business Directory for 1860–61.* Nashville, 1860.

Olmsted, Frederick L. *A Journey in the Back Country.* London, 1860.

Rosenburg, R. B., ed. *"For the Sake of My Country": The Diary of Col. W. W. Ward, 9th Tennessee Cavalry, Morgan's Brigade, C.S.A.* Murfreesboro, Tenn., 1992.

Rowland, Dunbar, ed. *Jefferson Davis, Constitutionalist: His Letters, Papers, and Speeches.* Jackson, Miss., 1923.

Speer, William S. *Sketches of Prominent Tennesseans.* Nashville, 1888.

Sutherland, Daniel E. *A Very Violent Rebel: The Civil War Diary of Ellen Renshaw House.* Knoxville, 1996.

Temple, O. P. *East Tennessee and the Civil War.* Cincinnati, 1899.

Tennessee Historical Records Survey. *Civil War Records of Tennessee.* 3 vols. Nashville, 1939.

Worsham, W. J. *Old Nineteenth Tennessee Regiment, CSA.* Knoxville, 1902.

Government Documents

Tennessee Supreme Court Reports. 3 Caldwell-1 Heiskell, 1866–70.

U.S. Bureau of the Census. *Eighth Census of the United States: 1860.* Washington, D.C., 1864.

————. *Seventh Census of the United States: 1850.* Washington, D.C., 1853.

U.S. Congress, *House Executive Documents.* 39th Cong., 2d sess. (Ser.1293).

War of the Rebellion: A Compilation of the Official Records of the Union and Confederate Armies. 128 in 70 vols. Washington, D.C., 1880–1901.

Newspapers

Athens (Tenn.) Post
Bristol (Tenn.) Gazette
Bristol (Tenn.) News
Bristol (Tenn.) Southern Advocate
Chattanooga Daily Rebel
Chattanooga Gazette and Advertiser
Chattanooga Times
Cincinnati Enquirer
Cleveland (Tenn.) Banner
Greeneville (Tenn.) American Presbyterian

Greeneville (Tenn.) Banner
Greeneville (Tenn.) Democrat
Greeneville (Tenn.) New Era
Greeneville (Tenn.) Tri-Weekly Banner
Jonesboro East Tennessee Herald
Jonesboro (Tenn.) Express
Jonesboro (Tenn.) Union
Kingston (Tenn.) Gazette
Knoxville Daily Southern Chronicle
Knoxville Journal
Knoxville Register
Knoxville Southern Citizen
Knoxville Whig
Knoxville Whig and Rebel Ventilator
Lebanon (Tenn.) Register
Loudon (Tenn.) Free Press
Maryville East Tennessean
Memphis Appeal
Morristown (Tenn.) Religious Intelligencer
Nashville Daily Press
Nashville Republican Banner
Nashville Union and American
Rogersville (Tenn.) Times

Maps

Atlas to Accompany the Official Records of the Union and Confederate Armies. Washington, D.C., 1891–95.
Cowperthwait, Thomas. "A New Map of Tennessee. . . ." N.p., 1850.
Johnson, J. "Johnson's Kentucky and Tennessee." New York, [1860?].
Mendenhall, E. "Railway and County Map of Tennessee. . . ." Cincinnati, 1864.

Secondary Materials

Books

Abernethy, Thomas P. *From Frontier to Democracy in Tennessee: A Study of Frontier Democracy.* Chapel Hill, N.C., 1932.

Abshire, David M. *The South Rejects a Prophet: The Life of Senator David M. Key.* New York, 1967.

Alexander, Thomas B. *Political Reconstruction in Tennessee.* Nashville, 1950.

————. *Thomas A. R. Nelson of East Tennessee.* Nashville, 1956.

Allerdice, Bruce S. *More Generals in Gray.* Baton Rouge, 1995.

Armstrong, Zella. *The History of Hamilton County and Chattanooga, Tennessee.* 2 vols. Chattanooga, 1931–40.

Ash, Stephen V. *Middle Tennessee Society Transformed, 1860–1870: War and Peace in the Upper South.* Baton Rouge, 1988.

Atherton, Lewis E. *The Southern Country Store, 1800–1860.* Baton Rouge, 1949.

Atkins, Jonathan M. *Parties, Politics, and Sectional Conflict in Tennessee, 1832–1861.* Knoxville, 1997.

Ayers, Edward L., and John C. Willis, eds. *The Edge of the South: Life in Nineteenth Century Virginia.* Charlottesville, Va., 1991.

Bailey, Fred A. *Class and Tennessee's Confederate Generation.* Chapel Hill, N.C., 1987.

Barney, William L. *The Secessionist Impulse: Alabama and Mississippi in 1860.* Princeton, N.J., 1974.

Bergeron, Paul H. *Antebellum Politics in Tennessee.* Lexington, 1982.

Biographical Directory of the American Congress, 1774–1961. Washington, D.C., 1961.

Brice, Marshall Moore. *Conquest of a Valley.* Charlottesville, Va., 1965.

Brooks, Cora Davis. *History of Morristown, 1787–1936.* Nashville, 1940.

Burns, Inez. *History of Blount County, Tennessee, 1795–1955.* Maryville, Tenn., 1957.

Campbell, Mary Emily Robertson. *The Attitude of Tennesseans Toward the Union, 1847–1861.* New York, 1961.

Campbell, Randolph B., and Richard G. Lowe. *Wealth and Power in Antebellum Texas.* College Station, Tex., 1977.

Campbell, T. J. *Records of Rhea: A Condensed County History.* Dayton, Tenn., 1940.

Carmichael, Peter S. *Lee's Young Artillerist: William R. J. Pegram.* Charlottesville, 1995.

Clark, Blanche Henry. *The Tennessee Yeomen, 1840–1860.* Nashville, 1942.

Cody, Annie. *History of the Tennessee Division of the United Daughters of the Confederacy.* Nashville, n.d.

Coulter, E. Merton. *William G. Brownlow: Fighting Parson of the Southern Highlands.* Chapel Hill, N.C., 1937.

Crofts, Daniel W. *Reluctant Confederates: Upper South Unionists in the Secession Crisis.* Chapel Hill, N.C., 1989.

Crow, Vernon H. *Storm in the Mountains: Thomas's Confederate Legion of Cherokee Indians and Mountaineers.* N.p., 1982.

Current, Richard N. *Lincoln's Loyalists: Union Soldiers from the Confederacy.* Boston, 1992.

Daniel, Larry. *Soldiering in the Army of Tennessee: A Portrait of Life in a Confederate Army.* Chapel Hill, N.C., 1991.

Davis, William C., ed. *The Confederate General.* 6 vols. New York, 1991.

Dorris, Jonathan T. *Pardon and Amnesty under Lincoln and Johnson: The Restoration of the Confederates to Their Rights and Privileges.* Chapel Hill, N.C., 1953.

Dunn, Durwood, *Cades Cove: The Life and Death of a Southern Appalachian Community, 1818–1937.* Knoxville, 1988.

Dykeman, Wilma. *The French Broad.* New York, 1955.

Eaton, Clement. *History of the Old South.* 3d. ed. New York, 1975.

Fellman, Michael. *Inside War: The Guerrilla Conflict in Missouri during the American Civil War.* New York, 1989.

Fink, Paul M. *Jonesborough: The First Century of Tennessee's First Town.* Nashville, 1972.

Fisher, Noel C. *War at Every Door: Partisan Politics and Guerrilla Violence in East Tennessee, 1860–1869.* Chapel Hill, N.C., 1997.

Folmsbee, Stanley J. *Sectionalism and Internal Improvements in Tennessee, 1796–1845.* Knoxville, 1939.

Foster, Gaines M. *Ghosts of the Confederacy: Defeat, the Lost Cause, and the Emergence of the New South.* New York, 1987.

Gallagher, Gary W. *The Confederate War.* Cambridge, Mass., 1997.

Godbold, E. Stanley, and Mattie U. Russell. *Confederate Colonel and Cherokee Chief: The Life of William Holland Thomas.* Knoxville, 1990.

Gray, Lewis C. *History of Agriculture in the Southern United States to 1860.* 2 vols. Washington, D.C., 1939.

Hahn, Steven. *The Roots of Southern Populism: Yeoman Farmers and the Transformation of the Georgia Upcountry, 1850–1890.* New York, 1983.

Hamblen County Centennial Celebration. *Historic Hamblen, 1870–1970.* Morristown, Tenn., 1970.

Hilliard, Sam B. *Hog Meat and Hoecake: Food Supply in the Old South.* Carbondale, Ill., 1972.

Hopkins, Anne E., and William Lyons. *Tennessee Votes: 1799–1976.* Knoxville, 1978.

Hsuing, David C. *Two Worlds in the Tennessee Mountains: Exploring the Origins of Appalachian Stereotypes.* Lexington, 1997.

Inscoe, John C. *Mountain Masters, Slavery, and the Sectional Crisis in Western North Carolina.* Knoxville, 1989.

Kinzer, Robert C. *Kinship and Neighborhood in a Southern Community: Orange County, North Carolina, 1849–1881.* Knoxville, 1987.

Kruman, Marc W. *Parties and Politics in North Carolina, 1836–1865.* Baton Rouge, 1983.

Lillard, Roy G., ed. *The History of Bradley County.* Cleveland, Tenn., 1976.

Lillard, Stewart. *Meigs County, Tennessee.* Sewanee, Tenn., 1975.

Linderman, Gerald F. *Embattled Courage: The Experience of Combat in the American Civil War.* New York, 1987.

McBride, Robert M. et al., comps. *Biographical Directory of the Tennessee General Assembly.* 5 vols. Nashville, 1975–.

McKenzie, Robert Tracy. *One South or Many? Plantation Belt and Upcountry in Civil War Era Tennessee.* New York, 1994.

McKinney, Gordon B. *Southern Mountain Republicans, 1865–1900: Politics and the Appalachian Community.* Chapel Hill, N.C., 1978.

Mitchell, Reid. *Civil War Soldiers: Their Experiences and Their Expectations.* New York, 1988.

Mitchell, Robert D. *Commercialism and Frontier: Perspectives on the Early Shenandoah Valley.* Charlottesville, Va., 1990.

Mooney, Chase C. *Slavery in Tennessee.* Bloomington, Ind., 1957.

Morgan, John. *The Log House in East Tennessee.* Knoxville, 1990.

Noe, Kenneth W. *Southwest Virginia's Railroad: Modernization and the Sectional Crisis.* Urbana, Ill., 1994.

Otto, John S. *Southern Frontiers, 1607–1860: The Agricultural Evolution of the Colonial and Antebellum South.* New York, 1989.

Parks, Joseph H. *General Edmund Kirby Smith, CSA.* Baton Rouge, 1954.

Pomerantz, Gary M. *Where Peachtree Meets Sweet Auburn: The Saga of Two Families and the Making of Atlanta.* New York, 1996.

Prindle, Paul W. *Ancestry of William Biencke.* N.p., 1974.

Rothrock, Mary U., ed. *The French Broad–Holston Country.* Knoxville, 1946.

Russell, James M. *Atlanta, 1847–1890: City Building in the Old South and New.* Baton Rouge, 1988.

Salstrom, Paul. *Appalachia's Road to Dependency: Rethinking a Region's Economic History, 1730–1940.* Lexington, 1994.

Seymour, Digby. *Divided Loyalties: Fort Sanders and the Civil War in East Tennessee.* 2d ed. Knoxville, 1982.

Shapiro, David. *Appalachia on Our Mind: The Southern Mountains and Mountaineers in the American Consciousness.* Chapel Hill, N.C., 1978.

Soltow, Lee. *Men and Wealth in the United States, 1850–1870.* New Haven, Conn., 1975.

Taylor, Oliver. *Historic Sullivan County.* Bristol, Tenn., 1909.

Tennessee Civil War Centennial Commission. *Tennesseans in the Civil War.* 2 vols. Nashville, 1964.

Thomas, Emory. *The Confederate Nation, 1861–1865.* New York, 1979.

Warner, Ezra J. *Generals in Gray: Lives of the Confederate Commanders.* Baton Rouge, 1959.

Warner, Ezra J., and W. Buck Yearns. *Biographical Register of the Confederate Congress.* Baton Rouge, 1975.

Widner, Ralph W., Jr. *Confederate Monuments: Enduring Symbols of the South and the War Between the States.* N.p., 1982.

Wiley, Bell I. *The Life of Johnny Reb: The Common Soldier of the Confederacy.* Indianapolis, 1943.

Wilson, Charles Reagan. *Baptized in Blood: The Religion of the Lost Cause, 1865–1920.* Athens, Tenn., 1980.

Wilson, Sandra S., and Dennis L. Snapp, eds. *Broken Hearts—Broken Lives: Jefferson County, Tennessee, 1860–1868: Civilian Life in the Civil War.* Jefferson City, Tenn., 1986.

Winters, Donald L. *Tennessee Farming, Tennessee Farmers: Antebellum Agriculture in the Upper South.* Knoxville, 1994.

Articles

Alexander, Thomas B. "Neither Peace nor War: Conditions in Tennessee in 1865." East Tennessee Historical Society's *Publications* 21 (1949): 33–51.

Archer, M. "A Southern Part of East Tennessee." *Tennessee Ancestors* 3 (1987): 199–200.

Barney, William L. "Towards the Civil War: The Dynamics of Change in a Black Belt Community." In *Class, Conflict and Consensus: Antebellum Southern Community Studies,* edited by Orville Vernon Burton and Robert C. McMath. Westport, Conn., 1982.

Bates, Walter Lynn. "Southern Unionists: A Socioeconomic Examination of the Third East Tennessee Volunteer Infantry Regiment, U.S.A." *Tennessee Historical Quarterly* 50 (1991): 226–37.

Bryan, Charles F., Jr. "'Tories' Amidst Rebels: Confederate Occupation of East Tennessee, 1861–1863." East Tennessee Historical Society's *Publications* 60 (1988): 3–22.

Buckwalter, Donald. "Effects of Early Nineteenth Century Transportation Disadvantages on the Agriculture of East Tennessee." *Southeastern Geographer* 27 (1987): 18–37.

Burnett, Edmund C. "Hog Raising and Hog Driving in the Region of the French Broad River." *Journal of Agricultural History* 20 (1946): 86–103.

Campbell, James B. "East Tennessee During Federal Occupation, 1863–1865." East Tennessee Historical Society's *Publications* 19 (1947): 64–80.

Crawford, Martin. "Confederate Volunteering and Enlistment in Ashe County, North Carolina, 1861–1862." *Civil War History* 37 (1991): 29–50.

Fink, Paul M. "The Railroad Comes to Jonesboro." *Tennessee Historical Quarterly* 36 (1977): 161–80.

Folmsbee, Stanley J. "The Beginnings of the Railroad Movement in East Tennessee." East Tennessee Historical Society's *Publications* 5 (1933): 81–104.

Gallman, Robert E. "Self-Sufficiency in the Cotton Economy of the Antebellum South." *Agricultural History* 44 (1970): 5–23.

Groce, W. Todd. "Confederate Faces in East Tennessee: A Photographic Essay." *Journal of East Tennessee History* 65 (1993): 3–33.

Holland, James W. "The Building of the East Tennessee and Virginia Railroad." East Tennessee Historical Society's *Publications* 4 (1932): 83–101.

―――――. "The East Tennessee and Georgia Railroad, 1836–1860." East Tennessee Historical Society's *Publications* 3 (1931): 98–101.

Hutchinson, William K., and Samuel H. Williamson. "The Self-sufficiency of the Antebellum South: Estimates of the Food Supply." *Journal of Economic History* 31 (1971): 591–612.

Inscoe, John C. "Mountain Unionism, Secession, and Regional Self-Image: The Contrasting Cases of Western North Carolina and East Tennessee." In *Looking South: Chapters in the Story of an American Region*, edited by Winifred B. Moore Jr. and Joseph F. Tripp. New York, 1989.

―――――. "Thomas Clingman, Mountain Whiggery, and the Southern Cause." *Civil War History* 33 (1987): 42–62.

Krick, Robert K. "'The Cause of All My Disasters': Jubal A. Early and the Undisciplined Valley Cavalry." In *Struggle for the Shenandoah*, edited by Gary W. Gallagher. Kent, Ohio, 1991.

Lindstrom, Diane L. "Southern Dependence Upon Interregional Grain Supplies: A Review of the Trade Flows, 1840–1860." *Agricultural History* 64 (1970): 101–14.

MacArthur, William J., Jr. "The Early Career of Charles McClung McGhee." East Tennessee Historical Society's *Publications* 45 (1975): 3–13.

McKenzie, Robert Tracy. "'Oh! Ours is a Deplorable Condition': The

Economic Impact of the Civil War on Upper East Tennessee." In *The Civil War in Appalachia: Collected Essays,* edited by Kenneth W. Noe and Shannon H. Wilson. Knoxville, 1997.

Noe, Kenneth W. "Toward the Myth of a Unionist Appalachia, 1865–1883." *Journal of the Appalachian Studies Association* 6 (1994): 73–80.

Owsley, Frank L., and Harriet C. "The Economic Structure of Rural Tennessee, 1850–1860." *Journal of Southern History* 8 (1942): 161–82.

Pudup, Mary Beth. "Social Class and Economic Development in Southeast Kentucky, 1820–1860." In *Appalachian Frontiers: Settlement, Society, and Development in the Preindustrial Era,* edited by Robert D. Mitchell. Lexington, 1990.

Queener, Verton M. "East Tennessee Sentiment and the Secession Movement, November 1860–June 1861." East Tennessee Historical Society's *Publications* 20 (1948): 59–83.

Rogers, William F. "Life in East Tennessee Near the End of the Eighteenth Century." East Tennessee Historical Society's *Publications* 1 (1929): 27–42.

Salstrom, Paul. "The Agricultural Origins of Economic Dependency, 1840–1880." In *Appalachian Frontiers: Settlement, Society, and Development in the Preindustrial Era,* edited by Robert D. Mitchell. Lexington, 1990.

Taylor, Jerome G. "The Extraordinary Life and Death of Joseph A. Mabry." East Tennessee Historical Society's *Publications* 42 (1972): 41–70.

Thornton, J. Mills, III. "The Ethic of Subsistence and the Origins of Southern Secession." *Tennessee Historical Quarterly* 48 (1989): 67–85.

Wallenstein, Peter. "Which Side Are You On?: The Social Origins of White Union Troops from Civil War Tennessee." *Journal of East Tennessee History* 63 (1991): 72–103.

Williams, Samuel C. "John Mitchel, the Irish Patriot, Resident of Tennessee." East Tennessee Historical Society's *Publications* 10 (1938): 44–56.

Wright, Nathalia. "Montvale Springs under the Proprietorship of Sterling Lanier." East Tennessee Historical Society's *Publications* 19 (1947): 48–63.

Theses, Dissertations, and Unpublished Manuscripts

Bellamy, James W. "The Political Career of Landon Carter Haynes." Master's thesis, Univ. of Tennessee, 1952.

Bryan, Charles F. , Jr. "The Civil War in East Tennessee: A Social, Political, and Economic Study." Ph.D. diss., Univ. of Tennessee, 1978.

Eubanks, David L. "Dr. J. G. M. Ramsey of East Tennessee: A Career of
Public Service." Ph.D. diss., Univ. of Tennessee, 1965.

Groce, W. Todd. "Mountain Rebels: East Tennessee Confederates and the
Civil War, 1860–1870." Ph.D. diss., Univ. of Tennessee, 1992.

Hsuing, David C. "Isolation and Integration in Upper East Tennessee,
1780–1860: Historical Origins of Appalachian Characterizations." Ph.D.
diss., Univ. of Michigan, 1991.

McGehee, C. Stuart, "Wake of the Flood: A Southern City in the Civil
War: Chattanooga, 1838–1878." Ph.D. diss., Univ. of Virginia, 1985.

Rosenburg, R. B. "Reconstructed Rebels: Tennessee Pardon-Seekers under Johnson's Plan." Seminar paper, Univ. of Tennessee, Knoxville, 1984.

Schumaker, Francis Young. "Confederate History of Hawkins County,
Tennessee." Typescript. Special Collections Library, Univ. of Tennessee, Knoxville.

Index